Eminent Europeans

QUEEN MARIE OF ROUMANIA

Eminent Europeans

Studies in Continental Reality

By

Eugene S. Bagger

With Portraits

Third Edition

Essay Index Reprint Series

 BOOKS FOR LIBRARIES PRESS
FREEPORT, NEW YORK

First Published 1924
Reprinted 1970

940.28
B14e
84688
Sept 1973

STANDARD BOOK NUMBER:
8369-1693-X

LIBRARY OF CONGRESS CATALOG CARD NUMBER:
71-121446

PRINTED IN THE UNITED STATES OF AMERICA

PREFACE TO THE THIRD EDITION

THE more than generous reception with which the press and public of the United States honoured this book eighteen months ago cheered its author not only for personal reasons, but also as a sign of the growing American interest in the affairs of Europe. Nothing is more essential to-day to the welfare of the world than the realization on the part of the American people that the Atlantic Ocean has been abolished as a political fact and survives only as a producer of revenue for steamship companies. If it is true that happy people have no history, the recent outburst of historical writing in itself is an indication that something is radically wrong with this world, and moreover that the world begins to know it. And in history, as in medicine, there is no cure without a diagnosis.

In writing these essays on contemporary European personages I have deliberately resisted the temptation to prophesy, and encouraged the reader to take his chances on drawing conclusions. Nevertheless it is a source of no little satisfaction that the lapse of two most agitated years has not rendered necessary the retraction of a single statement or

the reconstruction of a single perspective of what
was fundamentally a topical book. The few minor
guesses I have indulged in were obliging enough to
come true. Thus I predicted, despite the assurances
to the contrary of some of my Roumanian friends,
that M. Bratiano will outlast in power his greater
antagonists at Paris; and M. Bratiano is still
Premier of Roumania, though he may not remain
that long. I single out this instance of my foresight
not as a boast, but by way of taking the edge off a
confession. Whatever objections my critics levelled at this book, excess of charity was not one of
them; but I must admit that in appraising M.
Bratiano's régime I was unduly optimistic.

If there be a chapter of the original ten which
I should select for rewriting it is, however, not
that on M. Bratiano, but the one dealing with
Count Michael Károlyi. For in the meantime the
first volume of his memoirs has appeared; and not
only would this record enable me to broaden and
deepen the psychological presentation, but it also
impels me to re-affirm my admiration for a fine
spirit and a life nobly lived. Fortunately Count
Károlyi's book will soon be available in an English
translation, and to all those interested in one of the
most thrilling and least known phases of recent history and in a gripping human document, I recommend it most heartily. I am also glad to say that
Professor Jászi's book, to which reference is made
in the preface of the first edition, has just been
published, in a substantially enlarged English

edition, under the title "Revolution and Counter-Revolution in Hungary."

.   .   .   .

The three new chapters—one each on Mr. Ramsay Macdonald, M. Poincaré and Signor Mussolini—which are added herewith to the original assortment, require no apology for their existence, whatever may be said about their quality. True, they exceed the compass of a book devoted in the first place to eminences of the minor European nations. On the other hand it will be admitted that by no contraction of its meaning can the designation "Eminent European" be denied to my three new subjects. Moreover, while the rise of British Labour and the problem of reparations have been discussed *ad nauseam* in the American press, and while there has been no lack of "human interest" anecdotes on the entry of Mr. Macdonald and the exit of M. Poincaré, I do not think that the psychological background of either of these protagonists has been presented with such frequency and finality as to render my version supererogatory. To some readers my attempt to write about Mr. Macdonald and M. Poincaré without discoursing on British Labour policy and reparations may appear like going to Rome without seeing St. Peter's. To others it will be a welcome innovation.

A word apart as to the essay on Mussolini. To recount the story of the Fascist movement on its serious side seemed to me mere duplication of work

PREFACE TO THE THIRD EDITION

well done by Mr. Carleton Beals in his "Rome or Death." Still less did I want to produce another prospectus about Fascist uniforms and cohorts and centurions and all the rest of kleagle-and-klig-rapp, eia-eia-alala-rah-rah-rah stuff. What I tried to do was to draw an outline of the mind of Fascism as mirrored by the mind of its founder. Signor Mussolini may not like all I have said about him, but I trust he will approve of my attempt to treat him as a philosopher rather than the chief attraction of an Italian Wild West show.

E.S.B.

London, May, 1924.

PREFACE

MUCH publicity has called to life, too much publicity has destroyed Central Europe for the English-reading peoples. Prior to the World War those peoples had a vague notion, founded entirely on implicit belief in the honesty of mapmakers, that there were countries called Austria, Hungary, Roumania; a learned minority cherished schoolday memories suggesting the potentiality of a land named Greece, where marble ruins and archæologists led a dreary sort of symbiotic existence; and it was recalled of Bohemia that its most interesting feature was a seaboard which could not be found. The conflagration of 1914 illuminated, for a moment, the landscape stretching between the Rhine and the Black Sea; but the sense of reality thus evoked was presently wiped out by the vast black clouds of Propaganda. The lands whose main artery is the Danube became fixed in one's consciousness as mysterious caverns whence emanated atrocities, unpronounceable proper names, information bureaus, national councils, and pamphlets, pamphlets, pamphlets, pamphlets. Then followed the period of self-determination; and before long

PREFACE

the English-reading public self-determined that it
was sick of Central European pamphlets and whatever they stood for.

Yet to me, a native of the fair city of Budapest,
the causes expounded by those pamphlets indicated
realities—all the more real because I could view
them from the perspective of prolonged absence.
It is a commonplace to say that one discovers things
by getting away from them. When I lived at
Budapest—and I lived there the first twenty-one
years of my life,—I did not know that there existed such a thing as Central Europe. I had to
come to America to discover Central Europe. Like
all awakening to the obvious hitherto obscured by
its very obviousness, the discovery meant a revelation.

But what interested me in those pamphlets and
other printed matter was not the Causes—it was the
peoples behind them, or rather, people. I realized
that I knew from first-hand experience that which
most Americans and Englishmen accepted as an act
of faith: that those peoples, those people, *lived*.

Now, if the peoples of Central Europe became
unreal to Americans and Englishmen because they
were disguised as Causes, the personalities of Central Europe became still more unreal because they
were disguised as Symbols. There is less distance
between a People—itself a collective being, a
generalization—and a Cause, than between a Personality—something concrete, if only in the crudest
sense palpable—and a Symbol. My profession

PREFACE

thrust upon me the duty of reading hundredweights of literature—pamphlets, books, magazine and newspaper articles, dealing with the leaders of Central Europe. Some of these literary products were well-informed and informing; others were too-well-informed and misinforming; some were well-written, others were not; most of them may have served the specific purpose of the moment, usually connected with some sort of Drive; but whatever their other qualities may have been, they hardly ever made one suspect that the persons discussed had, among other things, souls. These persons were banners or at best standard-bearers; they were archangels or devils; they were vessels of political theories and principles, tokens of interests and preferences, sometimes dummies clothed in "human interest" anecdotes—human beings they were not. I read the biographies of a few—excellent specimens of political philology, warehouses of cold storage information—too many trees, of the forest not a trace.

In the following papers I have attempted to present some of the men, and one woman, who for the past eight years signified Central European history, as human beings, and not as symbols and political abstractions. I did not have to go very far before I realized the difficulties of my task—difficulties not specific, indeed, but generic—inherent in the drawing of "contemporary portraits" of a higher than the Sunday supplement plane. Its successful performance would have postulated a manifold

PREFACE

equipment, involving the arts of the journalist, the historian and the novelist. It would have required the journalist's sense for the topical, the trenchant detail, for the manipulation of the subtle threads with which things remote geographically and psychologically are embroidered upon the consciousness of the hurried reader. The historian was called upon to contribute perspective, the faculty of sifting evidence, and the sense of connections. At least as important as these would have been the novelist's gift of re-creating reality from mere material. Selection of the essential, suppression of the irrelevant: in this highest precept of all art the three requirements converged.

Such was the nature of my undertaking. I owe an apology for the result—not for the plan and the aspiration. If I missed my mark, at least it was because I aimed too high—not too low. That may be no excuse for the rifleman; but the writer may plead it in extenuation.

Comparisons are invidious—especially so for the weaker party compared. I am aware of the handicap that my book carries in its title. But the book had been written before the title was thought of; it was chosen because it covers what it should. No intelligent and fair-minded critic will charge me with the desire to outdo Mr. Lytton Strachey. It was only when most of my chapters were already typed that I awoke to two facts. First, that I tried to see and to present in a new light things whose poignancy had worn off by custom and repetition.

PREFACE

Second, that I tried to write fragments of contemporary history with the methods and intentions of, not the chronicler nor the special pleader, but the analytical novelist, only working upon historic fact and document instead of imaginary material. In other words, I was interested in psychology and environment rather than in plots and events. My book turned out to be a faint attempt at dealing with a problem in literary form which had been already so brilliantly solved. So much the worse for my book.

There will be those who object to the limitation of this volume to personalities from the comparatively unimportant countries of Central and Southeastern Europe. Now, treating an ignored subject, or the ignored aspects of a subject (and despite tons of wartime press output, Central Europe *is* ignored) may be quite as important as elucidating new shades of a known one. But that is a defence of my theme, not of my title. The fact is—and here I touch upon an idea which will recur in the subsequent pages—that in a sense Hungarians, Czechs, Roumanians are better Europeans, are more European, than Englishmen or Frenchmen. England is a world; so is France; but Hungary, or Czechoslovakia, or Roumania, are mere segments of the whole called Europe.

*   *   *   *   *   *

To the two chapters wherein printed sources were extensively used—those on M. Venizelos and King

PREFACE

Constantine—bibliographies are appended; in the others, quotations are credited in the text. As regards the two Hellenic chapters I must make special mention here of my indebtedness to Mr. John Mavrogordato, M.A., whose writings during and after the war, published in *The New Europe* and elsewhere, have helped me much toward an understanding of Near Eastern problems. For valuable suggestions for the chapter on President Masaryk, as well as for general encouragement, my sincerest thanks are due to Professor Herbert Adolphus Miller of Oberlin College, Ohio. There are practically no books in the English language dealing with the two revolutions and the counter-revolution in Hungary. For information on these subjects I am indebted to the files of the *Manchester Guardian* and the *Neue Zürcher Zeitung,* above all, to the excellently edited organ of the Hungarian bourgeois refugees in Vienna, the *Bécsi Magyar Ujság* (Vienna Hungarian Gazette). The facts relating to the Hungarian White Terror are set forth in the Report of the British Joint Labour Delegation, headed by Colonel J. C. Wedgwood, M.P., which visited Hungary in the spring of 1920. I take this occasion to convey my thanks to Colonel Wedgwood for his courtesy in supplying me with that most indispensable document.

But the two Hungarian chapters could never have been written without the guidance that I derived from the *œuvre* of Professor Oscar Jászi, the great intellectual leader of Young Hungary. My

PREFACE

obligation to him far exceeds the range of my quo-
tations from his brilliant book, *Magyar Calvary—
Magyar Resurrection,* unavailable, alas! in English.
It was he who taught me, like so many others of my
generation, to understand Hungary in terms of
European culture and modern political science.

The chapter on Queen Marie of Roumania treats
that very beautiful and spirited lady in a way which
our best people might possibly call unorthodox. I
wish to assure my numerous Roumanian friends—
who after all may not read the chapter very carefully—that whatever I say about their Queen is by
no means intended to bear upon their nation. I was
born in a country where preference for things Roumanian is not, to put it mildly, a common tradition;
but I am only glad to state that years of study and
personal contact have generated in me a sincere admiration of and affection for the spirit of Young
Roumania, that truly European spirit which is represented by men like M. Octavian Goga, poet,
statesman, humanist. If I have to confess to a bias
in the matter of Roumania, it is a distinctly pro-
Roumanian bias, born of my faith in Young Roumania as the outpost of Latinity at the eastern gate
of Europe.

E. S. B.

Baltimore, July, 1922.

CONTENTS

PAGE

I.—QUEEN MARIE OF ROUMANIA 1

Princess of Great Britain and Ireland, Duchess in Saxony. Born October 29, 1875. Daughter of Duke of Edinburgh and Saxe-Coburg-Gotha, second son of Queen Victoria and the Prince-Consort, Duke Albert of Saxe-Coburg-Gotha. Married to Crown Prince Ferdinand of Roumania January 10, 1893.

II.—KING FERDINAND OF ROUMANIA 25

Of the House of Hohenzollern-Sigmaringen, the elder, Roman Catholic, non-reigning branch of the Hohenzollern dynasty. Born August 24, 1865, at Sigmaringen. Succeeded his uncle, King Carol I, October 10, 1914.

III.—THE RISE OF ELEUTHERIOS VENIZELOS . . . 47

Eleutherios Kyriakou Venizelos. Born August 23, 1864, at Murniæs near Canea, Island of Crete, son of Kyriakos Venizelos, a merchant. Doctor of Laws, University of Athens, 1887. Chairman of Insurrectionary Assembly of Crete, 1897. Councillor of State, 1899. President of the Hellenic Council, October, 1910–March, 1915; August, 1915 –October, 1915. Head of Salonica Government, October, 1916–June, 1917. President of Hellenic Council, June, 1917–November, 1920. Married Helena Schilizzi in 1921.

IV.—CONSTANTINE AND THE FALL OF VENIZELOS . . 83

Constantine I, King of the Hellenes, Prince of Denmark. Of the House of Schleswig-Holstein-Sonderburg-Glücksburg. Born August 31, 1868. Married Princess Sophie of Prussia, sister of Kaiser Wilhelm, October 28, 1889. Succeeded his father, King

CONTENTS

PAGE

George I, March 18, 1913. Deposed June 12, 1917. Resumed power December 19, 1920. Deposed again Sept. 27, 1922. Field-Marshal-General of Prussia. Colonel-in-Chief of 88th Royal Prussian Infantry and of 2nd Royal Foot Guards.

V.—THOMAS GARRIGUE MASARYK 125
President of the Czechoslovak Republic. Born March 7, 1850, at Hodonin, Moravia, son of imperial gamekeeper. Lecturer on philosophy, University of Vienna, 1879. Professor, Czech University of Prague, 1882. Member of Austrian Reichsrat, 1891. Assumed office as First President of the Czechoslovak Republic, November 14, 1918. Re-elected for life, May 28, 1920. Married Charlotte Garrigue, of Brooklyn, N. Y., in 1878.

VI.—JOHN BRATIANO, JR 143
Born 1865. Educated in Bucharest and École Centrale, Paris. Premier of Roumania, 1907–1910; June, 1914–January, 1918; December, 1918–November, 1919; reappointed January, 1922. Married to Princess Elise Stirbey.

VII.—COUNT MICHAEL KAROLYI 163
Born March 4, 1875. Hereditary member of Hungarian House of Lords. Renounced seat in Upper Chamber and got elected to House of Representatives, 1906. Married to Countess Catherine Andrássy November, 1914. President of Hungarian Republic, November, 1918–March 21, 1919.

VIII.—IGNACE JAN PADEREWSKI 211
Born November 6, 1860, at Kurylówka, Podolia, son of a small noble land-owner. Professor, Warsaw Conservatory, 1879-81. First concert at Vienna, 1887; at Paris, 1888. Prime Minister of Poland, 1918-1919. First married 1879, to Rose Hassal, Warsaw, who died a year later. Second wife Hélène, Baronne de Rosen, 1899.

CONTENTS

PAGE

IX.—EDWARD BENES 237

Premier of the Czechoslovak Republic. Born 1884. Educated at Universities of Prague and Dijon, and at Sorbonne, Paris. Ph.D., University of Prague, 1909. Instructor in Sociology, 1912. Foreign Minister of Czechoslovakia, 1918. Premier, September, 1921.

X.—ADMIRAL HORTHY 255

His Serene Highness Nicholas Horthy de Nagybánya. Regent of Hungary. Born 1867 at Kenderes, County Szolnok. Educated at Imperial and Royal Naval Academy, Pola, and at Vienna. Naval Aide to Emperor Francis Joseph. In World War commander of Imperial and Royal Cruiser Novara, later Commander-in-Chief of Austro-Hungarian Navy. Commander-in-Chief of Hungarian National (White) Army, Szegedin, in spring of 1919. Elected Regent March 1, 1920. Married to Paula Purgly, daughter of apothecary at Nagyvárad (Grosswardein).

XI.—JAMES RAMSAY MACDONALD 285

Born 1866 at Lossiemouth, Morayshire, Scotland. Educated at village school. Joined Independent Labour Party in 1894. Journalist and author. Represented Leicester in Parliament, 1906-18. Re-elected at Aberavon, 1922. Prime Minister of Great Britain and Secretary of State for Foreign Affairs, January, 1924.

XII.—RAYMOND POINCARE 307

Born August 20, 1860, at Bar-le-Duc, son of a civil engineer. Elected to Chamber of Deputies, 1889. Minister of Public Instruction, 1893 and 1895; Minister of Finance, 1894 and 1906; Premier, 1911-13 and 1922-24; President of the French Republic, 1913-1920. Member of the French Academy; Senator. Married Henriette Benucci.

CONTENTS

PAGE

XIII.—BENITO MUSSOLINI 331

Born April, 1883, at Predappio, son of the village
blacksmith. Editor of *Avanti,* organ of the Italian
Socialist Party, 1912-14. Founded at Milan the
pro-war, pro-ally Syndicalist daily *Popolo d'Italia,*
1915. Organized Fascist movement, 1919. Elected
to Chamber of Deputies, May, 1921. Premier,
Minister of Foreign Affairs, Minister of Interior
and Commissioner of Air Forces, from October,
1922. Commander-in-chief of Fascist forces.

ILLUSTRATIONS

	FACING PAGE
QUEEN MARIE OF ROUMANIA	*Frontispiece*
KING FERDINAND OF ROUMANIA	28
ELEUTHERIOS VENIZELOS	50
KING CONSTANTINE OF GREECE	86
THOMAS GARRIGUE MASARYK	128
JOHN BRATIANO, JR.	146
COUNT MICHAEL KAROLYI	166
COUNT STEPHEN TISZA	178
IGNACE JAN PADEREWSKI	214
EDWARD BENES	240
ADMIRAL NICHOLAS HORTHY	258
JAMES RAMSAY MACDONALD	288
RAYMOND POINCARE	310
BENITO MUSSOLINI	334

But this I say, brethren, the time is short: it remaineth, that they that weep be as though they wept not; and they that rejoice, as though they rejoiced not; and they that buy, as though they possessed not; and they that use this world, as not abusing it: for the fashion of this world passeth away.

I. Corinthians 7: 29–31.

QUEEN MARIE OF ROUMANIA

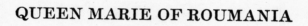

QUEEN MARIE OF ROUMANIA

I

SHE might have been Queen of England.

The story has never appeared in print. It was related to me by an English friend who had heard it on a visit to Bucharest, from one of the Queen's most intimate friends. The latter, in her turn, had it from the Queen herself. Princess Mary was sixteen then, the daughter of the Duke of Edinburgh, Queen Victoria's second son. It was on the Isle of Wight, and it was Spring. One day the young Prince George came to her and said in that inimitable casual English manner: "Missy, will you be my wife?" It should be recalled that he was the second son of the Prince of Wales. The Duke of Clarence was still among the living, and there was nothing to hint at his early death, nothing but the old habit of Anglo-Saxon fate which very often condemns to death the first-born. It is no bad arrangement, in a way. The system brings happiness to the eldest son by giving him the expectancy of his estate, and it brings happiness to the second son by giving him the estate, the more appreciated because unhoped for. Still, there was something to be said for being even the sister-in-law of the future King of England, and Princess Mary was sixteen. It is the age when girls love to be carried off their feet, when girls are not on the lookout for what the French call *un mariage de raison*. Why should she have refused?

Withal, my English friend doubted the authenticity of the story, and when he returned to London he asked Lord Knollys, King George's secretary, if it was true. It was. Princess Mary refused to marry her first cousin. Without looking for further, more subtle, reasons, perhaps that in itself explained the refusal. Girls at sixteen (and not only at sixteen) love the thrill of a new experience. It is difficult for a girl with a restless imagination to look forward to her first cousin for the thrill of a new experience.

As to King George, he seems to have lived down his disappointment. One of the best husbands in the universe, he hardly feels pangs of regret now. Perhaps Queen Mary occasionally teases her husband about the feeling which Queen Marie once inspired in him. And, in a subtle way, King George had his revenge. The Princess who refused to marry the second son of the heir to the English crown was known later to favour more than one *arriviste* commoner.

The months passed; then a year, two years—and Princess Mary was still unmarried. She was young; but she was not very happy in her parents' home, and when Prince Ferdinand, the Roumanian heir-apparent, asked her to become his bride she did not refuse.

Did she love him? It was adventure—of a kind. She was to go to Roumania. How wonderful all journeys are before you start! Every place is invested with glamour before you get there. To a foreigner, even Hoboken, or Highgate, may suggest romantic associations. To the young bride Roumania was a name—and a sonorous name. It derived from a common root with Romance. Then she arrived, and before long she felt very lonely with her husband, who appeared selfish and had confirmed habits like an old bachelor; with King Carol and Queen Elizabeth, who, in their childless life, had lost all understanding of youth, if they ever possessed any.

She had a child—a boy, as is proper in well-regulated royal families; and, twelve months later, a daughter. Then she rubbed her eyes, and looked around. Suddenly the woman of twenty-one felt a strong craving for life—to be bathed in, to drink experience.

It was not an especially complicated case. Princess Mary (or, as she now spelled her name, Marie) was heartily bored. She started highly unconventional friendships, and was harshly criticized because of them by her uncle and aunt, the King and Queen, and by her subjects-to-be who were nothing if not critical. She tried to ignore criticism, but her critics were too many and too strong for her.

All this happened at the royal court of Bucharest;

it might just as well have happened in a Paris or Copenhagen flat, in a suburb of London or Boston. Princess Marie was not the first wife in history who suddenly felt a desire to see some one other than her husband opposite her at breakfast. She had a will. In a flash, without consulting any one, she left her husband like Nora of the Doll's House and went off to Gotha, where her father was reigning as Duke. A few months later Princess Mignon was born.

There were those to whom her exit was not unwelcome. Queen Elizabeth was one of their number. To her the Princess Marie symbolized a defeat—one of the bitterest of her life. The Queen had desired to marry her nephew, the Crown Prince, to one of her friends, Mlle. Vacaresco. She failed. Princess Marie had no part in the affair; she appeared on the scene later, when all was over but the newspaper echoes. She was not the cause of the Queen's defeat, but she was its memento. The Queen hated her, and was glad to see her go.

Some of the Roumanian politicians, inveterate lovers of mischief, were equally gratified. But their satisfaction with what seemed to be a final break was thwarted by the birth of Princess Mignon. The Crown Prince, unlike his wife, possessed a heart. Unlike her, he also had a strong and real sense of duty. A *rapprochement* was engineered. Princess Marie returned to her husband and to the court.

This reconciliation, much more than her marriage,

was the turning-point in her life. When she married she embarked on a voyage of discovery. Now she surrendered to a routine. It was a surrender in a rather complete sense. With this young princess of twenty-two, locked up in the petty pleasures and sorrows of Roumanian court life as in a gaol, one had the impression that hers was a case of arrested development: that her life had run up against a wall. That wall she was never to surmount. She could not go on—but she could go around in a circle, she could go back and forth. That restlessness which had made her decline her first cousin was still in her blood. It found an outlet in a continuous, untiring activity, an activity regardless of results and consequences and not always particular as to means.

II

She began to paint. My English friend was in Bucharest when the Arts were wooing her. She said to him: "I am only happy on days when I have painted for two hours and been on horseback for two hours." Painters disliked that remark, but for the psychologist it was a gem. Painting, for her, was simply another form of exercise, a drain for her bursting vitality.

Nor was painting the end of it. The Roumanian court was a young court, but it already had its traditions. One of these traditions was that of the literary Queen. Under the pen name Carmen

Sylva, Queen Elizabeth had written a number of books, and those books were not only published, but they also sold. They delighted many a snob and many a sentimentalist, in Roumania and abroad. Surplus of energy, boredom and jealousy of the older woman began to hatch a conspiracy in Princess Marie; and one fatal day the conspirators thrust a weapon into her hand—a pen. Queen Carmen was avenged at last. It was her example that turned Marie into an author.

The relationship of kings and queens to the Arts is rather a pathetic one. It is not only that they want so terribly to be successful. They *must* be successful—in their exalted position they cannot afford failure. They might, of course, try anonymity; but on that term success would not be worth having. They crave fame. Being sentimentalists, *ex officio,* as it were, they hate taking chances; they shrink, as Meredith says somewhere, from the awful responsibility of the deed done; they are unaccustomed to, and abhor, the idea of paying a price. Kings and queens of the twentieth century may don disguise when they sail forth in quest of the grosser pleasures; but when they are out for literary fame they wear their full regalia; for they know the publicity value of their crowns, and are loath to sacrifice it.

Some fifteen or twenty years ago a friend of mine, a clever Frenchman, was introduced, in Paris, to King Oscar of Sweden, then on a visit in the French capital. The King seemed to like him, and he was quite pleased, even a little proud, when he received word that His Majesty wished to see him. He felt sure that the King sought the benefit of his knowledge of Paris and the world; that he intended to discuss with him the relation of Sweden to Norway, or the problem of Russian aggression, then the bugbear of Scandinavia. One little thing he forgot: that His Majesty was also a poet, and that he had just published a volume. He was reminded of it soon enough. When he arrived the monarch greeted him most cordially, and drew quite close to him. He was, in all humility, preparing for his initiation into the holy of holies of European diplomacy, when suddenly the question came from the sovereign lips,— coaxingly, almost shyly:

"Do you think that my book will sell?"

Dr. Johnson said that women preaching reminded him of dogs walking on their hind legs— they did not do it well, but the wonder was that they did it at all. Queen Marie started writing books in English, and thus accomplished one of the miracles of her life; for she does not completely master the English language, nor any other for that matter. Yet she neglects no opportunity to proclaim to the world that she is an English princess; on the slightest provocation, without any provocation at all, she will tell you that she is English, and how English she is. A thoroughbred Coburg, she hasn't a drop of English blood in her veins.

Every religion has its martyrs, even the one

whose Bible is the Book of Snobs. There are
people—I have known them—who conscientiously
buy every book of Queen Marie as soon as it is off
the presses. I assume that some of these zealots also
try to read her books, though I doubt if any one
ever succeeded in reading them, as Daisy Ashford
would say, to the bitter end.

For Princess Marie literature was not a vehicle
of self-expression, not even, primarily, a road to
fame, but just a safety valve, like her painting,
like her horseback-riding. She went out riding
every morning, and on his visits to Bucharest my
English friend repeatedly had the pleasure of ac-
companying her. He felt the honour keenly, but his
pleasure was not unmixed. For she rode her horse
for hours and hours at a stretch, absolutely careless
of the creature's fatigue. No Englishwoman could
ever do that. My friend was told that no horse
lasted in the royal stables over three or four months.
"I did not check up," he adds, "the mortality
among the stenographers to whom Her Majesty
dictated her books, but it must have been high."

III

Then the Princess became Queen; and by a coincidence the war broke out almost at the same moment. For Marie it was a fortunate coincidence.
She found herself. At last here was an adequate
outlet for her boundless energy, a field that could
absorb all the cloudbursts of her activity. She

could now be "up and doing" twenty-four hours a day if she chose. She could achieve things—more than that: she could achieve things that really mattered. She could manage men; she could mould events. Heretofore she had to enjoy, in a degree, action vicariously in her fairy tales; now she could play a part in making real history. She wanted to be on the bill all the time—a "headliner," as Americans say.

"I have never been so happy as during the war." If Queen Marie never said that, she might have said it; if anybody ever said it, it was a woman. One of the women who, "fed up" on the strenuous futility called social life, could now address mass meetings, organize relief societies and vigilance committees, direct war loan campaigns, prepare Red Cross supplies, even nurse the wounded—anything. No woman had a greater opportunity in the war than Queen Marie. She lived up to it.

One of the first tasks the war thrust upon her was a removal. A removal, from one city to another, means no small thing even in the ordinary middle-class household. It is an epoch-making event in the life of a court. A long time before the Germans pierced the Roumanian front a confidential report on the military situation was demanded from head-quarters. "Is Bucharest menaced?" asked the court. "Not in the least," answered the generals, in chorus. Queen Marie is a shrewd woman. "We must pre-pare to go to Iassy," said Her Majesty.

And to Iassy they went. There was a shortage

of munitions at the front, of food in the towns, because there was a shortage of rolling stock. There were no cars to accommodate the refugees from the devastated areas. But trains were commandeered to transfer to the royal palace at Iassy all the contents of the Cotroceni household. All kinds of mediocre furniture, worn-out polar bears' skins turned a murky grey with age, cracked Persian pottery, embroideries and silks snatched up at Liberty's during hasty stays in London. True, Roumania was at war; but the *Stimmung* of the Bucharest court had to be recreated at Iassy at any cost.

In the evening little intimate concerts were given. Richly painted shades or heavy pieces of silk covered the lamps, and a Roumanian violinist, Enesco, or a pianist, Mme. Cella Delavrancea, played everything from Bach to Debussy. Missions came from Allied governments, Albert Thomas from France, Gutchkoff, the Minister of War, from Russia, to stimulate Roumanian resistance. They were welcome but not needed. The King and Queen had made up their minds. The Roumanian armies would fight on to their last drop of blood.

A great friend of Her Majesty once said to me: "No woman was ever so gifted as she—none, not even Sarah Bernhardt or Mrs. Fiske."

A curious comparison—a Queen and two actresses. A truer comparison than would appear at first glance. Queens and actresses have many parts to play. At Iassy Queen Marie, clad all in white, with a diamond cross on her breast, a cross of the colour of blood on the white veil that covered her forehead, visited the hospitals every morning. In the afternoon she gave audiences, either to native politicians in need of a coaxing word, or to foreign diplomatists. To the French Minister, Count de St. Aulaire, later Ambassador in London, she explained what a wonderful Queen she was—it was she who dragged her hesitant husband, her reluctant Premier, into the war.

Count de St. Aulaire, being the envoy of a mere republic, was convulsed with the delights of such intimate relation with a real Queen. He flashed across Europe enthusiastic dispatches; he said, adapting the famous *mot* of Mirabeau, that there was only one man in Roumania, and that was the Queen.

All of which was delicious, and Her Majesty enjoyed it to the dregs. Now I don't want to be misunderstood. I don't mean to say that the tragedy of the war did not affect her. She did not remain unmoved by its horrors. But contact with the war, and not the least with war's horrors, made her a different, and, morally, a richer woman. She tasted power. She liked it, and in a weak and respectful country she was able to hold on to it.

In a sense her choice was justified at last. As Queen of England she would never have had the opportunities to rule, to control and initiate, that now literally poured into her lap. The court was managed by polished but inefficient gentlemen. The generals were not much better. One, Mavrocordato,

was appointed to a mission with the Allied General
Staff at Salonica; but the French were advised
never to let him reach his destination, and they
wisely heeded the counsel. Another, Catargi, was
appointed Minister to Belgium, and was now safe,
in more than one sense, with King Albert's court
at Le Havre. Two men gained the special confidence of the Queen. The one was Prince Stirbey, a descendant of former rulers of Roumania.
The other was a man in khaki, the Canadian Colonel
Boyle.

Prince Stirbey was not only a real prince—he
was the Prince Charming. He was very handsome
and very rich; he did not speak much, but the little
he said was good. He was all the time engaged in
far-reaching schemes—his one ambition in this
world was to become richer every day; but he kept
his schemes to himself. They were not in evidence.
The one thing that was in evidence was his charm,
and even about that he had to exercise restraints.
Who would have thought that the Prince Charming
had a wife somewhere, and an innumerable host of
daughters? However, in the Orient women know
their place and keep it. In any event, his wife and
his multitudinous daughters did not prevent Prince
Stirbey from accomplishing, in the briefest time, a
most brilliant military career. In a few months the
Lieutenant was promoted to Colonel. No recom-
pense is too big for charm. Not only did Prince
Stirbey become the *éminence grise,* the power behind the throne, of Roumania—as the Prime

Minister's brother-in-law he was an ideal go-be-
tween from court to the world of politicians. But
his position had its risks—grave ones. Many a
Roumanian lip at one time fell into a shape that
made you believe that you had just heard or were
just going to hear the word Rasputin. But in the
Orient, where intrigue was invented, they have also
perfected the art of directing public attention
where it belongs. Perhaps Prince Stirbey prayed
to the Almighty that He would send some one to
deliver him from being the butt of popular interest.
Perhaps Prince Stirbey invented Colonel Boyle.

IV

Who was Colonel Boyle? His admirers called
him the Colonel Lawrence of Roumania, local version of the Oxford archæologist who became statesman, strategist and cavalry hero in Arabia. But
Colonel Boyle's relations with Oxford were less
patent, and although at one time he may have had
something to do with excavating, he was no archæologist. He came from Canada. Behind Canada
lay Alaska, land of the midnight sun, of gold, of
prospecting, of tangled lawsuits about clashing
claims. In Roumania nobody asked for details.
All he was asked was, "Who are you?"

"A Colonel, at any rate," answered Boyle.

"Why not become a hero?"

"I am prepared for any job that you may give
me."

It was at the beginning of the Bolshevik upheaval in Russia.   Colonel Boyle was entrusted with the task of freeing a certain number of Roumanians from the grasp of the Bolsheviki.   At that early stage the prestige of khaki was still considerable. They will tell you in Roumania that Colonel Boyle saved five, fifty or five hundred lives in Russia.   In cases like that it is always a question of appreciation rather than of fact.   Whatever else his mission accomplished, one result was obvious.   Colonel Boyle became the Queen's slave.

"When I saw her I felt like Paul on the Damascus road," he is reported to have said.

From that moment on the Queen utilized him— sent him on missions that required tact and discretion as well as energy and resourcefulness.   She sent him to rescue her son, the Crown Prince, from the clutches of—but that is another story.   She sent him to try to get for her sister, wife of the Grand Duke Kyril, the throne of Russia.   Why not?   The Czar of all the Russians was not only dead—he had been buried and lamented in an article by Her Majesty the Queen Marie.   And had she not the blood of Catherine the Great in her veins?   Once she was passing a column of Russian soldiers.   One exclaimed: "There—what a good Empress she would make for us!"   But she was engaged elsewhere.   Her sister had been the Duchess of Hesse. She had divorced her husband in order to marry the Grand Duke Kyril of Russia.   They were both alive, and although handicapped, in Orthodox eyes,

by the matter of the divorce, still the nearest claim-
ants to the Russian throne.

Boyle had once had a stroke in an airplane, but he
was fond of flying nevertheless. He was sent to the
Wrangel front to ascertain how long it would take
for Wrangel to reinstate the Romanoffs. He returned with the message that it was a question of
six months. Six days later General Wrangel was
floating quietly toward Constantinople, and the
coronation of the Grand Duke Kyril was postponed
sine die.

There is no use crying over spilt crowns. A
French proverb says, *"Un amant de perdu, dix de
retrouvé."* In a period of great upheavals if you
miss a throne you may find another if you only look
around quickly enough. Venizelos was tottering in
Greece; the exchange of Constantine was rising.
Constantine's son suddenly became a good match.
Prince Stirbey—or was it Colonel Boyle?—was
dispatched to Switzerland to negotiate the marriage
between the Prince Georgios of Greece and the
Princess Elizabeth of Roumania. The mission was
crowned with success.

But that is rushing too far ahead. The war was
still on. The Germans were advancing, they were
menacing the Roumanian rear. The court was prepared for any emergency. Elaborate plans were
made. The King and Queen would take refuge in
a Russian town. The Roumanian army would withdraw to the Caucasus, if need be, but it would fight
for every inch of ground. . . .

The Roumanian government signed the separate peace on May 7, 1918. Small countries have to play safe even when they embark on an adventure. Some of the great Scottish families had sons both in the Jacobite and the Whig camp, so that they might keep their estates whichever side won. Similarly, small countries whose fate hinges on the pleasure of the Great Powers, usually have two sets of politicians ready to change places according to the ups and downs of international rivalry. Roumania had a set of pro-Ally statesmen that had brought her into the war. She also had a set of pro-German politicians who were prepared to come into power as soon as their rivals went out. The Premier who signed the separate peace in Bucharest was M. Marghiloman.

V

Half a year passed, and Germany was defeated. The Marghiloman ministry went out; the Bratiano ministry—the old pro-Ally war cabinet—came back. Once more peace, officially so called, reigned in Europe.

The Queen journeyed to the West. The war had ended; but not her war-born activities. Her trip was one of pleasure combined with business. She did not cease to work for her country. She was asked by Roumanians to buy locomotives and rolling stock, to sell wheat and maize for them. In Paris, beside attending innumerable social engage-

ments and buying almost as innumerable dresses
she found time to discuss with leaders of industry
and finance the needs of Roumania.   She was ever
on the verge of concluding big transactions; but
they seldom came off entirely.   Hitches occurred.
They couldn't be helped.   The Queen had an imagination that was all the more apt to run away with
her as it had been fed the richest of foods for the
past three years.   Be that as it may—the fact remains that Queen Marie unfolded a skill as a press
agent for her country that any professional might
envy.   She "sold" Roumania to the West.

But Paris, after all, is a comparatively easy place
for royalty.   After forty years of the Republic a
queen—any queen—cannot help being a social success.   Dinners are given for her by the Comtesse de
Béarn, the Comtesse Aynard de Chabrillan, the
Marquise de Flers and others.   Often at these
dinners a strange hissing sound may be heard above
the din of conversation and laughter, the ruffling of
silks and the clinking of hand-cut glasses.   It is the
sound of little private axes being ground by a prudent and ambitious hostess.   But it takes an experienced ear to perceive that discreet noise.   They
still know how to make guests happy in the grand
style at Paris.

London is different.   The acid test of twentieth-
century royalty is its reception in England.   One
might almost say to a king, "Tell me with whom you
associate in England and I tell you what kind of a
king you are."

To begin with, the attitude of the British aristocracy even to their own King is a peculiar one. They worship the institution of monarchy with an almost religious zeal. But their respect for the office does not preclude indifference, or worse, to its incumbent. That King Edward—who really was an excellent ruler, but who had had his escapades in his youth and spoke English with a German accent —did not have a very happy time of it with a certain section of the British aristocracy is well enough known. Who can be more royalistic than the Duke of Buccleuch? Yet it is possible for a Montagu-Douglas-Scott to look down upon a mere Saxe-Coburg—not to mention their recently acquired name of Windsor—as a kind of, well, upstart. To a degree it is nothing but self-defence—love of comfort. The presence of a King or Queen adds nothing to the glory of an English or Scottish duke, but it does constrain him, and dukes do not like to be constrained.

And if some of these great houses are mildly reluctant to associate with a King of England, it is only what one may expect if they refuse point blank to consort with what they call minor royalty. Snobs of all nations, if they have been good on earth, go to England when they die, and good English snobs remain there—it's safer than Heaven.

Consequently, to say that the position of a "minor royalty" in London is none too pleasant is an understatement. As to their relations with His Britannic Majesty—a member of the Household once said that they might almost as well be mere Americans. This, of course, is an exaggeration; yet great is the day, and correspondingly rare, when they are bidden to a short informal meal, or to a long formal function, in the company of the King. They are treated at Court as an exalted kind of poor relation. If they are out for a "good time," socially, they are left to their own devices.

Yet they are not altogether forlorn even in London. All over the world, from Punta Arenas and Johannesburg to Moscow, there are branches of the international organization known as the Fraternity of Social Climbers. Their motto is, "If you can't have the sun and moon to play with, content yourself with the stars." Around each of the minor royalties visiting in London there is a fairly large and quite brilliant—too brilliant—court of what are called *vieux nouveaux riches,* ambitious Jews whose fortunes were founded in the comparatively ancient times of, say, the Boer War, of foreigners who want to become, or at least pass for English.

When the King and Queen of Roumania come to London they are, and are not, at a loss for company. They are invited to a number of official and quasi-official functions and entertainments dutifully given for them by members of the Cabinet, the Prime Minister, the Master of the Horse—and beyond that they have to accept, and even be grateful for, the association of a little inner circle of first, or, at the best, second generation millionaires who have everything in the world they can wish for except

security of social tenure. Their greatest friends are
the Lord and Lady Astor, and Lord Astor's sister,
Mrs. Spender Clay, of whom Queen Marie is particularly fond.

How little Queen Marie, who claims to be English, knows about Britain is attested by the
rumoured fact—I must give it as such—that she
attempted to marry off her daughter to the eldest
son of the haughtiest of Scottish dukes. It was
simply out of the question. German princes, before
the war the most reliable and abundant supply of
mates for female royalty, were somewhat out of the
fashion; so the Queen finally picked for the Princess
Elizabeth's husband a Prince whose German origin
was passably overlaid by a few coats of Danish and
Greek tradition. It was an ambition easy enough
to fulfill. True, the Crown Prince Georgios was a
nephew of the Kaiser; but he also was Crown
Prince of Greece. He became Queen Marie's
son-in-law.

VI

All things considered, European capitals—the
important ones—offer a rather slippery ground for
the feet of Queen Marie. With Western Europeans she always has a sense of insecurity. But
there is a land of promise for her—the land of
promise for all uprooted: America.

All her uncertainty vanishes, as by touch of the
well-known magic wand, in her contact with Ameri-

cans. Then she is in her element. She is a live
woman—she is very beautiful, she has "pep" and
imagination; she would cut a figure even were she
not a "crowned head," as American newspapers
wistfully put it. But she is a queen; and for Americans she represents the eighth wonder of the world,
the Shulamite, the fulfilment of a hundred and fifty
years' republican dreams, the Queen. She is the
fond union of legend and reality; she, the author of
fairy tales, is a fairy tale herself, and also a live,
honest-to-goodness fairy who will come to lunch if
asked. La Rochefoucauld said: *"Le plaisir de
l'amour est d'aimer."* The Queen is not only loved
by Americans: she loves Americans. Never is she
more conscious of her charm than when she is with
Americans. She ought to be a happy woman, for
she need not take chances on Heaven. She can look
forward to beatification on this earth. On the day
when she lands in America a whole continent will
turn into an altar where the smell of newsprint will
substitute incense.

At the beginning of the war she was represented
in a German paper—was it "Simplicissimus?"—as
saying: "Now we have to mobilize the photograph-
ers." Of course she did not say that; but if she had
said anything of the kind she would have said movie
camera men. Yes, for Queen Marie, America is the
Land of Opportunity. But even in America she
ought to be warned against little social mistakes.
Every once in a while she sends letters to the American press; but she usually selects the wrong news-

papers. Once, on the eve of one of her several visits to the United States that did not come off, she sent out 435 photographs—one to each Congressman.

VII

Still, one must not be unfair to her. She writes letters that make excellent reading and have a real literary quality; and she adores her children—she was prostrated by the death of her son Mircea in the dark days of the war. But one cannot forget her treatment of horses. She rides them to death in three months.

KING FERDINAND OF ROUMANIA

KING FERDINAND OF ROUMANIA

I

THE French statesman Cardinal Mazarin was wont to ask candidates for appointments in his service, "Are you happy?" *Siete felice?*——

The query was a wise one, and the adjective well chosen; for *felice* means more than happy; it implies the idea of good luck. A connoisseur of men, Mazarin knew that unhappy people—people, that is, born with a heavy, brooding temperament, habitual worriers, are usually the unlucky ones—as if Fate took a malicious pleasure in seeking out the thin-skinned, those who feel pinpricks as stabs and scratches as sabre cuts. *"Ce sont toujours les mêmes qui se font tuer,"* says the French proverb. And German slang has a most picturesque expression for these *mêmes,* for the person in whose pursuit misfortune goes out of its way—it calls him a *Pechvogel,* a "pitch bird" literally. He is an inverted Midas whose touch turns gold into lead.

If externals alone determined people s lives King Ferdinand of Roumania might, indeed, be called a happy man, and a lucky one, too. He reigns over a peaceful country of seventeen million inhabitants, potentially one of the richest lands in Europe, just doubled by a victorious war; he is not unpopular; he has a lovely wife, good shooting, and, in his library, many fine books, among which those by Anatole France are even cut. Still, if one looks a little more closely at the chart of his life, it becomes apparent that he has not been favoured by Fate as much as he could desire. There was a little joker, as American slang has it, concealed somewhere in almost every one of the gifts bestowed upon him by a squint-eyed Providence.

To begin with, he might be called good-looking, but for—That "but for" has pursued him all his life like a second shadow. He is slim and fair; he has well-shaped hands and a small head, with a long nose that might express character; but his forehead is narrow to the extreme, the forehead of a man who is shy as well as obdurate. That, however, is not the worst of it. When he was born it was found that his ears protruded like the wings of a windmill; as if an impatient teacher had precociously pulled them, anticipating by years some childish trespass. A nurse was instructed to flatten down the rebellious flaps by the application of bandages. During the first months of a baby's life that defect is corrected easily enough. But the nurse forgot about the bandages, and Prince Ferdinand was marked for life by ears the shape and size of which were not compensated for by any special acoustic capacity.

KING FERDINAND OF ROUMANIA

It is a commonplace to speak about the relation of people's character and their exterior. A physical trait will infallibly influence a sensitive and self-conscious youth such as Prince Ferdinand of Hohenzollern-Sigmaringen grew up to be. For him it is to pass through life full of a good will toward men and things which he vainly struggles to express adequately. He has a kind heart; he has a genuine sense of duty. But over the council of his mental and moral traits shyness presides, a relentless chairman. He is the King with the Inferiority Complex.

When in 1866 Prince Charles of Hohenzollern-Sigmaringen—of the elder, Catholic, non-reigning branch of the House of Zollern—was offered the throne of the then Principality of Roumania, he was at first inclined to refuse. He consulted Bismarck, who advised him to accept, but in a rather flippant spirit. *"Cela vous fera des jolis souvenirs de jeunesse,"* the Iron Chancellor remarked. For once Bismarck guessed wrong. Charles accepted, and before long Prince Carol became King—a wealthy and important King at that, whose friendship was sought by Czar and Emperor. He established in Roumania the House of Hohenzollern—and today Roumania is the only country where a Hohenzollern still reigns.

Thus one of Charles's dreams was fulfilled. He became the founder of a dynasty. Another dream —to become the founder of a family—remained unfulfilled. He ardently hoped for a son—his wife gave him a daughter, and this daughter died young.

But he had nephews, and one of these, Prince Ferdinand, was elected Principe Mostenitor, heir-prince, by the Roumanian diet.

"Lives of crown princes remind us. . ." They remind us, in the first place, of the tribulations of Frederick the Great when he was not great as yet. He led, as everybody knows, a dog's life, while his father was still alive and kicking—very literally so. But even at its best a crown prince's position is anything but enviable, if judged by the standards of his own class. Firstly, there is the usual feeling of the heir to a great fortune, the "too good to be true" feeling: "I shall never come into my own." Then, they have to contend with the natural jealousy and distrust on the part of the monarch, whose death in their heart of hearts they cannot help hoping for. That jealousy and distrust, just as naturally, breed in them a spirit of antagonism, a critical attitude with a strong emotional accent, as Freudians would say. Queen Victoria steadfastly refused the co-operation of her eldest son, and even declined to share with him the knowledge of political and diplomatic affairs which she accumulated during her unusually long and eventful reign. It so happened that his mother's jealousy was for the Prince of Wales a blessing in disguise. It turned him loose on life at large, and his contact with unexpurgated reality, maintained through the long years of his waiting, made him a very wise King indeed, one of the most human and humane in modern times.

II

In a sense, the lot of the Crown Prince Ferdinand was somewhat better. King Carol did not keep him at arm's length. He consulted his prospective successor, taught him, treated him much as the head of a big commercial concern would treat an earnest and ambitious son. But Ferdinand was labouring under what is perhaps, short of that lack of restraints which makes the criminal, the greatest of moral handicaps—an exaggerated shyness, a lack of self-confidence. His subjects-to-be did not make things easier for him. Roumanians have a great many defects, but one of the qualities of these defects is an overdose of cleverness. They are too clever to be good. Now here was this young and timid foreigner who did not speak their language, whose mental processes were obviously slower than their own, who was not "in" on the great many personal intrigues, animosities, *ad hoc* alliances, log-rolling constellations that make up ninety per cent of the political life in small countries (as in great ones), and who was, nevertheless, destined to rule them eventually. They were far from accepting that eventuality, those potential subjects. Worse even, Prince Ferdinand himself had his doubts as to the happy ending. His uncle the King was healthy and strong. The King's mother was still alive, a very energetic lady of ninety. Ferdinand felt that his chance would never come, that his uncle would outlive him.

Most of the mischief that mars this best possible
of worlds is not the doing of evil people. Hundred
per cent wickedness is a rare phenomenon, as rare
as genius; there is not enough of it to go around. It
is the sentimentalists who are responsible for the
majority of our messes. Intent on the right, but
with too little judgment, they occasionally blunder
their way to justification; but most of the time they
merely act as section hands on the line of com-
munication to hell. Bad people commit crimes,
but sentimentalists commit mistakes, which, as the
French rightly say, are much worse.

Queen Elizabeth of Roumania, better known under her pen name as Carmen Sylva, was a sentimentalist. The most conspicuous thing about her
was her heart. She was one of those beings who
not only feel everything with the deepest intensity,
but who make no secret of the fact. She quivered
and throbbed and sighed and loved all the time.
Emotional strain was for her what water is for a
fish. Superlatives were the only words she used,
and she talked a good deal, and wrote as much.
Her favourite preoccupation was being at the mercy
of somebody or something. She was not only at
the mercy of her own loves; she was at the mercy of
the loves of other people, of the first comer. She
was, in a word, what in the language of the United
States is somewhat rudely but graphically described
as an easy mark. One of her maids-of-honour,
Helene Vacaresco, rather a clever and gifted person, conquered her completely. Mlle. Vacaresco

wrote. Prose, poetry, anything. She paid Her Majesty the subtle compliment of translating her works into French. The Queen regarded her as her best friend. One day the Queen had an inspiration.

Roumanians, notwithstanding their German rulers (wags said, because of them) were even then a strongly Francophile people. The King was sneered at as a Prussian. The Queen had a poet's imagination; also, a poet's lack of practical sense. She wanted to help the King in overcoming the general antipathy against things German which included the dynasty. The Crown Prince, true enough, was a German. But let this German Crown Prince marry a Roumanian woman, and then—In a word, Carmen Sylva conceived the brilliant idea of a marriage between the Crown Prince Ferdinand and the translator of her works into French, Mlle. Vacaresco.

The Queen lived in Roumania, but she thought in a vacuum. One of the trifles she forgot was her own *raison d'être*. She forgot how she had come to be Queen in Roumania. The Roumanian statesmen chose a foreigner to rule them because they would never choose a Roumanian. Charles of Hohenzollern-Sigmaringen was King of Roumania not so much by grace of God as by grace of the mutual jealousy of the great Roumanian clans. And the Roumanian politicians did not go to Germany for a King merely in order to be saddled with a Roumanian Queen.

Meanwhile Ferdinand and Helene were left to themselves a good deal. They were photographed together. Suddenly Queen Elizabeth sprang Carmen Sylva's idea on the Cabinet. She announced the engagement. The Cabinet, for once, put down its foot like one man. Mlle. Vacaresco would never do. The Cabinet won. The Queen was deeply mortified. Mlle. Vacaresco had to leave the country. She went abroad in quest of solace and found it in collecting newspaper clippings about herself and, after a while, in publishing a book on "Kings and Queens I Have Known." Ferdinand also went abroad, in quest of a bride. After a while he found one.

He found a wife who might have been Queen of England, and who now was willing to live with him in his distant and comparatively unimportant country. Princesses of the Blood usually marry because it is the easiest escape from being bullied into marrying somebody else. The second suitor often has a good opportunity prepared by the refusal of the first. In 1893 the Crown Prince Ferdinand married Princess Mary, daughter of the Duke of Edinburgh, and brought his wife home to Bucharest.

III

He was happy. But his bliss was not unmitigated. The eternal "but for" arose again. We know the story of the poor man who quite unexpectedly inherits a huge fortune from some long-forgotten second cousin in the Antipodes. He who has led a quiet, solitary life, reasonably contented in fulfilling his simple wants, is now infested by a host of friends whose emergence was just as sudden as that of the heritage. His door is besieged by beggars, amateur and professional; his mail is swamped by wonderful offers of infallible investments. His life is poisoned, and he ends by wishing back his poverty. The story of the man who marries one of the most beautiful women in Europe is rather analogous. Exceptional beauty in one's wife is a mixed boon. One enjoys it to a degree, of course. But then, one seldom sees the face of a person one has lived with for years. One is envied; but one does not envy oneself. Those who envy you have almost more fun than yourself; for they enjoy vicariously a happiness that for you has become, more or less, a mere routine.

And Princess Marie, as she called herself, was as audacious as her husband was shy. Her adventures on the Riviera are remembered—daring though, in the event, harmless escapades at masque balls and the like. Then there was the stranger who saw her in front of a milliner's window and asked her permission to buy her the hat she was admiring. "Certainly," she said and stepped into the shop, followed by the man whose ardour materially cooled when she gave her name and address. Such anecdotes could be multiplied.

But this one will give a taste of her husband's difficulties.

One of these difficulties was geography. The poet Ovid wrote his Tristia because he was exiled to Tomi by an angered Cæsar; and Tomi was in Roumania. Every married woman sooner or later in life passes through the phase of Ibsen's heroine Nora, though most are not conscious of what is happening to them, and resign after a brief and futile flurry. It is one thing to see, for a short interlude, another man opposite one at the breakfast table; quite another to shed the chains that have been forged forever. One day Princess Marie left Roumania for her mother's home, resolved never to return. Months passed, advisers were consulted, and some of them were of opinion that the departure was not only final but also for the ultimate good. Princess Marie, they said, knew not a good thing when she saw it. She had had the privilege of living in Roumania, and did not appreciate it. M. Maioresco, who later became Premier, was especially unrelenting, and was supported by Queen Carmen, who had forgotten nothing. But more months passed, and at last a baby was born to the Crown Princess. Prince Ferdinand, as always, shrank from a violent decision. He was good. He forgave. It is difficult for courtiers to be *plus royaliste que le roi,* especially when the king appears in his *rôle* of husband. There is a Chinese proverb which says, "You always get your own food in a chipped bowl." Prince Ferdinand, he of the inferiority complex, had long ago resigned himself to the chipped bowl. His forgiveness was part intrinsic kindness, part surrender to fate, part a sense of duty as future ruler. It was not only his domestic happiness that was served to him in cracked china.

Like a real feudal lord, like a true gentleman, he was extremely fond of hunting. It was his great relaxation from the very tiring occupation of a king which is not unlike that of a managing editor of a great newspaper; it consists of signing a few state papers and reading a great many newspapers. The greatest sport for a Roumanian gentleman is the bear hunt. One was organized for the Crown Prince. He had been looking forward to it for weeks. He was thrilled with expectancy. For two full days he climbed difficult mountain passes, yearning for the encounter. At last the bear appeared. The Prince shouldered his rifle. Suddenly the bear rose on its hind legs and danced. It had been commandeered by an all too obliging host, anxious lest his princely guest should not have good sport. The Prince went home, furious. The story swept Roumania like a cataract.

Another of his subjects asked him to a pheasant shoot. It was a bad year for pheasants, so a train-load of birds, in boxes, was imported from France and Germany. They were let loose in the woods, but when the great moment arrived they refused to rise. The beaters were at a loss. They performed extra antics to no avail—the pheasants stood, or rather lay, pat. It was very pathetic indeed. Poor Prince! His bear had risen; his pheasants did not. It was wrong all around. It was Fate.

IV

Another pleasure of Kings is the war game. For that Prince Ferdinand inherited a taste from thirty generations of Hohenzollern ancestry. More directly, he inherited it from his uncle and predecessor, King Charles, who was a good soldier and achieved great distinction in the Russo-Turkish war of 1877. Ferdinand had had his share of manœuvres. He yearned for the real thing. In 1912 Bulgaria and Serbia fought shoulder to shoulder against Turkey. Having been friends and allies for such a long time—six full months— they decided it was getting too much for them, and fell on each other's throats. Roumania had interests at stake. She intervened. At last, a war! Prince Ferdinand was appointed in command. His mouth watered. The great moment! He conceived strategic plans, envisaged great battles, dreamed victories. Alas for him! the Bulgarians refused to fight. They surrendered with their whole army. The bear had risen. It was wrong. The Bulgarians lay down. Wrong again. Meagre though the Roumanian victory was, it was bought at a Pyrrhic price. The Bulgarians had cholera, and they infested the victors. The farce all but turned into tragedy.

In the war of 1913 the Roumanian generals had
not tasted blood. But they smelt it a little, and
decided it was good. They looked forward to their
next chance. The world war was lurking below
the line of the horizon. At the end of 1914 it
seemed as if there had been a turn in the fortunes
of the Crown Prince Ferdinand. His uncle, whom
he had believed imperishable, died, and the Crown
Prince became King. He also became Commander-
in-Chief of the Roumanian army. He lived up to
the exigency of the moment. He designed a
new uniform. It was one of the great achievements of his life. But still greater ones were in
the offing.

The world war was on. It was only a question
of time—Roumania, with her army clothed in the
brand-new uniform devised by the King, was to
step in at the right moment. With her powerful
allies staunchly on her side, she was sure to win.
Just who these powerful allies would be, whether
the Entente or the Central Powers, was for the
moment undecided; but that was a secondary consideration. On paper Roumania was a kind of
non-resident member of the Triple Alliance; but
Italy had been a regular member, and still . . .
The majority of the Roumanian people were
pro-Ally; and Ferdinand inherited from his uncle
King Carol among other pleasant and useful
heirlooms a very keen hatred of his kinsman the
Kaiser.

In the spring of 1916 the fateful hour struck.

The Russian government assured King Ferdinand that the Bulgarians would desert the German cause as soon as they saw that they would have to fight against the Russians who were to be sent to aid Roumania. Marshal Joffre telegraphed that Austria was as good as beaten, that Roumania would not meet with any resistance on the road to Budapest, that she was on the eve of realizing her long-cherished dream of annexing Transylvania. Roumania was swept into the war on the side of the Allies by a tidal wave of hope and enthusiasm. The Commander-in-Chief was happier than anybody else.

This time the adventure of the dancing bear was not repeated. Germany realized that she was staking all. Troops were rushed east from Verdun and hurled against the Roumanians. The Russian army ran true to form; that is, it ran. The Roumanian government, headed by the King, had to evacuate Bucharest and transfer to Iassy. For another year resistance dragged along. Then came the *débâcle,* and King Ferdinand was compelled to sign the separate peace. He had to dismiss his pro-Ally ministry and to surround himself with the old pro-German clique.

Another turn of fortune's wheel, and Germany was downed. The King and Queen returned to Bucharest in triumph. The incredible came to pass: Roumania emerged from a lost war with her territory and population doubled, with her national dream completely realized. She gained far more,

comparatively, than either France or England. It
was nothing short of a miracle.

Nor did the wheel of fortune, once started in the
right direction, stop at this one winning number.
Roumania had her share of the spoils; now she was
to taste military triumph, all the sweetness of revenge over the hereditary enemy. The Soviet Government of Hungary was nearing its end; but it
was for the Roumanian army to administer the
death blow. Ferdinand could now enter Budapest
at the head of his victorious troops. But the chance
came too late. The King had lost zest in military
adventure. He disliked the idea of a war which
was seventy-five per cent politics and only a quarter
fighting. Riding in triumph over the little Jew
Béla Kun did not whet his fancy. He stayed at
home while his regiments marched into the Magyar
capital.

Suddenly he felt a thirst for Life, with a capital L. Now it was he who passed through the
stage of Nora. He wanted to see the world. He
was past fifty, and he had never seen Paris. He
craved Paris. It took him a year to carry out his
plan. But at last it was realized. He was in Paris.
He placed a wreath on the monument of the Unknown Warrior of France; he visited the tomb of
Napoleon at the Invalides. In a very substantial
sense, this was more than a pleasure trip. It was
a great victory that he scored at last in an old
family feud. He was a Hohenzollern; and he was
in Paris. Where was his kinsman the Kaiser,

where was the Crown Prince? They could never, never, never hope to enter the earthly paradise called Paris. No Hohenzollern of the Protestant, imperial branch could. The Sigmaringen branch, which now was the only ruling one, the royal house of Roumania, had always regarded itself the true, the elder line of the Hohenzollern family; but for centuries they were overshadowed by the younger line, the upstart Brandenburgians, who had achieved their greatness simply because their ancestor, a monk, broke his vow and stole the estates of his order. For once in his life, there in Paris, Ferdinand felt like a conqueror . . .

V

In this twentieth century of ours what one might call the fairytale view of kingcraft and kingship is still a popular one. Newspapers and magazines of the order euphemistically termed yellow picture the rulers of this world as childish persons impossibly happy in their resplendent uniforms, with their breasts covered with no end of ribbons and stars. Nor are their heads forgotten—albeit drawn as mere pegs to hold their crowns. Kings in newspapers always wear their crowns to breakfast. There is something to be said for that version. Resplendent uniforms are actually worn at not a few court ceremonies, ribbons and stars are treasures coveted even by those who have the right to bestow them and thus ought to know what they are worth; and as to the heads surmounted by crowns that in real life are mostly metaphoric, in most cases the less said the better.

And yet behind the unreal glamour of their anachronistic existence the few kings and queens still extant lead an anxious and cramped life, desperately struggling to keep pace with a time that is running away from them. First of all—not that this is put forward as a revelation—there is the daily risk of attempts on their lives. Secondly, there is the political danger, ever-growing, of revolution. The spectre of unemployment haunts sovereign dreams oftener than ordinary mortals would think. Some years ago an attempt was made on the life of the King of Spain as he was riding in a carriage up the Champs Élysées on the side of President Poincaré. When all was over the latter asked his guest how he felt. "Oh, I am getting used to it," Alfonso replied. "This is the third incident of its kind. There were two attempts made on me before I was twenty-one. *Ce sont les risques du métier.*"

There are other risks connected with the trade. The same King Alfonso was, in the days after the Armistice, asked by a friend of the writer whether opposition to his reign was strong in Spain. "Since 1914," the King replied, "thirty-nine dynasties have lost their thrones. One must always be ready for everything."

That wonderful London institution, Lloyd's, is, as the reader knows, prepared to insure one against any kind of risk. The premium quoted on Spain continuing a monarchy is very high indeed. Even higher is the rate of the life insurance policy paid for by the King of Spain. The risks of the trade, as he himself put it, are held against him. Bankers are reluctant to lend him money—his personal income is not very great, and a republican régime may repudiate the debts of a deposed king.

Protective mimicry is a weapon of the weak, and kings are not above taking a leaf from the book of the squirrel whose fur turns white in winter. American dowagers at Paris and Philadelphia may be more royalist than the Duke of Orléans, but kings are sometimes less monarchistic than their office. The King of Italy has declared repeatedly that he was a Socialist. One of the chief republican leaders in Spain relates that King Alfonso once said to him: "If I were not King I would be a republican." According to certain malicious reports in the household of one of the major European monarchs still undethroned rehearsals for a revolutionary emergency are held at intervals, like fire drills in a department store. And yet, with all its difficulties and extra risks, the king game still finds its amateurs. They are recruited from among the class which the English, with their divine snobbishness, describe as "minor royalties," princes of the blood whose status corresponds to that of the sons of second sons within the peerage.

When sovereigns write letters to their colleagues they address them as *"Mon très cher frère."* But this is a mere manner of speaking. There are no brotherly feelings lost between kings. They know one another little, love one another less, and they don't try to please one another as much as they might. In the unreal universe of the royal courts one of the important realities are the little pieces of ribbon. They are coveted not only by professional courtiers, war profiteers, young visiters from the States and other climbers. Even the kings themselves adore them, that is, those bestowed by other kings, much as beautiful and idle women adore jewellery. One of Prince Ferdinand's great ambitions in life was to possess the two highest-prized pieces of ribbon in Europe, the Order of the Garter and the Order of the Golden Fleece, respectively distributed by the King of England and the King of Spain. Prince Ferdinand never received either.

One of the most pronounced characteristics of a king is his extreme touchiness in the matter of rank. This is a trait seldom perceived by his subjects—just because they are subjects. But it is all the more apparent in the intercourse with his equals, other royalty.

Poor King Ferdinand! He could never forget an experience he had as Crown Prince. At the funeral of King Edward VII. Prince Ferdinand followed the cortège in a brougham which he shared with the Crown Prince of Serbia. It was awful.

A King of England is not buried every day, and Ferdinand had looked forward to this occasion. All his fun was spoiled. On that day his inferiority complex received its hallmark.

THE RISE OF ELEUTHERIOS VENIZELOS

THE RISE OF ELEUTHERIOS
VENIZELOS

I

EUROPEANS whose memory reaches beyond the Great Divide of modern history, August 1, 1914, may remember a quaint word that greeted them with fair regularity at their breakfast on windy Spring mornings from Page 1 of their favourite newspaper. It was a composite word, a sort of linguistic chimæra: comitadji. It was an extremely expressive word, for its very derivation and structure were symbolic of its meaning. The first half of the word was, of course, the French *comité*. To this was tacked the Turkish suffix—*dji*, denoting connection or occupation. In other words, literally the comitadji was nothing more thrilling than a committeeman. Actually he was a hundred times more thrilling than a committeeman. For the committee which originally gave the name to the comitadji was the Supreme Committee of Macedonia and Adrianople, headed by the redoubtable Bulgar, terror of European chancelleries, Boris Sarafov. Later the name was applied to the membership of any political organization of

Christians in European Turkey. Thus one spoke
of Serb comitadjis, and the common term used in
Continental newspaper parlance for members of
the Greek irredentist society, the *Ethniké Hetairia,*
too, was comitadji.

Now this hybrid word covered an amphibious
specimen of humankind. Of course, comitadjis of
the lower ranks were plain peasants of the Balkan
type, accustomed to transmute their plowshares
into swords at a moment's notice. But their leaders, or at least some of them, were different. One
day you would meet, in a Vienna or Paris café, a
gentleman in a top hat, frock coat, white waist-
coat and patent leather shoes. He would speak
perfect French or German, as the case might be;
he would have conventional manners, and perhaps
the only unusual features about him would be a
fiery black moustache of extra length and a no
less fiery look in eyes of extra blackness. You
would learn on inquiry that the distinguished gentleman was a lawyer or professor from Sofia or
Filippopoli or Athens, and naturally you would
refrain from examining his hip pocket, which as
likely as not would contain a sixshooter. But then,
three or four days later you might meet the same
gentleman somewhere in the Macedonian hills, and
you would be justified in not recognizing him at
once. For now he would be dressed in a cotton
shirt, wide breeches tucked into boots, a flat round
cap, cartridge straps crossed on the chest, and a
belt harbouring a couple of pistols and a yataghan

ELEUTHERIOS VENIZELOS

or two. You would, even more punctiliously than
before, abstain from investigating his pockets, one
of which might or might not contain a novel by
Anatole France or a handy edition of Plato's
dialogues.

And this fierce-looking warrior would shoot a
cigarette out of your mouth from a distance of
ten yards with the same ease as the frock-coated
lawyer of the Paris hotel lobby would have, a few
days earlier, delivered a learned disquisition on
the historic dispute detween the Bulgarian Exar-
chate and the Oecumenical Patriarchate. Man is
a creature of adaptation; and strange conditions
produce strange variants. The noun comitadji,
with its French front and Turkish rear, expressed
the double-faced necessities of the life from which
it sprang.

The comitadji season usually began late in
March or early in April. For twenty years prior
to the Great War the news of the thawing of snow
in the Balkan passes was a signal to editors in
Vienna, Budapest, Berlin, Paris and London to
bring up reinforcements to the telegraph desk; for
the comitadjis might go on the rampage any moment, and there was no telling what that might
lead to. Comitadji field activities were classed
under two principal headings. "Fighting for the
liberty and rights of Christians" was one. This
meant killing as many Turks as possible. "Read-
justment of the ethnical balance" was the other.
This meant, for the Bulgars, killing as many Serbs

and Greeks as possible; for the Serbs and Greeks, killing as many Bulgars as possible.

All this, of course, was done by the Turkish half of the comitadji. The French half wrote articles and letters to Western newspapers, negotiated loans in more or less delicate ways, and generally pulled such wires as were within reach. The two activities converged in causing headaches to the diplomatists of Europe. Theirs was a strenuous life, full of change and surprise and danger. To be a good comitadji one must be a person of versatile gifts and great endurance. To be a very good comitadji one must be a genius. Very good comitadjis were accordingly rare.

II

In reading Mr. Robert Lansing's chapter on Eleutherios Venizelos in his volume "The Big Four and Others of the Peace Conference" one is struck by the notion that the word comitadji was performing little antics in the subconscious section of the otherwise so orderly mind of America's Foreign Minister. To Mr. Lansing the personality of the Greek Premier was the most perturbing among all the strange phenomena of that unusual foregathering. And the worst of it was that he could not satisfactorily account to himself for the reasons of his disquietude. He knew that M. Venizelos was a great man—he was told so from all sides, and he had the evidence of his own eyes. He believed

that "the views of M. Venizelos were given greater
weight by the Big Four than those of any other
single delegate at Paris." In consideration of
which, and also of his own first-hand impressions,
it seemed to him "almost heretical" to have a feeling of uncertainty as to M. Venizelos's real character. Nevertheless Mr. Lansing, with his usual
painstaking honesty, did not balk even at the moral
risks of heresy, and refused to accept M. Venizelos
at his current exchange value.

The misgivings which thus drove Mr. Wilson's
conscientious Secretary of State to the verge of a
spiritual abyss, were two. First, he knew that M.
Venizelos had been, in an earlier period of his career,
"in repeated revolts against constituted authority
and had lived as an outlaw in the mountains of
Crete." This was bad enough; what was much
worse was that M. Venizelos did not look the part.
He was,

. . . in appearance, in manner, and seemingly in temperament,
the opposite of a typical revolutionist, especially of a Greek
revolutionist whom popular imagination pictures as a swarthy,
passionate brigand bristling with weapons.

To an observer thus sharing the orthodox conception of what a man who had been in repeated
revolts against constituted authority ought to look
like, nothing could be more disappointing and per-
plexing than the exterior of M. Venizelos.

His appearance was, on the contrary, that of a sensitive

student. He might have been a professor in some great European university spending his days in interpreting the unearthed treasures of Crete's prehistoric civilization or in poring over faded manuscripts containing the Hellenic philosophies of ancient days. Of medium height and with little superfluous flesh, with hair and beard white and thin suggesting premature old age, M. Venizelos was not distinguished in form, feature or bearing. His complexion was ruddy, his eyes bright and clear, and his mouth gentle with generous mobile lips. He stooped in walking and his attitude in standing was shrinking, almost apologetic. One could hardly avoid the feeling that here was a man too modest, if not too timid, to be a great intellectual force in world affairs, too simple of soul to mingle in the jealousies and intrigues of European politics, and too idealistic in thought to pit his mind against the materialism and cleverness of the trained diplomats and political leaders assembled at Paris to draw a new map of Europe.

Nor was this all. This mildness of appearance and manner, continues Mr. Lansing, was further enhanced by M. Venizelos's smile and voice.

When he smiled, his whole face lighted up with benevolence and friendliness. His smile was his great charm, a charm that was emphasized by the soft and gentle tones of his voice. Everything about him seemed to diffuse goodness. He appeared to be living in an atmosphere of virtuous thought and kindly purpose.

His whole personality, concluded Mr. Lansing, contradicted this record.

Mr. Lansing's doubts and apprehensions were not shared by his chief. President Wilson—so M. Venizelos's biographer, Mr. S. B. Chester notes on the authority of Secretary Josephus Daniels, "was said to have placed Venizelos first in point of personal ability among all the delegates" at Paris. Mr. Wilson's admiration of the Greek statesman's brilliant qualities dated from their very first meeting, to which reference is made by Dr. Dillon in his "Inside Story of the Peace Conference."

M. Venizelos [writes Dr. Dillon] hastened to call on President Wilson as soon as that statesman arrived in Europe, and, to the surprise of many, the two remained a long time closeted together. "Whatever did you talk about?" asked a colleague of the Greek Premier. "How did you keep Wilson interested in your national claims all that time? You must have—" "Oh no," interrupted the modest statesman. "I disposed of our claims succinctly enough. A matter of two minutes. Not more. The rest of the time I was getting him to give me the benefit of his familiarity with the subject of the League of Nations. I was greatly impressed by what he said.

Notwithstanding the respect and sympathy which from the time of this conversation he conceived for the champion of the Hellenic cause, and with the expressions of which he was not sparing, Mr. Wilson to the very last supported the Bulgarian claims against Greece. The President was noted for his happy faculty of dissociating personal likes and dislikes from considerations of State.

III

In all fairness to Mr. Lansing it should be said

that his perplexities were shared by not a few. The character of Greece's Prime Minister and quasi-dictator was, and has remained, if not an enigma, at any rate a controversial subject. Largely, there were in the West of Europe three groups, or rather layers, of opinion concerning him, graded according to information and sophistication, and decreasing proportionately.

In Allied lands the large majority of newspaper readers naturally swallowed what Mr. Lansing would call the orthodox view, promulgated officially and semi-officially by the newspapers and the innumerable information bureaus and other propaganda agencies. According to this version, Venizelos was perfection itself, one of the great men of the period, the saviour of his country.

As the one criterion by which this judgment was arrived at was obviously the usefulness of M. Venizelos for the military purposes of the Allies, a goodly section of liberal opinion both in England and America was anti-Venizelist, holding that the Greek statesman was a militarist and imperialist, an exceedingly clever but also exceedingly unscrupulous politician, willing though hardly blind tool of the Entente. This "heterodoxy" was substantially reinforced by the high-handed methods employed by the Allies to curb Constantine. One weakness of liberals is their *a priori* sympathy for the under dog, quite frequently uninquisitive as to whether the dog in question deserved his nether position or not, and what he would do should he get uppermost. Thus there arose among British Liberals and Labourites, and a certain section of American intellectuals a tender regard for Constantine unwarranted, in the eyes of the initiate, by his record, and explicable only as a reaction to too much governmental affection for Constantine's antagonist.

The third, and smallest group consisted mostly of officials and specialists who had opportunity either to come into personal contact with the Greek Premier, or else to study his character and activities from close range. Some of these men had approached him with an open-minded expectancy not entirely untinged by diffidence, determined partly by the reasons just dissected, and partly by a prejudice somewhat akin to Mr. Lansing's apprehensions. In all honesty it must be stated that there existed in the West a distrust of Greece in general and of Greek politicians in particular, a distrust which broad-minded and cultivated Greeks deplored, but could not, in their heart of hearts condemn as altogether unjustified.

M. Venizelos conquered this distrust. There were in him, below the layer of his most obvious qualities,—his eloquence, his tremendous intellectual *élan,* his somewhat cool sweetness of temper, and his unswerving directness of purpose,—qualities evoking admiration rather than affection,—a certain simplicity, an unusual moderation—infallible mark of the imaginative—and an indifference to personal advantage that inevitably struck those who grew familiar with him or his record. If these traits, labelled by Mr. Lansing as Venizelos's idealism, and distrusted by him as disingenuous, constituted a mask, it was a mask that fitted perfectly and behind which no one ever peered. If this idealism was not genuine, it was at any rate never betrayed.

IV

What was the record of this remarkable man which, in Mr. Lansing's wistful words, so contradicted his personality?

Eleutherios Venizelos was born at Canea, in Crete, on August 23, 1864. His father was a well-to-do merchant who had suffered persecution for his Greek patriotism from the Turkish rulers of the island. His advent was ushered in by a cycle of legends—how many invented *ex post facto* it is impossible now to tell. One modestly relates how little Venizelos was born in a cattle-shed, in fulfilment of his mother's vow to the Virgin. According to another his mother had dedicated him to St. Eleutherios, the patron, not of liberty, but of delivery. A third tells us that the priest who baptized him said: "I baptize thee Eleutherios, for thou shalt deliver Crete from the Turkish yoke."

A fourth story, not the least interesting one, is authentic. Three children of his parents had died before he was born. So the couple decided to follow with him the one safe procedure, which, ac-

cording to Cretan belief, consisted in pretending
that little Eleutherios was a foundling. He was,
shortly after his birth, "deposited comfortably on
dry leaves outside of his father's house," and duly
found by a friend of the family who "happened"
to pass by. The friend carried the infant into the
house and "persuaded" M. and Mme. Venizelos
to adopt him. No more appropriate *début* could
be imagined for one destined to become a past master in the fine art of diplomatic expediency.

To be sure, the story carries a slight suggestion
of the Moses myth. That Venizelos is a reincarnation of the sun-god is not on record, but one
cannot vouch for the rumours that will circulate
a thousand years hence. Besides, there is something just, or almost, as good. M. Caclamanos,
Greek Minister to the Court of St. James, relates
that when in 1899 M. Clemenceau returned from a
visit to Greece he told the Comtesse de Noailles that
he had found a man—one M. Venizelos—or was
it Venezuelos?—of whom "the whole of Europe
will be speaking in a few years."

Old M. Venizelos was a good Greek. But he
also was a wise father and a shrewd merchant. He
gave his son such education as the facilities of
Canea afforded. When these were exhausted he
wanted him to enter the ancestral firm. Young
Venizelos said he preferred to continue his studies
at Athens. But the father would not hear of it.
For a Cretan Greek it would never do to have too
much education. Too much education gave one

cravings that one could not fulfill, pretences that one could not live up to. It made one restless. Cretans who went to Athens for an education usually ended by becoming revolutionists. That was bad both for them and their families. The place of a well-to-do young Cretan was in the home. Of course, Turkish rule was a nuisance and a disgrace and all that. But it had its good side; for the Turks cared little about trade, and knew less. If one only kept one's peace and paid one's taxes one was allowed to thrive and prosper.

A bitter dispute between father and son ensued. It was settled by the intercession of a friend, M. Zygomalas, the Greek Consul at Canea. Zygomalas recognized the unusual stuff that was in young Venizelos, and induced the father to allow him to go to the University of Athens. Young Venizelos went, and in due course of time returned with the degree of LL.D., and set up to practice the law at the Cretan capital.

He did not remain long at it. Old M. Venizelos was a wise man. In Crete, like in other countries, the law is the jumping-off board to politics for the ambitious. But in Crete, unlike lands of less troubled historic climes, being a politician was merely an incidental phase to a larger, more exciting and more dangerous game: that of revolution.

Young Venizelos had no illusions. Neither had he fears. From the outset he had seen his road clearly. He knew that he was sent to bring not peace, but a sword—for there could be no peace

in Crete as long as the Turks remained there.
There wasn't much of a choice.

> I had to decide [he said later] whether I would be a lawyer
> by profession and a revolutionary at intervals, or a revolu-
> tionary by profession and a lawyer at intervals.

He chose the profession of a revolutionary.

V

It was in the seventeenth century that Crete,
ancient land of Minos, cradle of Ægean civilization, had come, after a rather chequered past under
Byzantine, Latin and Venetian domination, under
the yoke of the Turk. A number of the natives
adopted Islam in order to avoid persecution; there
was some very slight Turkish military coloniza-
tion; but the majority of the population remained
Greek in sentiment and Orthodox in religion, and
even the Moslem converts retained their Greek language. In the second half of the nineteenth century the Christian majority gained rapidly. By
1900 the Moslems shrank to a mere handful.

Between 1821 and '27 Crete participated in the
Greek insurrection, but when in 1830 Greece
achieved independence, the Protecting Powers,
England, France and Russia, decided with that
half-heartedness which was to remain the curse of
Near Eastern politics for another eighty years, that
the largest and most important of the Greek islands
should remain under Turkish rule.

Until 1852, under the exceptionally decent and
enlightened rule of Mustapha Pasha, an Albanian
appointed from Egypt by Mehmet Ali, Crete enjoyed comparative quiet and prosperity.   But in
1852 Mustapha Pasha was rewarded by promotion
to Grand Vizier.   Four years later a rebellion
broke out, and thenceforth until 1912 the history of
Crete is a series of revolts tempered by intermittent
truces.   These outbreaks usually culminated in a
declaration—not of independence, but of union with
the Kingdom of Greece—"Mother Greece" the
Cretans called her; and more than once the Cretans
would have had their way but for the interference
of the Protecting Powers, so called.

The record of the Powers in the Cretan Question
forms one of the stupidest and meanest chapters
in that book of stupidity and meanness, nineteenth
century diplomatic annals.   For any one not utterly
devoid of vision and of a sense of fair play, it must
have been evident that the Cretan problem admitted
of but one lasting solution, and that was union with
Greece, ardently desired by a substantial majority
of the natives.   But the doctors of Europe decided
that the Sick Man was to be preserved on his sick-
bed, and while his estate was suffered to go to the
dogs, his dependents were expected to pay the bills
of physician and apothecary, not to mention the
upkeep of the policemen needed to exact payment.

It is unnecessary here to inquire into the reasons;
in ultimate analysis there weren't any, for the
motives of the Great Powers cannot be dignified

by that name. About the nearest approach to an
excuse for not allowing Crete to join Greece was
that the Moslem minority needed protection;
though why the powers should have preferred to
"protect" the Christian majority under Turkish
government to safeguarding the Moslem minority
under a Greek administration no one not born and
bred a diplomatist can fathom.

Details of the endless squabbles and fights cannot be entered here. But there was a side-issue
that mirrored the main problem in its full glory,
even as the tiniest dewdrop mirrors the mighty sun.
Since the days of Pasiphaë Crete has been the home
of strange yearnings; and in the second half of the
nineteenth century, and the first decade of the twentieth, the governing passion of Cretans was for not
possessing a flag of their own. They said they
were Greeks, and the blue flag of Greece with its
white St. George's Cross was good enough for
them. But the Protecting Powers, ever intent on
protecting the Cretans against themselves, insisted
that if the islanders objected to the Crescent and
Star, they must have a flag of their own.

Accordingly, after much squabble and some experiment, a Cretan flag was devised—a white cross
on a blue field, with a white star on a red field in
the canton. One can imagine the four Ambassadors
(at this time Italy had joined the Protectors)
seated around a table, contemplating the design
just finished, and beaming upon one another in
silent congratulation over their ingenuity and tact.

For not only were the colours of the flag borrowed
from the Greek and Turkish ensigns respectively,
with even the numeric proportion of Christians and
Moslems expressed in the relation of blue and red,
but the Christians could rejoice in having no crescent to wave over their heads, and the Moslems in
having the star.

It was a very pretty flag, and in a way it was
a perfect solution. Its only drawback was that it
did not solve anything. For the Cretan Greeks
refused to swallow, as it were, the new flag. The
moment the Admirals and Consuls, representatives
of the might and majesty of the European concert,
looked the other way, down went the Cretan emblem on the flagstaffs of the public buildings at
Canea, and up went the standard of Greece. After
a while the Admirals discovered in horror what had
happened, and issued orders to strike the Greek
flag and rehoist the Cretan. Sometimes the orders
were obeyed. At other times they were not. In the
latter case the "protecting" fleets of Europe fired
a few shots at the "rebels," and a few Cretans died,
and the Greek flag went down, and a good time
was had by all, including the Grand Vizier at Constantinople, and the editors in Vienna and Berlin,
who for the day were spared the trouble of digging
up topics for special articles from Meyer's Con-
versationslexicon.

And in the meantime Turkish tyranny and corruption and sloth continued under the protection
of the naval guns of His Britannic Majesty and

the French Republic, not to mention the Czar of all the Russians and the King of Italy. Occasionally—and the intervals tended to grow shorter—there were massacres of Cretan Christians by Cretan Moslems, immediately followed by massacres of Cretan Moslems by Cretan Christians, both followed by ambassadorial luncheon discussions, and a note or two, and an *iradé* or two, and a dozen editorials in European newspapers, solemnly stating that a final settlement of the Cretan Question is more desirable and also further off than ever.

VI

In 1896 there was a new insurrection. The *Ethniké Hetairia* of Greece, the organization of the irredentists, smuggled arms and supplies to the rebels; the Greek Colonel Vassos, a brave and resourceful soldier, landed at the head of a semi-official expeditionary force. In February, 1897, Canea was set on fire by the Moslems. It was during that conflagration, says Mr. Chester with an ominousness he seems to be unaware of, that Venizelos rose to the front rank of Cretan leaders.

By May the Cretan events precipitated war between Greece and Turkey. It was a short war—the Greeks were utterly beaten in a month and a day, and sued for peace. But the Cretan revolt continued for a few months longer, although Colonel Vassos and his little army had been recalled to the mainland to serve with the Greek army.

5

For the Cretan insurgents the campaign meant fighting not only the Turkish regulars and their native Moslem confederates, but also the troops of the "protecting" Powers garrisoned in Crete. Venizelos, the young lawyer of Canea, was at war with Europe. When in 1916 Venizelos, as head of his home-made Salonica government, declared war on the Central Powers there were those who could not help perceiving the humour of the situation and smiled at such exuberance of private enterprise. For Venizelos it was *vieux jeu;* for as early as 1896-'97, and later in 1905, he had been fighting England, France, Russia and Italy—not to mention Turkey. It was a mere accident that he did not meet with his death when the Protectors of Crete shelled his headquarters at Akrotiri.

All the qualities which in his later career called forth such admiration were already in evidence during the Akrotiri rebellion; his reasoned, unemotional eloquence, his *sangfroid,* above all, his moderation—most unusual trait in a revolutionist on field duty. A British naval officer who was sent to negotiate with the rebels was struck by nothing so much as by the respectability of their leader. He described Venizelos as a "quiet, reasonable young man" who fully realized the predicament of the Powers.

"Go slow with the Porte," Venizelos said. "Make a feint of coercing us if you have to—I shall restrain my men."

"Why don't you trust us implicitly?" countered the British representative, "instead of forcing our hand?"

Venizelos's answer is the classic statement of
the case of Near East Christians against the
Powers of Europe.

"The European policy," he said, "is invariably the maintenance of the status quo, and you will do nothing for the subject races unless we, by taking the initiative, make you
realize that helping us against the Turks is the lesser of the
evils."

"Damn it, the beggar is right!" wrote the Englishman.*

The story of the Akrotiri revolt condenses in a
strangely graphic way Venizelos's subsequent career. It presents his tendency to rise, skyrocket-
like, to sudden splendour, and vanish again in utter
darkness. In August, 1897, he was elected President of the Insurrectionary Assembly. He was
uncompromisingly in favour of union with Greece;
but things did not go well with the revolutionists,
and by one of those lightning reversals of sentiment which seem to be a feature of Greek politics,
the party opposing outright annexation and content with autonomy under Turkish suzerainty
swelled into a majority overnight. Venizelos was
not only forced to resign from the chair, but was
formally excluded from the Assembly.

Now in Western Europe a blow like that would
be enough to kill a politician, figuratively. In the
primitive, though not unsophisticated, Near East,
where armed force is not the symbol and *ultima*

* Quoted by Dr. Herbert Adams Gibbons.

ratio, but the immediate executor of political power, it is almost enough to kill a politician bodily.

> Eleutherios Venizelos [wrote Biliotti, the British Consul-General at Canea, to Constantinople], whose appointment as President has been cancelled by the General Assembly, and his partisans, twelve in number, were kept prisoners during eight hours in a house at Archanes, which the mob threatened to set fire to, and they were stoned nearly everywhere during their twelve days' return journey to Akrotiri.

And Admiral Harris, the British naval officer in command, reported that Venizelos "narrowly escaped being killed by the populace." The Admiral's report is noteworthy because it brings into relief a highly significant trait of Venizelian strategy. The Admiral accuses Venizelos and his annexationist friends of secretly encouraging the Turks to remain on the island, as autonomy, by curing the worst evils, would delay union with Greece, while continuation of the Turkish tyranny would hasten that event.

The insurrection, like the Greek campaign on the mainland, ended in defeat. Nevertheless Crete —and here for once the Protecting Powers deserve some credit—emerged with important gains. Union with Greece, voted as a matter of routine by the Assembly, was of course nullified; but autonomy was granted, and Prince George, second son of the King of the Hellenes, was appointed High Commissioner under Ottoman suzerainty. The population clamoured for the withdrawal of the Turkish

troops. Fulfilment of this wish might have taken
some time, had not the Moslem hotheads of Canea
committed the indiscretion of massacring a handful of British bluejackets. Thereupon the Powers
ordered the Porte to evacuate the island, and the
last of the Turkish soldiery embarked in November.

VII

Venizelos was defeated, for the first time in his
life—not for the last. Within a year he was on
his feet again. His career resembles that of the
Greek flag on Crete. He could not be kept down
for any length of time. A few months passed, and
he was elected one of the Executive Committee of
five, in charge pending the arrival of Prince
George. A little later the new High Commissioner
appointed him one of his seven Councillors—Ministers of State in everything save title. Venizelos
dominated the Council. Although he held the port-
folio of justice, he was practically Foreign Minister, and negotiated with the Powers concerning
domestic reform and financial assistance.

His relations with the Prince were strained from
the first. George was inexperienced—he was
haughty, rash and vain, self-willed and officious.
In his first interview with M. Sphakianakis, ven-
erable dean of Cretan leaders, the Prince found it
opportune to announce that he had the blood of
Peter the Great in his veins.

"I hope that your Highness will at least spare us

the executions," replied M. Sphakianakis in the
suavest tones.

According to Mr. Chester, Prince George combined the appetite for intrigue with a marked lack
of talent for it. He was constantly touring the
European courts—he was closely related to the
Kings of England and Denmark, and to the Czar.
The expenses were borne by the Cretan people.
But it was all for their good, said the Prince. He
was sure he would achieve results by virtue of his
family connections.

Before long the Prince's administration degen-
erated into a petty tyranny hardly less odious than
that of the Turkish valis of old. Oppression, chicanery, favouritism, corruption were rampant. In
1901 Venizelos was dismissed. He at once took
the lead of the opposition in the Assembly.

During the following four years Prince George's
rule assumed more and more the character of a
minor brand of White Terror. Cretans despaired;
public opinion in Greece was scandalized; nevertheless the "family connections" set through the
renewal of the Prince's mandate for another term.
The opposition, though teased and terrorized in a
hundred ways, limited itself to parliamentary chan-
nels. But in March, 1905, the news was flashed
across Europe that M. Venizelos, at the head of a
little army, had taken to the hills.

This time it was not against the Turks. There
were no more Turks left in the island. It was
Venizelos vs. the House of Glücksburg—prelim-

inary skirmish of a much more famous battle to
come. Venizelos charged that Prince George had
overridden his mandate, nullified the constitution,
and had become the leader of a political party.

The insurrection of 1905 is known as that of
Therisso. There was the usual squabbling, some
desultory fighting between insurgents on the one
hand and international troops on the other. There
was the usual declaration of union with Greece, first
by the insurgents, then by the Assembly at Canea,
under the very nose of the Prince and the European
admirals. Up went the Greek flag—down it went
again. The rebels needed money. Venizelos tried
to borrow 100,000 francs in Greece. He failed.

His ascendency over his countrymen was now
unquestioned and unassailable. His statesmanship
again evoked admiring comment from his opponents, the international agents. The French Consul-
General, like the British naval officer eight years
ago, was struck, above all, by his moderation. M.
Maurouard noted in one of his dispatches that in a
speech made at Therisso before the insurgents
"M. Venizelos was not responsible for a single
violent remark."

Violent remarks were left to the exclusive use of
Prince George, who in various communications addressed to the European chancelleries and in his
statements to the press spoke with extreme bitterness of the mis- and malfeasances of M. Venizelos,
attributed his insurgency to vanity and thwarted
ambition, protested his own innocence, and even

accused some of the Consuls and international
military officers of collusion with the rebels.

But then, the Prince's patience was sorely tried.
His very Ministers deserted him, and joined the
insurgents. The Assembly at Canea demonstrated
its loyalty by adopting a series of reforms, providing for restrictions of the High Commissioner's
prerogative, extending the suffrage, and abolishing
press censorship—all carefully copied from the bill
of grievances with which the insurgents had taken
the field.

By November the Therisso revolt collapsed.
Venizelos and his supporters, having obtained
amnesty from the representatives of the Powers,
surrendered their arms.

Once more Venizelos was knocked out. Once
more he fell—upwards. Within a few months he
was back at his old job negotiating with the Powers
for additional reforms. Within a year his opponent,
Prince George, descendant of Peter the Great and
cousin to half the monarchs of Europe, found it
advisable to board a Greek warship in a hurry and
with omission of music and flowers. He was sup-
planted by M. Zaimis, an experienced and decent
politician, nominated with European authority by
the King of Greece.

M. Zaimis found in Venizelos a willing co-
operator. By the middle of 1909 the situation was
consolidated to such extent that the Powers agreed
to withdraw their troops from the island. Venizelos,
says his biographer, was sufficiently satisfied to

make an eloquent speech in honour of the departing internationals. Lack of a sense of humour was never one of the defects of Venizelos's qualities.

With the removal of the European troops Crete was, in everything but name, a part of Greece. Henceforth justice was administered, decrees were promulgated, in the name of the King of the Hellenes. Greek officers trained and commanded the gendarmerie. Formally, however, the union was not proclaimed until the outbreak of the Balkan war in 1912, and even then the Powers withheld for another eight months their recognition of a status that had obtained for five years.

There is a story of the New York Jew who wandered into a delicatessen store, and, pointing to a juicy ham, demanded a pound of "that cheese." "I beg your pardon," said the dispenser of viands, "that is ham, not cheese." "Are you here to wait on me or to argue with me?" snapped the customer. "I say I want a pound of *that cheese.*" He got it. One of the great traditions of European statecraft was to call a *de facto* ham a *de iure* cheese, whenever required by its ritual.

VIII

By 1909 Venizelos achieved everything there was to be achieved in his native island. Crete, like Macedon for Alexander, had grown too narrow for him. But the wider opportunity was already in the offing.

On January 10, 1910, Venizelos landed at

Piræus. He was forty-six years old. For the next
ten years, remarks his biographer, the story of
Venizelos is the history of Greece.

He was invited to act as official peacemaker in the
dispute between the Military League and King
George. The dispute was the aftermath of nothing
less than a *coup d'état*. Half a year earlier the
officers who had formed the League marched out
to Goudi Hill, near Athens, encamped there and
sent an ultimatum to Premier Rallis. The ultimatum demanded reforms in military and civil
administration. Above all, it demanded the resignation of the Crown Prince Constantine as Commander-in-Chief, and the removal of his brothers
from the army.

Princes of the Blood are seldom popular in
armies. They are too lively a reminder of the un-
equal distribution of duties and rewards in this
world. The officers' corps of a European army is
like a club. However snobbish and narrowly exclusive it may appear to the undesired outsider,
usually full equality reigns within. Now in the
democracy, genuine though restricted, of an officers' corps Princes of the Blood, as a rule, constitute an anomaly of insufferable prerogative. In
peace time they are a nuisance; in war they may
amount to a positive danger. Eugene of Savoy,
the ablest general that ever served the Hapsburgs,
himself a Prince, never accepted a command without stipulating that Archdukes would be strictly
kept at home.

The Greek Princes were numerous. They came from an unusually overbearing breed. Routine promotion was slow. The country was poor. Pay cheques for the officers were not infrequently a few weeks behindhand. The cases of champagne for the Princes were always on time. Some of the officers were patriots; others may have been firebrands; the majority were just plain human beings with a grievance. They discovered certain delicious secrets, well known to carpenters and stonemasons, but as a rule without the scope of the more aristocratic professions. They formed a trade union and struck. They established strike headquarters on Mount Goudi. Unfortunately for their employer, the government, it was impossible to send the army against them; for in this case the strikers happened to be the army.

The effect of the officers' ultimatum was overwhelming. M. Rallis resigned almost before he had read it to the end. The Princes, including the Commander-in-Chief, followed suit. M. Dragoumis was named Premier at the head of what on the continent is called a *cabinet d'affaires*. He had the backing of the Military League.

At the court consternation reigned. The King feared revolution. Uncertainty followed the first shock; for the *coup* did not prove a settlement. The officers had talked politics for years—Greeks hardly ever do anything else. But now the officers tasted acting politics, and found it good. Soon their saner leaders perceived that measures to prevent trees from growing to the sky were in order. There was one man, and one only, in the Hellenic world to handle the situation. The leaders of the Military League sent a delegation to Crete to fetch Venizelos.

Venizelos arrived, and called on the King with the *plein pouvoir* of the officers. King George had no reason to like the man who had spoiled his son's sojourn in Crete so effectively. This man now came as the ambassador of rebels. "I hope," said King George to a friend "that M. Venizelos will soon be hanged from the mast of a battleship."

The pious wish was not fulfilled, and before long the King had occasion to mend his opinion. The devil is never so black as he is painted—not even a Cretan devil. M. Venizelos brought with him to Athens the gift that had earned him in Crete the respect and admiration of the European representatives. It was moderation. If he was a revolutionary adventurer, his manner strangely resembled that of a conservative statesman. If he was a gambler, he gambled with such perspicacity that the game was undistinguishable from legitimate business. He knew that if you only give Time a chance it will work for you. He possessed one of the rarest as well as most effective faculties—mastery of the fine art of waiting. To be able to sit still with a nonchalant dignity; not to shoot until you see the whites of Opportunity's eyes, is the key to success in diplomacy and war, also in that combination of diplomacy and war, love. Marlborough had that faculty, and Cavour; so did Casanova. It is a gift indispensable to snipers—and to makers of history.

Venizelos succeeded in appeasing the old King. A revolutionary who has mended his ways makes the best minister, a French statesman once remarked. The King was scared out of his wits by the prospect of a National Assembly, demanded by the Military League and by Venizelos. The King, as amateur Freudians would say, had a complex on National Assemblies. He had seen one in his youth. It was the foregathering which deposed his predecessor, Otto of Bavaria, and set him on the throne of Greece.

King George, unlike his sons, was a very astute diplomatist. But he was no match for Venizelos. In the end the Cretan had his way. His winning move was a *bravoure* in the best Venizelian manner. He told the King that on the day when the National Assembly convened the Military League would be dissolved. Never has a single stroke killed two flies more thoroughly. Venizelos won the King's heart. He also got rid of the Military League. The Cretan, too, had a good memory. He remembered the fate of Colonel Lapathiotis, the officer whom the League had set up as Minister of War in August and pulled down in December for being too independent in his appointments. "Sometimes a dead ally beats a dozen live enemies," says a Malay proverb.

IX

In October, 1910, Venizelos was appointed Premier. He had a very substantial majority in the National Assembly, and he ran the business with a smooth efficiency that was a novelty at Athens. He immediately started general housecleaning— reorganization of home government, finances, army, navy. And he began to lay the foundations of that foreign policy which culminated in the two victorious wars of 1912 and '13.

Within half a year of his appointment Venizelos sprang a surprise. He rehabilitated the Crown Prince Constantine. In the first transaction that brought these two men together Venizelos played the *rôle* of Santa Claus and guardian angel combined.

Constantine's first appearance before European publicity was in the ill-starred war of 1897, in which he held a command. A chronicler, commenting on his qualifications for the post, remarks that Constantine's cuisine was the best prepared sector of the Greek front. Fortunately for Greece, the war was over in thirty days and one. Returning home from a lost war belongs with the less pleasant features of a Prince's routine. Napoleon III, himself an expert, declared with envy that Francis Joseph was the only monarch in Europe whom his people cheered after a defeat in the field. The campaign of 1897 did not make Constantine very popular in Greece.

In 1909 Constantine, yielding to the ultimatum of the Military League, resigned from the post of Commander-in-Chief and went to Berlin to find solace.

What could be Venizelos's motive in restoring Constantine to good standing in the army? The answer, though a complex one, may be guessed at. Constantine was unpopular with the officers, who despite the disbandment of the Military League still formed Venizelos's mainstay. The Premier incurred grave risks in championing the Crown Prince. But Constantine was not nearly so unpopular with the officers as Venizelos was with the Elder Statesmen of Athens. These politicians had been efficient only in running the machine of their own ascendency. Venizelos wrecked that machine. The politicians perceived that as long as he stayed among them the machine could not be repaired; also, that he had come to stay. This provincial shyster—this Highlander who tucked his trousers into his boots—this professional rebel—this ex-comitadji—presumed to beat them at their own game. The politicians despised him as a backwoodsman and a parvenu; they hated him as the Anti-Christ.

Did Venizelos need an ally? With all his faults, Constantine had his good qualities. He was a good fellow, in his way; he was not over-intelligent. Venizelos discerned in him the makings of a splendid figure-head. The first rumblings of the coming Balkan war were just growing audible. Venizelos, coldest-blooded of men, was generous not so much by impulse as by reasoned conviction. When the Archbishop of Canea, prompted by Prince George, excommunicated him as the leader of the Therisso rebellion, he countered the move by advising the people of Crete to respect and obey the church. What could the Archbishop answer to that?

He saw that sooner or later he would have to deal with the heir to the throne—why not disarm him before he even had a chance to arm himself?

Venizelos trusted his own ability to restrain the undue growth of trees toward the sky. He introduced a bill creating the post of Inspector-General of the army. The bill was passed. Constantine was appointed.

The two Balkan wars were fought, and the peace of Bucarest was concluded. It was in the course of the negotiations of the London treaty, preliminary to the second war, that Venizelos was recognized as a star of the first magnitude on the firmament of European politics. To the Great Powers Venizelos was the conference. M. Clemenceau's prediction was fulfilled.

It was in October, 1910, on the eve of his appointment to Premier, that Venizelos said to King George:

If your Majesty consents to leave me full liberty of action and to ratify my program, I promise to present you in five years with a renovated Greece, capable of inspiring respect and of supporting her rights.

Moderation of statement was always a dominant trait in Venizelos. He promised to the King a renovated Greece in five years. Within three he presented with a doubled Greece, not George himself, for the old King had been assassinated at Salonica, but his son and successor, Constantine.

Yet there was one thing that the Cretan statesman who had fought four Great Powers and survived it, who within a year brought two wars to triumphant conclusion, who even managed to overcome the camarilla of the Elder Statesmen of Athens, could not conquer. It was the inborn diffidence of the House of Glücksburg. Old King George had said to M. Caclamanos: "Venizelos is by far the ablest statesman Greece has produced during my reign." Nevertheless—or shall I say consequently?—the King summoned his old confidant, M. Streit, then Greek Minister in Vienna, to enter Venizelos's cabinet. "M. Venizelos will bear watching," said the King.

There never was any love lost between Eleutherios Venizelos and the House of Schleswig-Holstein-Sonderburg-Glücksburg.

6

CONSTANTINE AND THE FALL
OF VENIZELOS

CONSTANTINE AND THE FALL
OF VENIZELOS

I

WERE the making of history entrusted to writers of motion picture scenarios, they could not devise a more dramatic, even melodramatic, contrast than that separating the antagonists in the duel which was destined to be Greece's contribution to the annals of the Great War. Constantine, scion of a North German princely house, huge, fair, sanguine, shrewd though not too intelligent, bellicose and proud, with a joviality only too often swept away by flashes of temper, amiable on the surface, cruel and self-centered at bottom, wilful rather than strong-willed, is the typical aristocrat—if we accept the blond beast as a definition of aristocracy. Venizelos, the thoroughbred Levantine, small, wiry, undistinguished of feature, as supple physically as mentally, with a lightning intellect, a will like a Damascene blade, at once lithe and ruthless, a manner of extreme suavity screening a cold glow of passion, is the ideal of the man risen from the people —but a people whose plebeian tradition is two thousand years older than the heritage of the proudest Northern aristocracy.

This contrast is in no wise weakened by the paradox that temperamentally Constantine is the more democratic of the two. In Europe a certain spirit of good fellowship, the quality which Americans describe as being a good mixer, is more often found in the politician of aristocratic antecedents than in the leader of democracy; for, while the former, on account of his independence, can afford to be a democrat, in the latter years of solitary struggle engender an intellectual contempt for the human material that is only too apt to be reflected in outward behaviour as aloofness. Indeed, this aloofness was ever one of Venizelos's most marked characteristics—and one which, as both his enemies and friends agree, contributed in no mean degree to his phenomenal fall.

No one is likely to challenge the definition of Constantine as an aristocratic type. After all, that type has its variants no less than democracy. General Gordon was an aristocratic type—so was George Gordon, Lord Byron; so are the Duke of Northumberland and Lord Robert Cecil. The range is wide enough.

But there will be those who object to the description of M. Venizelos as a leader of democracy. Is not his record, these protestants will point out, one of militant imperialism, of exclusive nationalism? True enough. The democracy of which M. Venizelos is a leader and a prototype is the democracy, not of the Russian, but of the French revolution; and the democracy of the French revolution was

KING CONSTANTINE OF GREECE

militant and imperialistic. It was not narrowly national; but it was the father of modern nationalism. The democratic ideal of M. Venizelos is a Greater Greece, uniting within its boundaries all the redeemed groups and segments of the Hellenic race, governed by an all-Hellenic parliament. It is a political, as distinguished from a social, concept of democracy; its stamp is of the year 1848 rather than of 1922.

Mr. Justice Brandeis once referred to Secretary Hughes as one of the most enlightened minds of the eighteenth century. One may call Venizelos one of the greatest statesmen of the early nineteenth century,—perhaps the greatest statesman of the spirit, born of French parentage in the Germany of Stein and Hardenberg and Körner, carried at once to victory and defeat by the Allied arms at Leipzig, stifled by the Congress of Vienna, resurrected and downed again in 1849. Of all European countries that spirit rose to full fruition in Italy alone. The Balkan war of 1912, which brought M. Venizelos to European prominence, was the last wingbeat but one of the national *risorgimento* of the nineteenth century. The last was the phase of the World War which liberated the oppressed races of Austria-Hungary and restored Poland. The difference between the democracy of President Masaryk of Czechoslovakia and that of Premier Venizelos of Greece is the difference between the economic development of Western and Eastern Europe respectively, A.D. 1918.

With their characteristics, physical and mental, presenting such glaring antithesis, is there any wonder that partisanship, in no issue of the war bitterer, should have indulged in conceiving the duel of Venizelos and Constantine as that of Good and Evil, of Light and Darkness, of Ahuramazda and Ahriman? The files of the Constantine-Venizelos polemics furnish the supreme instances of what may be called the demonological interpretation of history. In this case Ahuramazda and Ahriman are interchangeable. According to one school, there is no virtue of which Venizelos is not the incarnation, there is no vice, no depravity of which Constantine is not the horrible example for all ages. Turn the names around, and you have the exegesis and apologetics of the other religion. In the heat of this theological controversy the very characteristics of the opponents are exchanged; to Constantinists their hero appears vested in all the glory of typically Venizelian virtues, and vice versa. One of Constantine's American apologists raises lack of humour to the nth power by seriously asserting that Constantine—that 100 per cent Nordic Teuton, if there ever was one—is a more genuine Greek than Venizelos.

There is perhaps one quality that both hold in common. It is stubbornness. Yet the very agreement spans an abyss of difference. Constantine's will is like a Teutonic knight in full armour, riding his chain-mailed mount to charge. That of Venizelos is visualized by a Japanese wrestler. Or else, to change the figure,—which is the more stubborn —a block of concrete or a girder of steel?

II

There is significance in the fact that each man lacks the most striking quality of the other. The most obvious, also the most effective attribute of Venizelos is his intellectual superiority: of Constantine, his personal magnetism.

The greatest tribute to Venizelos's intellectual power was rendered by Constantine himself. "When he is with me I confess that his arguments are so convincing that I quickly begin to imagine that they are my own," he said once. On the other hand, no one who ever came into contact with Constantine, not even the wildest American correspondent bursting with the ambition to tell him what an unspeakable traitor he was, could remain unaffected by the charm emanating from that kingly personage. A Venizelist lady who wrote a rather vituperative book about him said that no woman could possibly resist the smile of his blue eyes. It would seem that the only mortal, male or female, who did not melt away in Constantine's radiance is M. Venizelos himself.

Certainly the saying, "Every inch a king," has never applied more strikingly to a ruler—and that means a good deal, for Constantine measures six feet six inches. The highest compliment to his splendid physique was probably paid by the American visitor who, issuing from an audience with him, burst into a sigh: "What a wonderful guard for the Harvard eleven was wasted to make a king!" Another admirer from the States declares that Constantine is the "personification of majesty."

On occasions of state, in full dress uniform, with blue and white plumes on his head and his marshal's baton (he has two: a Greek one, and also a Prussian) in hand—verily, no finer specimen of the Blond Beast can be imagined. Much of his charm is explained by the contrast between his majestic appearance and the amiable directness of his manner. How could an American resist when this Scandinavian war god in blue and silver offers him a cigarette and lights it to boot?

We are told that he talks much and well, rather vivaciously, pounding the table now and then, or twirling his silky moustache with his fine long hand. He affects *sangfroid,* but at the same he "registers," like an actor in the movies, every emotion that crosses his system—he is an actor whose favourite *rôle* is pretending that he isn't one.

Perhaps the best symbol of his personality is that tchako with the blue and white plumes about which Mr. Paxton Hibben is so enthusiastic. M. Venizelos, indoors, always wears a little black silk skull cap—reminiscent of Mr. Pickwick and an orthodox Rabbi from Galicia. He and Constantine could no more exchange their respective headgear than their heads.

American visitors adore Constantine. So do his soldiers. Some one has said that the King, though

not a good general, is a good soldier. Why not?
Soldiering is his one passion, his vocation and avocation. He learnt the art in Prussia—a fact of which
both he and his enemies made much, though at different junctures,—at the Staff College, and he was
an officer of the Imperial Foot Guards. But in one
thing he surpasses his Prussian masters. He loves
to go forth among his soldiers and fraternize with
them, and he knows how to do it. He has an excellent memory, and knows hundreds of his soldiers
by their first names.

In the Balkan war of 1912 he distinguished himself by taking Salonica. The inside story of that
feat is intriguing. For one reason or another (to be
unearthed, possibly, some day in the archives of
Berlin or Vienna) Constantine was not anxious to
enter Salonica, and did so only under heavy pressure from Venizelos, who telegraphed to King
George not to allow the Crown Prince to divert the
army into the direction of Monastir. Constantine
was also hailed as the conqueror of Ianina, the
Epirus fortress. Here, again, he received efficient
help from General Danglis, assigned to the task by
Venizelos.

But the greatest military feat that attaches to
Constantine's name, apart from the victory over
the French marines, related below, is connected with
the baptism of his youngest child. Constantine
made the entire army and navy godfather. This
established a direct family tie, considered very
strong in Greece, between him and every soldier and

sailor, the mutual appellation between father and godfather being *"koumbaros,"* equivalent of the French *compère.* Never was an act of courtesy better rewarded. The soldiers and sailors went hysterical with delight. After reviews Constantine is wont to mingle with the soldiers; he shakes hands with them, and calls them by their first name, and they address him, not as "Your Majesty," but as *"koumbaros."* Sometimes democracy, like honesty, is good business.

Constantine always, or at least of late years, understood better than Venizelos how to be on good terms with a crowd. Venizelos could impress a crowd—he could convince a crowd—he could even whip a crowd into a fit of enthusiasm—but Constantine knew better how to play on their affection in the long run. With all his six feet and a half, his Teutonic cast and his gorgeous trappings he was more like a member of a Greek crowd—of any crowd—than the homely but distant Venizelos. After all, the advocate who asserted that Constantine was a more typical Greek than Venizelos, was right in the sense: Constantine was a more typical *man* than Venizelos, who would be set apart in any mass of men by the cold intellectual glow of his genius.

Constantine not only speaks Greek perfectly, but he speaks the familiar idiom of Athènians, whilst Venizelos prefers a puristic, classicized speech. More is revealed by this one detail than by half a ton of propagandist literature.

There is a story how Venizelos, after his arrival in Greece in 1910, made a speech from the balcony of his hotel to a crowd assembled below. The issue that agitated the public mind at the time was: should the National Assembly, elections for which were pending, be a Constituante, or should it merely revise the existing constitution? The difference was vital. A constituent assembly would have mooted the question of the dynasty, of the form of government. A revisionist assembly would occupy itself with reforms of detail, not touching on the form of government at all. The hotheads of the Military League clamoured for a Constituante. The King and the court party sat up nights praying to the Almighty for a revisionist assembly. Venizelos (one of whose chief principles was ever not to allow trees to grow to the sky) sided with the King.

In the course of his speech from the balcony of the Grand Hotel Venizelos remarked, *en passant*: "The Assembly, of course, will be a revisionist body." From every direction shouts came: "We want a Constituante." Venizelos, without raising his voice, repeated with slow emphasis: "I say, the Assembly will be a revisionist body." Reinforced shouting from the crowd: "Down with revisionism! We want a Constituante!" The politicians on the balcony watched Venizelos intently. In a sense that moment marked the parting of roads. Had the Cretan given in to the crowd there's no telling where the affair might have ended. It might have ended in revolution, in a republic, anything. The

popular mood was ripe. Without visible emotion
Venizelos repeated for a third time: "The Assembly
will be revisionist." The crowd was nonplussed.
Never had Athenians been treated like this. There
was an ominous hush—then wild cheering for Venizelos. He won.

The incident, like the matter of the idiom, reveals
much. It gives a flashlight photo of the man of
Akrotiri and Therisso who in the very act of waging
war on four Great Powers of Europe—a Quixotic
act, to say the least—impressed the representatives
of those Powers with his sound respectability, with
his quiet, almost bourgeois, manner. Here was the
rebel leader, who had risen to leadership because he
could shoot as well as talk straight, turned conservative—not in betrayal of his original purpose, but
in strict adherence to it. He had changed his
method, not his end. And that scene on the balcony,
by disclosing a very important aspect of Venizelos's
character, lifts for a second the curtain off his
future. That was not the manner of a Greek
speaker to treat a Greek crowd. The average Greek
politician would have yielded to the crowd—or he
would have argued with it, or harangued, or cajoled,
or threatened it. He would not have ignored it. It
might have been less effective—but it would have
been more Greek. Detachment is not a quality that
a Greek crowd expects from its leaders. A de-
tached Greek is almost a contradiction in terms—
like a spendthrift Dutchman.

Now detachment, if it be a virtue at all, is es-

sentially a lonely, an un-social virtue—the very
word implies loneliness. His detachment would
have set Venizelos apart as a solitary man even
among an unsocial people like Englishmen or Nor-
wegians. But the Greeks are not an unsocial
people—they are social with a vengeance. They
could, and did, admire a man like Venizelos—they
could follow him, even love him—but they could
hardly regard him as one of their own number. And
Venizelos was not an Athenian—not even a Greek
in the strictest sense: he was a Cretan.

In 1910, when Venizelos was first elected to the
Greek chamber, the Turkish government protested
violently his admission on the ground that he was
an Ottoman subject, and when he was seated nevertheless he was, *in contumaciam,* sentenced to death
by an Ottoman court for high treason. The incident
nearly led to a declaration of war. And if the Turks
could never forget that Venizelos was born under
the Ottoman flag, there were not a few Athenians
who could not forget it either, and they took care to
remind the rest. Venizelos was forty-six years old
when he landed in Greece. That detail must not
be lost out of sight.

III

As a speechmaker, King Constantine was less
restrained than his Prime Minister. He was an
emotionalist, apt to run away with his feelings—
sometimes even with those of his audience. There
was the little matter of his speech at Potsdam, in

1913, when he received the baton of a Prussian field marshal from his imperial brother-in-law. The honour, and the recollection of the grand old days when he had been attached to the Prussian Staff College and the 2nd Prussian Foot Guards, made him eloquent.

> I am proud of being a Prussian officer [he said]. We Greeks owe the magnificent victories of our army to the principles of warfare which I and my officers acquired through intercourse with the Prussian General Staff. To the General Staff I owe the knowledge that brought me such brilliant successes in the war.

Now this was both an exaggeration of his own part in the war with Turkey, and a grave act of discourtesy. Constantine may or may not have owed his knowledge to the Prussian Staff College. But with the brilliant successes of the Greek arms the French military mission, called to Greece by Venizelos to reorganize the army, also had something to do. To this Constantine made no reference.

Within twenty-four hours pandemonium was loose in the Paris press. Venizelos (who may or may not have owed his knowledge of how to treat the indiscretions of a sovereign to intercourse with Prussian chancellors) promptly telegraphed that the King was not accompanied by a responsible minister, and that the foreign policy of the Greek government remained unchanged. The pandemonium subsided.

But Constantine was scheduled to visit Paris next. A festive reception, after what had happened, was out of the question. To drop the visit altogether would have created an international scandal worse than the speech itself. The old diplomatic expedient of incognito travel was chosen. Now, an incognito visit by a sovereign does not mean that the city thus visited must not know of his presence. It means only that the city should pretend not to know of his presence. In this particular case Paris refused to pretend. A crowd assembled in front of the terminus. Its attitude was so threatening that Constantine was hurried to the street through a side exit. Some one recognized him—it would be about as easy to conceal a polar bear on a Paris street, on any street, as the six feet, six inches of Teutonic masculinity that is the King of the Hellenes. A throng gathered, and Constantine was hooted. He was rushed to his hotel—a throng awaited him at the entrance. He had to sneak in through a back door.

It is in small events like this that the inexorable consistency of Fate manifests itself most vividly. Constantine could never forget that side exit of the Paris terminus, that back door of the Paris hotel. He had never been fond of the French. From this moment he hated them with the unforgiving obstinacy so characteristic of his unimaginative mind.

Though an excellent linguist otherwise, Constantine's French is not flawless. For some unexplained reason he learned to speak French late in

7

life. Now, in the ordinary routine of court education, it came to pass that a French tutor was employed for his children. Queen Sophie—Kaiser
Wilhem's sister—was furious. She detested the
French all her life. She told her children not to
attend the French lessons.

The tutor was perplexed. He tried to expostu-
late with the Queen, who turned her back on him.
The tutor appealed to the King.

"I did not learn how to speak French until I was
thirty-seven," said Constantine, "and then I needed
it but a few weeks in Paris. It will be the same with
my children."

That was the end of the French lessons of King
Constantine's children. However, the King himself received, a little later, a French lesson, from
one Senator Jonnart—and he isn't likely ever to
forget it. Of which more anon.

IV

The story of the Constantine-Venizelos duel has
been told and retold many times. A bare summary
here will suffice.

Practically from the first day of the World War
Venizelos advocated Greek intervention on the side
of the Entente. He pointed out to the King, in
conversations and in memoranda, that Greece was
bound by her defensive alliance with Serbia to send
troops to the latter's aid; that apart from considerations of honour, to assist Serbia was vital for Greece,

for a crushed Serbia could only mean an enlarged Bulgaria and a strengthened Turkey; that the victory of the Central Powers would re-establish Turkish hegemony in the Balkans, and that a Turkey thus bolstered up first would crush its own Greek subjects and then attack Greece; that Greece, with her disproportionately long coast line, her wide-flung island possessions and her dependence on sea-borne trade, was at the mercy of British naval power.

He also argued that it was important for Greece to get in ahead of Italy—he had little doubt that Italy would ultimately side with the Allies—because only in that manner could Greece obtain British and French sanction for her claims in Northern Epirus and the Dodecanese, claims that were in violent conflict with Italian aspirations.

On the other hand, he declared, by joining the Allies Greece would gain an opportunity, unlikely ever to recur, to settle accounts with Turkey for good; to unite under her sovereignty all the unredeemed sections of the Hellenic race—those of the coast of Asia Minor, of Thrace and of the islands, perhaps even Cyprus; to safeguard herself permanently against the danger of Bulgarian encroachments; to secure, finally, the friendship and assistance of England and France, the powers that, owing to their obvious mastery of the seas, would probably win the war.

King Constantine, on his side, was determined from the outset to remain neutral. In various communications addressed to the Kaiser, his brother-in-law, to Greek diplomatists abroad, to the Bulgarian government, and in his many and bitter discussions with Venizelos himself, he declared categorically that Greece would not fight. That his resolution was essentially sentimental, that it was predetermined by his sympathy for Germany, or rather the Imperial house, and by the loyalty of an alumnus to his *alma mater,* the Prussian Staff College, is established beyond doubt. There was a time when he boasted of this sympathy and this loyalty, even though later on he found it diplomatic to deny it. For a while he could rationalize his emotion by pointing to the military preponderance of the Central Powers in the Balkans; but the wish was father to the argument.

The first definite issue occurred in January, 1915. King Carol of Roumania, friend of Germany and Austria, had just died; there were hopes at Paris and London that Roumania would "get in line." Sir Edward Grey addressed Venizelos. If Greece, he said in effect, would join the Allies, she would obtain the coast of Asia Minor as compensation. Venizelos was delighted.

Preparations for the Gallipoli expedition, suggested by Mr. Winston Churchill in September, were in progress at London. No one realized more keenly than M. Venizelos the tremendous import of the undertaking. He asked for the mobilization of an army corps, to be dispatched presently to Gallipoli. It was denied. He asked for a single division. Constantine's Prussian-ridden General Staff refused, and Venizelos was dismissed by the King.

The consequences of missing this opportunity were later summarized by M. Venizelos himself.

Five days after the decree of mobilization [he said] the army corps which I asked for would have been mobilized. In another nine days, with the abundance of material which we and our Allies had at our disposal, we should have found ourselves with our army corps, or with our one division, in occupation of the Gallipoli peninsula, which was unguarded, ungarrisoned and unfortified. . . . Within ten or fifteen days, a part of our Gallipoli forces, especially if we had had an army corps, would have advanced to Constantinople and found it abandoned by the Turks.

This was not the vision of a dreamer. By the end of February, wrote the American Ambassador, Mr. Morgenthau, every measure was taken by the Turkish government and by the German and Austro-Hungarian Ambassadors to leave Constantinople to its fate. Trains to rush the high dignitaries, the archives and the gold in the Turkish and German banks to safety were kept in readiness.

But the opportunity, perhaps the greatest the Allies had in the whole war, was missed. The continued neutrality of Greece enabled the German General Staff to fortify and garrison the Straits. By the time the British forces effected their landing everything was ready for their reception. The enterprise ended, despite the unprecedented heroism of the British, in a bloody *débâcle*. Constantinople was not taken—and the war was prolonged by three years.

His refusal to assist the Allies in the Dardanelles venture established Constantine's standing in the Valhalla of German heroes. Temporarily, that is. One wonders, in this year of the Lord nineteen hundred and twenty-two, if there are many Germans whose gratitude to the sovereign of the Hellenes has remained unshaken. For three thousand years, ever since the days of the wooden horse contrived by a Greek King, there lingered in this world a suspicion of Danaic gifts. In the twentieth century a Greek King's contribution to the German cause were the war years 1916, 1917, 1918.

V

It was on the issue of Bulgaria's attack on Serbia that the next round of the Venizelos-Constantine duel was fought.

The Gounaris cabinet, which superseded the Cretan in the spring of 1915, restated Greek neutrality in the best manner of Constantinian diplomacy. Its appointment followed by a flaring-up of German propaganda at Athens, under the very able direction of Baron Schenk. These were the days when some of the biggest war fortunes were made in Greece. They were founded on the exportation to Germany of Greek morale, Greek sentiment, Greek flattery—above all, of Greek vows of neutrality. Private enterprise in these lines prospered under encouragement from the State. On the other hand, the supply of fuel and other provisions to German submarines was reserved for a State monopoly, operated by Constantine's naval staff.

Despite the wholesale purchase of Greek newspapers and the wholesale bribery of Greek politicians by Baron Schenk, despite governmental terrorism unprecedented even in Greece, the elections in June, 1915, returned a substantial majority of Venizelists. In August Venizelos was asked to form a new cabinet. But previously Constantine secretly gave assurances to Germany that Greece would not abandon neutrality even though Bulgaria attacked Serbia.

On September 24 Venizelos learned that general mobilization had been ordered by the Bulgarian government. He immediately demanded that Greece should join Serbia under the defensive alliance concluded in 1913. For a few days Constantine equivocated. He harped upon the military superiority of the Germans and on the dangers of intervention, but he dared not to refuse point blank. At last Venizelos confronted him with the choice. He said that he had the majority of the Greek people with him, and that by thwarting his policy Constantine virtually set the Constitution aside.

At last Constantine showed his hand. "I am responsible to God alone," he said. Venizelos obtained a vote of confidence in the Chamber. Next day he was dismissed.

One of the gravest charges brought against Constantine by his opponents is based on his attitude toward the Serbian treaty. One of the weakest points of his defence is his answer to the charge. This answer is defined by the note addressed by Venizelos's successor, M. Zaimis—the ex-High Commissioner of Crete—to Serbia. The gist of its many words is that the treaty of 1913 limited Greece's obligation to aid her ally to the case of a Balkan war only.

This is flatly contradicted by Venizelos, who negotiated the treaty himself. He says that it was expressly understood at the time that the *casus foederis* was not limited to a Balkan war in the strict sense.

Another argument, not contained in the Zaimis note, but stated manifoldly by Constantine both previously and afterward, was that Greek military assistance to Serbia was contingent on the latter country's putting 150,000 men in the field to co-operate with her ally. On every occasion Constantine carefully refrained from mentioning the fact that England and France had repeatedly offered to substitute the army of 150,000, as Serbia was unable to supply it.

But, damning though the evidence be on these two points, the verdict of history upon Constantine's good faith in the matter of the Serbian alliance will not rest on them. It will be founded on the fact that two days before Bulgaria declared war on Serbia Constantine had notified the Bulgarian government that Greece would not fight.

A few days later Venizelos defeated the Zaimis government on a vote of confidence. Zaimis resigned. M. Skoulloudis was appointed Premier. The Chamber was dissolved, a writ for new elections was issued. Venizelos directed his followers to abstain from voting, in protest against the King's unconstitutional procedure. The result was that in the stead of the 720,000 votes registered in June of the preceding year, only 230,000 were cast. Needless to say, the government won a splendid victory.

The period between October, 1915 and October, 1916 marks the total eclipse of Venizelos, and the zenith of Constantine. It is the period of rolling German gold, of secret service *à la* Metternich, of newspapers bought up or silenced by raids and confiscation, of the wholesale prostitution of Greek public life. Constantine became one of the most popular men in Germany. In this period falls his refusal to allow the Serbian army transit through Greek territory. His reasons for the refusal were set forth in beautiful diplomatic prose, but, if one can believe the usually trustworthy Mr. John Mavrogordato, the Allies had the last laugh in the affair, for the whole agitation to obtain Constantine's permit for the transit on land was a screen behind which the Serb troops were safely transported by sea.

In this period also fall the invasion of Greek territory by Bulgars and Germans; the surrender of the important Fort Roupel to the Germans (a little matter which cost Greece Northern Epirus, promptly claimed by Italy as a punishment), the capitulation of the Hadjopulos army corps of 8000 at Kavalla; wholesale delivery of Greek cannon and supplies to the Germans; and the blockade of Greece by the Allies. Although it was plain that under no circumstances would he fight, Constantine maintained the Greek army on full war footing— and full war footing implied wartime allowances to officers. Queen Sophie took over the management of all charitable organizations at Athens. She managed them with German thoroughness. Thousands of reservists, drawn to the capital from all parts of the country, were sent about to shopkeepers and homes to solicit contributions for the united charities. The reservists were vigorous young men. Contributions were rarely refused. The reservists were fed from the soup kitchens maintained by the charities. They also received a generous pocket-money. Constantine was very popular in Athens. So was Queen Sophie.

VI

On September 25, 1916, Venizelos left Athens, late at night, in utter secrecy. He boarded a small steamer and went to Crete—thence to Samos and Mytilene and other Greek islands. On October 5, the anniversary of his dismissal by Constantine, Venizelos established the Salonica government. On November 24 Venizelos declared war on Germany, Austria-Hungary and Turkey. Once more he was fighting half Europe. It was a homely, cosy feeling—a memory of his fading youth come to life again.

This time Constantine's answer was not words, but a deed. On December 1 the Royalist troops at Athens, whipped to a frenzied loyalty by the speech-making and fraternizing Princes, ambushed two thousand English and French marines who had landed to secure the surrender of arms and ammunition, agreed to by Constantine. The King had assured the French admiral in command that the Allied troops would not be attacked, and the admiral relied on the royal word. The result was the massacre of a large number of the French and Englishmen. The admiral and his staff themselves were taken prisoner, but were released afterward. It was the greatest victory of Constantine's military career, achieved without a coach. For several days anti-Venizelist pogroms raged. Scores were murdered, hundreds imprisoned, thousands of stores and homes looted. Constantine was more popular than ever with the reservists.

He was more popular than ever at German General Headquarters, too. On January 26, he telegraphed to the Kaiser:

We send you from the depth of our hearts the most cordial wishes on the occasion of your birthday. We are following with admiration the great events on land and sea. We pray that God grant you very soon a glorious victory over all your infamous enemies. We have been honoured by the landing of forty Senegalese soldiers intended to guard the French legation. What a charming picture of civilization.

Another charming picture of civilization was, three days later, the saluting of the Allied flags by royalist troops in the Zappeion. This was by way of expiation for the little mistake of December 1.

The tragicomedy lasted until June. On the eleventh of that month the French High Commissioner, Senator Jonnart, presented an ultimatum demanding the abdication of Constantine, on the technical ground that he had violated the constitution guaranteed by Great Britain, France and Russia. Constantine had his French lesson. He proved a docile student. In twenty-four hours he was on his way to Switzerland. His son Alexander was proclaimed King. Two weeks later Venizelos was reinstalled at Athens. Once more Greece was united. From this moment the Hellenic Kingdom was a full-fledged Ally. For the next three years and five months Venizelos was virtual dictator. We have had a glimpse of him at the Paris conference. With the Treaty of Sèvres, which gave Greece the last of the Greek-inhabited regions of what was once the Ottoman Empire, he reached his zenith. There were no more heights to be scaled.

VII

In November, 1920, Venizelos was at Nice on a well-earned vacation. It was exactly ten years after his memorable landing at Piræus. In the meantime he had elevated Greece from a small poor country of the darkest Balkans into a European power—restored Hellenic territories beyond the wildest dreams of the nationalists—won three wars —played an important *rôle* at the greatest international conference ever held. His career was phenomenal—unheard-of—Napoleonic. Professor Herbert Adams Gibbons draws the chart of those ten years in terms of graphic contrast:

In 1910 Kaiser Wilhelm could ask contemptuously, Who is this man Venizelos? In 1920 Venizelos had a leading *rôle* in deciding the destiny of the Near East, while the Kaiser was sawing wood in a Dutch garden with a sentry watching him.

A naked man jumps far, says a Serbian proverb. Ten years earlier Venizelos had arrived in Greece, a naked man—unencumbered by family ties, parish considerations, clique loyalties, party fetters. He jumped, and jumped very far indeed.

But when a naked man falls after the far jump he is apt to fall hard.

In October, 1920, King Alexander died from a monkey-bite. Venizelos summoned Prince Paul, who was living at Lucerne, to the throne. Admiral Coundouriotis assumed the regency. On November 14 the general elections took place—the first since June, 1915. Next day the world was astounded by the news that Venizelos was defeated by an overwhelming majority. Most of the Athens dispatches added that the Greek people decided for the return of Constantine.

In more than one way that was an exaggeration.

When the first excitement cooled down it appeared, as Mr. Mavrogordato points out, that the "overwhelming majority" for Constantine was sixty per cent of the total as against forty per cent of Venizelist vote. Moreover, the sober truth was that the sixty per cent majority was not so much *for* Constantine as *against* Venizelos—an important difference. But for the moment subtleties like that were drowned in the exultation of the Constantinists. Mm. Rallis and Gounaris, with their excellent sense of political *coup de théâtre,* flooded the world with accounts of their victory, and announced that a plebiscite would be held in a month to decide over Constantine's return.

The Venizelists at once gauged the scope of this announcement. They knew only too well that at that particular moment of anti-Venizelist elation it would be very easy for the Royalists to manipulate a plebiscite so as to make the demand for Constantine appear unanimous. They declared, therefore, that they regarded the vote of November 14 as binding and final, and submitted to the people's will. But the Royalists were not thus to be deprived from a cheap and spectacular triumph. The plebiscite was held in due course. The result did not disappoint. Out of 1,013,724 votes cast 999,954 were for Constantine. The Royalist claim that the vote was practically unanimous was correct—as far as it went. Minor details were overlooked. They included military supervision of the voting; an ingeniously contrived ballot, which did not show any express alternative to Constantine; and the circumstance that Royalists were permitted to vote as many times as they liked.

The Greeks are a notoriously continent race as far as alcohol is concerned. But human nature will not be cheated, not even in Hellas. Human nature craves intoxicants. The favorite intoxicant of Greeks is politics. One hardly ever sees a drunken man in the streets of Athens. But the cafés are always crowded—with wild-eyed, gesticulating, passionate men who sip Turkish coffee from diminutive cups—and gulp down politics by the gallon. The evening of the day when Constantine was recalled by a majority of one million votes will be remembered as the greatest political orgy in Hellenic history. In Athens strangers wearing the royalist badge embraced and kissed one another in the streets, and smashed the heads of such candidates for suicide who wore no badges. White-haired Colonels in full dress uniform emulated St. Simeon Stylites on top of lamp-posts, shouting *"Zito Basileus"* until they fell, exhausted, off their perch.

VIII

Constantine was not remiss in improving on the occasion. He did not wait even for the plebiscite— reasonably enough—but ordered a special train to take him from his Swiss retreat to the South Italian port of embarkation. And he took pains, now that he was vindicated, to tell the world at large that, though abused and mortified beyond endurance, he bore no grudge. His mouthpiece was *Le Matin* of Paris, which obliged him by rushing a correspondent to his side.

First of all, Constantine asserted, it was a malicious as well as absurd lie that he had been pro-German. Had he not offered aid to the Allies five times, and had he not been politely refused? As to the Serbian treaty—why, Serbia was obliged to send 150,000 men to aid Greece, and she didn't have them. The army corps of 8000 which at Kavalla had surrendered to the Germans and was interned at Goerlitz—why, they were isolated, completely cut off. He—Constantine—ordered them, through Sir Francis Elliot, the British minister, to await the ships that were sent to fetch them home, but this order somehow never reached them. What could they do but surrender, as the alternative would have been to rebel against their anointed King? Nor was Fort Roupel surrendered to the Bulgars by choice. It was completely isolated, and the only order sent from Athens was not to open hostilities with the Central Powers.

The story about the Massacre of the First of December had been distorted. For one thing, there were only 800 royalist troops in Athens, against 2000 Allied marines. Nobody gave orders to fire on the French—some one, perhaps a Frenchman, fired a shot—the garrison became excited—there were casualties—it was regrettable. Besides, the Allies had promised, through M. Benazet, certain concessions in exchange for the surrender of arms.

These promises were never ratified, still less kept. The Allied demand thus was illegal.

Not a very convincing defence, on its face. Mr. Mavrogordato, ablest of the Venizelist spokesmen in England, points out that the King's best reply to the accusation that he had been pro-German was not denial, nor protestation of his pro-Ally sentiments, but simply the question: why shouldn't he be pro-German? In 1914, the treaty with Serbia notwithstanding, there was no moral, even less a legal, obligation for a Greek to be pro-Ally. The only obligation of a Greek was to be pro-Greek. If the interests of Greece demanded neutrality, or even siding with Germany, it was not only the right but the duty of the King of Greece to remain neutral, or to side with Germany. The issue, at least, was debatable. But Constantine ran true to form. It seemed safer—it certainly was easier—to prevaricate than to argue.

One point of his pleading should be noted. He asserted that on December 1, 1916, eight hundred Greek soldiers had been drawn, unwilling, into the skirmish with the French. It is established as a fact that the Greek troops outnumbered manifoldly the Allied marines; and there are witnesses who have heard the Princes' harangues against the "treacherous Entente," repeated day in, day out, in the barracks and cantonments of the royalist regiments.

A rising star never lacks enthusiastic astrologers to proclaim its glory. Constantine always had his

8

partisans in the West; now that he was rehabilitated by his people a whole host sprang forward to paint the lily white.   Most interesting among the arguments produced at this juncture was the assertion of the British Admiral Sir Mark Kerr, who had been head of the naval mission to Greece, that Greece was not obliged in 1915 to go to Serbia's aid, because Serbia herself had broken her engagement when in June, 1913, she refused to back up Greece in her conflict with Turkey.   Mr. Mavrogordato finds two faults with this defence. Firstly, he says, it was not thought of in 1915—the Zaimis note, which repudiated Greece's obligation, made no mention of it.   In fact, it emerged for the first time in 1917, in a pamphlet by Mr. G. F. Abbott, entitled "The Truth about Greece."   But being manufactured *ex post facto* was the lesser flaw in Sir Mark Kerr's claim.   Worse it was that it wasn't true.   For not only did Serbia in June, 1913, stand loyally by Greece, but M. Streit, the Greek Foreign Minister, himself conveyed the Greek government's gratitude to Belgrade.*

IX

Venizelos received the news of his defeat calmly. "I hope that the Allies will not punish Greece because of Constantine," he said.

Was his detachment a pose?   That question will have to be settled between M. Venizelos and God.

* M. Streit, with General Dousmanis and Colonel Metaxas, formed the so-called "invisible government" at Athens in 1916.

Never since has he said or done anything to justify doubt as to his sincerity in the moment of his downfall.

His views concerning the causes of the *débâcle* were characteristically clear. "Suppose," he said to an English visitor, "your army had been mobilized, not in 1914, but in 1912—and had remained under colours until 1920. Suppose Mr. Lloyd George had then appealed to the country. He would have been defeated. The soldiers who had been away from their homes for eight years—all their friends and relatives—would have voted against *any* government."

Venizelos, as he was himself only too willing to admit, was in the eyes of the Greek people identified with war. He had led them through three wars —1912, 1913 and 1916—18. For the Greek popular mind the three wars merged into one. For Greece, as for Serbia, the World War began in 1912.

Then there were his mistakes—undeniable and undenied. "He was," says Mr. Mavrogordato, "singularly unhappy in his choice of subordinates, many of whom were competent only in the persecution of their political and private enemies." To be sure, he had to work with the material he found on the spot. He did not introduce corruption, nepotism and petty oppression into the Greek government; but he did not exert himself sufficiently to eradicate those evils. With all his mastery of statecraft, and his skill in reorganizing the army and navy notwithstanding, Venizelos was not a good administrator. Rather, he was not an administrator at all. He thought, writes an American defender of Constantine, "that as long as he devoted himself to the service of the Hellenic national interests beyond the frontiers of the realm, all questions of internal character would have only a secondary importance." He committed, in an aggravated form, the mistake of President Wilson in going to Paris. His prolonged stay abroad was more inevitable than Mr. Wilson's; it was also more prolonged. His absence lasted, not a few months, but three years.

The most tragic trespass of his government was one for which he was not responsible at all. It was the outburst of terrorism with which his supporters avenged the unsuccessful attempt on Venizelos's life by a Constantinist fanatic at Paris. The pogroms enacted by Constantine's reservists in December, 1916, were now duplicated by the opposing camp. Among the victims of these lamentable excesses was M. Ion Dragoumis, son of the former Premier and most brilliant and substantial literary figure of Young Greece. According to the official version, he was stabbed to death by a soldier "while resisting arrest." His death, says Mr. Mavrogordato, inflicted an irreparable loss on Hellenic life.

X

Analogy between Venizelos and Mr. Wilson is not limited to the external and accidental connection between their absence from home and their defeat at the polls. With all the enormous differences of mentality and temperament the two had one quality in common—aloofness. In M. Venizelos the trait is not so all-pervading as in the American President—it is also much less obvious, for Venizelos's manner is suavity itself, and he is past master of an art of which Wilson was utterly devoid—that of ingratiating himself with strangers, and with journalists. He is also capable of securing the allegiance and co-operation of gifted men—a capacity not shared by the fancier of rubber stamps. But Venizelos was hardly more than Wilson the man to inspire lasting personal affection on a large scale. He had no magnetism—none, at least, of the brand that works upon the masses. He himself recognized Constantine's superiority in this respect.

This aloofness, defect of a preponderant intellectuality, was capitalized by his enemies. Their strongest weapon was branding Venizelos a foreigner. His origin told against him. With the "first families," with the political clique of Athens, antipathy and envy took the form of snobbishness abusing the parvenu, the *homo novus,* the Cretan comitadji. "He is a nobody—he is not of the great family of Venizelos" said M. Rallis to Mrs. Kenneth-Brown. "So much the worse for the great family of Venizelos" came the appropriate answer.

As regards the common people, the cry of "foreigner" proved most effective. When in 1915

Venizelos was considering to placate Bulgaria by
ceding the Drama-Kavalla region (a loss amply
compensated for by the British promise of the
coast of Asia Minor) the politicians of Athens said
to the crowd: "Look at this foreigner—he wants to
sell out Greek land and Greek souls to the Bulgars."

His main support came from New, rather than
from Old, Greece—from the redeemed provinces,
Macedonia, Thrace, Crete, the islands, not from the
original kingdom.

XI

But he was not only a Cretan—he was altogether
un-Greek. He introduced and championed an entirely new element in Greek life. This Cretan
mountaineer was the apostle of Western civilization. Greece, shut off by history and geography
from the main currents of European life, remained
a world unto itself even after the liberation, even
after the importation of a Western varnish with
the Bavarian and Danish dynasties and the development of trade with the West. Greek ideology
showed all the terrible effects of inbreeding and
inward growth, of the lack of constant comparison,
of the absence of tests.

Some small nations have an international, cosmo-
politan touch about them that is denied to the great
ones. Conscious of their material smallness, they
seek to broaden their spiritual outlook. In a sense
Danes and Swiss and Roumanians are better Euro-

peans than Englishmen or Frenchmen, who live in self-sufficient national universes. In this respect Greece carried the murderous handicap of her own glorious past. Wasn't Hellas the fountainhead of European civilization? Europe owed a debt to Greece and Greeks were too content to live on the hope that the interest would be paid some time. Greece—one must remember the Greeks call their country Hellas, and themselves *Romeoi,* Romans— was the centre of the universe. She was perfect. If the rest of Europe refused to shape their culture, their politics, their whole life on Greek lines—why, so much the worse for the rest of Europe.

Venizelos, inveterate revolutionist, declared war on this deadly provincialism. He represented the West. He told Greeks that theirs was a small and poor and backward country, that their megalo- mania was absurd, and if they wanted to survive at all they had to learn everything from bottom up, to reform their political and economic life, their educa- tion, their manners, their whole mentality, on Euro- pean models. He could not open his mouth without reminding the Greeks of their worst faults, without exposing their Hellenocentric phantasmagories to ridicule. France and especially England always haunted his words.

To the multitude nothing could be more odious. Some of the elder statesmen—men of the highest personal culture—knew how right Venizelos was; but they recognized the tremendous propaganda value of the unpopularity of his views, and they were unscrupulous enough to raise the issue of 100 per cent Hellenism. This Cretan, this foreigner, was a traitor to Hellas. What did he want with his new-fangled ways, his alien—French and English —notions? Greeks were accustomed to do things in their own way for three thousand years—they were good enough ways, too, for were they not the ways of Pericles and Alexander? If Venizelos did not like it, why, let him chuck it.

The vote that brought about Venizelos's downfall was the vote from the country districts of Old Greece, the peasant vote. His following came from the larger cities. There is a curious, though not surprising, analogy between the return of Constantine and the triumph of Horthyism in Hungary. The Hungarian White Terror was a reaction against the Red Terror only in a superficial, chronological sense. It was, in reality, a reaction against Károlyi, not against Béla Kun—against the Westernism, the "new-fangled ways, alien—French and English—notions" of the Budapest intellectuals. The hundred per cent Magyarism of the country districts, manipulated by the officers of the army and the clique of Budapest politicians, put Admiral Horthy into the saddle. The hundred per cent Hellenism of the Old Greek peasantry, manipulated by the officers of the army and the clique of Athens politicians, brought Constantine back. It is no accident that in both countries the reaction represented the triumph of those elements which in the late war had been extremely pro-German.

XII

To allege that Constantine was brought back solely by the unpopularity of Venizelos would be unfair.   In a sense his victory was *his* victory, not only his opponent's defeat.   Venizelos was not only a foreigner himself.   He had been hoisted into power by foreign bayonets.   The best of rulers cannot live down that taunt.   "We don't want you to govern us well—we want you to get out" said the Venetian patriot, Daniele Manin, to the Austrians.   He summed up the inevitable choice of any spirited people between good government and self-government.   And Venizelos's government wasn't even a very good government.

Venizelos committed perhaps the greatest mistake of his life when he, in June, 1917, came down from Salonica to Athens on board an Allied warship. Had he, instead, fought his way down by land, the Constantinist troops would have joined him *en masse,* and he would have been hailed as the liberator.   This he admitted himself to Mr. V. J. Seligman.

Now, if Venizelos stood for alien rule by grace of alien bayonets, Constantine was the martyr of his Hellenism.   He had all the emotions of a singularly emotional people on his side.   He was, as Mr. Mavrogordato aptly puts it, the "King over the water." Never is a king so popular as when he is over the water.   A narrow strip of the salty liquid made even that dullest of small tyrants, James II., into a hero.

Constantine was a great and good man—he did not want to drag Greece into the war—he was a friend of the people, said the Epistrates who were fed from Queen Sophie's soup kitchens—he was one of ourselves, said thousands of military godfathers.

Moreover, all the petty and great chicaneries of the period October, 1915, to June, 1917, were overshadowed by the more recent transgressions of the Venizelist bureaucracy and the encroachments of the Allied military representatives.

"Absence makes the heart grow fonder," said Venizelos to a friend who discussed with him the outbreak of Constantinomania at Athens in December, 1920. Barring his death, Constantine's return was foreordained by the manner of his departure.

Much was made by certain journalists of the myth attaching to Constantine's name. They quoted an ancient Greek legend to the effect that Constantinople, lost when the Turks defeated and killed the last Emperor of the East, Constantine Paleologos, in 1453, would be recovered to Hellenism when another Constantine reigned over the Greeks. Nothing could be more romantic. Mr. Mavrogordato was unromantic enough to investigate. Careful search of Greek folklore failed to reveal the existence of the alleged Byzantine legend. Careful search of the Athenian press revealed the origin of the invention. On the other hand, there existed a Byzantine tradition that Constantine Paleologos was not killed by the Turks, but escaped and was hidden in Hagia Sophia by an angel. He would return, like Barbarossa, when his people needed him. However, not even Athenian editors have the courage to assert that Constantine of Schleswig-Holstein-Sonderburg-Glücksburg is the reincarnation of Constantine Paleologos.

XIII

In 1919 the Greek troops fighting in Asia Minor picked up some Cretan Moslems, expatriated from their native island after the withdrawal of the Turks. "You call yourselves Greeks," said one of the Moslems, "you have only got here because of a Cretan."

The taunt was true. It was the truth of it that the Greeks could never forgive Venizelos.

BIBLIOGRAPHY

Robert Lansing	The Big Four and Others at the Peace Conference.
S. B. Chester	Life of Venizelos.
Herbert Adams Gibbons	Venizelos.
Paxton Hibben	Constantine I and the Greek People.
Demetra Vaka	In the Heart of German Intrigue.
E. J. Dillon	The Inside Story of the Peace Conference.
John Mavrogordato	Greece, Constantine and Venizelos. Edinburgh Review, January, 1921.
V. J. Seligman	M. Venizelos on the Greek Situation. Fortnightly Review, April, 1921.

THOMAS GARRIGUE MASARYK

THOMAS GARRIGUE MASARYK

I

IN one of his letters to President Wilson Ambassador Page expresses surprise over the fuss made at the Court of St. James *à propos* of the visit of King Christian of Denmark, "a country with less population and smaller area than New Jersey."

There you have the typical American attitude toward small countries. To Mr. Page it matters little that Denmark has a better educational system, a more evenly diffused material prosperity, better sanitation, more advanced methods of agriculture, than any other country in the world; that there are fewer murders committed there in a year than occur in a day in Chicago; that, all things considered, Denmark is probably the most cultured, best governed, the happiest of modern nations. And if such is the attitude of the American Ambassador to Great Britain, what can be expected from the man in the street at Peoria, Ill.? Yet to-day this quantitative standard of America has conquered the world. Only in a century which measures the greatness of a nation in square miles of territory, gauges its culture by the number, per capita, of automobiles, and expresses the citizen's worth in dollars and cents, is it possible that a man like Thomas Garrigue Masaryk should not be universally recognized as one of the age's greatest.

Not that he has failed to attain recognition altogether; for his own nation idolizes him, and knowing foreigners are aware that his name will endure like that of only a few contemporaries. But the number of the knowing, in Western countries, in America especially, is limited to a handful of students and specialists; and this comparative obscurity is due solely to the fact that he is the son of a small nation. For, entirely disregarding for the moment his moral and intellectual stature, his achievements in the field of practical statesmanship are among the most amazing in this age of political portents. If ever the resurrection of a people was the work of one man, the resurrection of the Czech people after three centuries of quasi-extinction is the work of Masaryk. And never has a fight for freedom been waged and won against more formidable odds. The Athenians at Marathon were a safe bet in comparison.

At the outbreak of the world war Masaryk, then a member of the Austrian Reichsrat, fled from the Dual Empire and began to work for the liberation of Czechoslovakia. This was at a moment when most prudent people in Allied countries, the Battle of the Marne notwithstanding, would consider an eventual draw, even a moderate German victory,

THOMAS GARRIGUE MASARYK

as an extremely favourable outcome. Masaryk believed in Allied victory, and staked his all on it. He said that he would align the Czechs and Slovaks on the side of the Entente. Now, as a matter of military geography, this was about as sound a proposal as aligning, in an American-Japanese war, the State of Indiana on the side of Japan. Some people thought Masaryk was bluffing; others, that he was crazy. But a few influential and farsighted Englishmen and Frenchmen took him seriously.

Masaryk disregarded the sceptics and the scoffers, and went to work. Four years passed—and in the summer of 1918 the Allies recognized the Czechoslovak Provisional Government as one of the actual belligerents. It was a government without a country, as yet, for Czechoslovakia was in the very heart of the Teutonic empires; but it had an exchequer, and it had an army. In September its gold coins were circulating in Bohemia, and Czechoslovak legions were fighting in France and Italy. The end of October brought the end of the Hapsburg empire. After three centuries of slavery Czechoslovakia was free once more, and Masaryk, elected first President of the Republic while still in New York, entered Prague in triumph.

That was an achievement of which it is impossible to speak otherwise than in superlatives. And yet his statesmanship is not the supreme fruit of Masaryk's greatness; it is rather the background against which his greatness ought to be viewed.

o

For, like that of all truly great leaders, Masaryk's is a moral leadership above all; his greatness is moral greatness; his tremendous hold on his people is not merely that of the successful politician, but that of an apostle of religion.

II

He spent his life in fighting official Christianity, and fighting it, within his domain, very successfully. His name is anathema not only with the Church, but also with the churches; he is as outspoken an opponent of stereotyped Protestantism as of Popery. The conventionally religious regard him as the Anti-Christ, the incarnation of rationalism and free-thinking. And yet he stands out as perhaps the one real Christian among the practical leaders of the age.

In one of his writings he asks: "Has there ever been a better, more exalted, more divine life than that of Christ?" And he answers with Rousseau: "If Socrates suffered and died like a philosopher, Christ suffered and died like a God." In the next sentence he gives the clue of his religion. "Christ's whole life is Truth. God's Son is the highest simplicity, he shows purity and sanctity in the true sense of the word. Nothing external attaches to him and his life, no formalism, no ritualism; everything comes from the inner being, everything is thoroughly true, thoroughly beautiful, thoroughly good."

Masaryk's life is devoted to the quest of truth as the highest simplicity, the disentangling of the substantial living thing, of reality, from the maze of the external, the incidental; his battle is against that formalism which stifles the essence of life. He calls himself a Realist. The political party which he founded and which ultimately achieved the liberation of his country was called the Realist party—the party seeking the salvation of the nation through recognition and moulding of realities rather than in glamorous dreams of past and future.

Almost every person carries in his soul the image of some event or other, rising in an uncanny clarity from the mist of childhood's half-memories—a central impression, a kernel around which later experiences crystallizes, something that gives colour and direction to his whole life. Sometimes it is what Freudians call a complex; but it is not necessarily pathological; sometimes it is a trifling detail that acquires a disproportionate, and to other people often unintelligible, emotional emphasis. Masaryk tells of two such epochal occurrences in his childhood. His father was a gamekeeper on one of the imperial estates in Moravia, and they were very poor. Once in a year the emperor came down with a retinue of nobles and generals and diplomatists, to shoot hares, partridges and pheasants. The company deposited their resplendent cloaks and fur-lined overcoats in the cottage of the Masaryks; and the whole neighbourhood, poor peasants all of them, foregathered while the shoot was on, to behold and admire those fabulous garments, every one of which represented an unattainable fortune. Little Thomas alone refused to look at the display. "I did not like to see those things," the President of the Czechoslovak Republic once related this experience of the cottager's boy. "I felt there was something radically wrong. Just what, was not clear to me. But such a hate I had! That hatred lasted till today."

The other career-shaping episode happened when he was fifteen. Being barely able to read and write he was, at the urging of his parents, about to take employment with the village blacksmith. But he disliked the idea. It was not interesting; he yearned to see the world, for knowledge, for adventure. So he packed his little bundle, went to Vienna and became 'prenticed to a locksmith. He stood on the threshold of his dreams. He was in the imperial capital; the wide world lay around him; and the trade of locksmiths—how it attracted him! Locksmiths were magicians—they opened doors forbidden to others, doors behind which were stored he did not know what treasures of knowledge—locksmiths solved mysteries wrought in steel and iron. His fancy was aflame. Then came the disappointment. Instead of being initiated into the wizardry of locks he was put by his master to operate a machine of some sort or another—operate it day and night, twelve, fourteen, sometimes sixteen hours at a stretch. It was one single movement repeated thousands and thousands of times, turning out some minor piece of hardware. At the age of fifteen Masaryk got an object-lesson in modern industrialism which he never could forget, as little as that earlier one in the difference between rich and poor.

Hatred of injustice and hatred of the machine, the soullessness and inhumanity of it, became Masaryk's dominant passion, the pivot around which his *Weltanschauung* turned. Later in life he fought the Hapsburgs and the Germans because they represented injustice. He fought the Roman church and official Protestantism because he saw in them the incarnation of the machine, the lifeless thing that demands living sacrifice. He fought capitalism because capitalism was the tyranny of the industrial machine; but he also fought Marxian socialism because it also was of the machine, a deadly symmetry that would crush the soul of man. And the quest of his life, the quest of reality, is nothing but the supreme form which his hatred of injustice and of the machine has taken; for he holds that through the recognition of reality, and reality alone, can man free himself from bondage.

The locksmith's apprentice fled from Vienna to his parents' cottage, to the gloomy existence of the village failure. But fate watched over young Masaryk. With the aid of a benevolent priest who perceived the spark that glowed in him he succeeded in acquiring an education. He studied at Prague and at Vienna, later in the University of Leipzig; and, still a young man, he was appointed Professor in the University of Prague.

III

It is characteristic that the first act which concentrated public attention upon the personality of the future founder of the Czechoslovak independence was what most people regarded as an attack on Czech patriotism. Mournful over the tragedy that for three centuries had weighed upon the nation, the Czech scholars and poets turned for relief to memories of its glorious past. Greatest among these was the so-called Manuscript of Königinhof, the charter of Bohemia's historic grandeur. Masaryk turned the spotlight of his scholarship on this treasure of national lore, and exposed it as a forgery. All Bohemia was incensed; he was denounced as a traitor, a blasphemer and a German agent. Masaryk stood the fire without wincing. He took the offensive, and ridiculed those who thought it necessary to bolster up Bohemian greatness with unhistoric lies. "A nation that is not founded on truth does not deserve to survive," he said.

From that time onward Masaryk never ceased to pour scorn on romantic nationalism and to preach a realistic conception of national needs and duties. He contrasted patriotism, the living substance, to patrioteering, a mere ritual and empty formalism.

He exhibited the same strain of civic courage, the same contempt for the popular prejudice, the same love for truth as carried him through the Königinhof affair, in the celebrated case of Hilsner, the Jew accused of ritual murder. Everybody in Bohemia believed the charge; all clamoured for Hilsner's head. Masaryk alone stood up for the Jew, and proved the accusation of ritual murder absurd in general and Hilsner innocent in particular. This cost him a good deal of his popularity, and one day, when he entered his class, he was received with hooting and catcalls. He faced the turmoil for a moment, then stepped to the blackboard and wrote one word on it—"Work." Silence fell, and Masaryk addressed the students. "Don't drink, don't gamble, don't loaf, but work—that's what the Jew is doing and you have to do it, too, if you want to beat him." Thereupon he proceeded with his lecture.

Never again was he disturbed. When he related this story to me, he added, with his peculiar self-conscious, deprecatory smile, as if forestalling praise: "God knows, I don't like Jews." He meant to imply that he, too, had his prejudices, that he was not better than the rest; it never occurred to him that his very dislike made his attitude all the more admirable.

After all, it was as it should be that the man who restored the Czech nation was not a soldier nor a politician, but a moralist and a philosopher. Nations are known by the heroes they honour; and the greatest and most revered character in Czech history is not a general nor a statesman, but a thinker and a martyr, Jan Hus, the reformer treacherously burnt at the stake by order of the Emperor Sigismund at the Council of Constance, in 1415. His personality stamped forever all that is the best in Czech character; and the greatest tribute ever paid to Masaryk was the saying that he was lineal descendant and re-incarnation of Jan Hus.

The martyrdom of Hus is the climax of Czech history; it was a moral victory as great as the annihilation of the Armada was for England. For Masaryk the Reformation, which in Bohemia assumed the form of Hus's teachings, stands out as the greatest event not only in Czech history, but also in the history of the world. Religion is uppermost in his mind; but religion to him means Reformation. But the Reformation, as he conceives it, is not a definite and finite fact of the sixteenth century. It continues to this very moment. He writes:

History is often called a teacher and a judge. It is, above all, an obligation. The significance of our reformation determines the trend of our entire national being. Every conscious son of the Czech people finds in the story of our reformation his own ideal. Every son of the Czech people who knows Czech history must decide either for the Reformation or for the Counter-Reformation, either for the Czech idea or for the Austrian idea. . . . Like all genuine reformation, that of our country is still incomplete. Reformation means an incessant re-forming, uninterrupted renewal, a striving for heights, a constant process of perfection; it means growth.

It speaks well for the intellectual and spiritual level of the Czech people that Masaryk's teachings have won a tremendous hold over them. There is, perhaps, no other instance in our age of one personality stamping his nation as that of Masaryk stamp his own. Even deeper, naturally, and more conspicuous is his influence over his pupils in the university. A friend of mine, an American scholar who knows Bohemia well tells me that he can single out Masaryk's pupils—they have an ethical attitude toward life's problems, a seriousness and a striving for simplicity that marks them.

Masaryk's part in the spiritual growth of the Bohemian people has been compared with that of Tolstoy in the evolution of Young Russia. In drawing this analogy, however, one should bear in mind the fundamental difference that separates the two thinkers, a difference that is not merely individual, but also national. It is the difference that defines Russia from the rest of Europe, that is dwelt upon by Masaryk himself in his monumental work on the spirit of Russia, the greatest, perhaps, written on the subject by a non-Russian. It is the difference between the individualistic, activistic West, growing from a subsoil of Roman civilization, Roman law, Roman religion, and the communistic-anarchistic, passive, contemplative East, heir of the Byzantine tradition.

The central concept of Masaryk's religion is the idea of humanity, of universal brotherhood. "Brotherhood was the name and also the ideal of our national Church, the Church of the Bohemian Brethren. The idea of humanity is the fundament of our reformation."

There was a Czech philosopher in the fifteenth century, Peter Chelcicky, who preached the idea of humanity. But Chelcicky's humanitarian ideal implied the doctrine of non-resistance; he held that the use of force was evil under any circumstances, even in self-defence. Masaryk tells of the astonishment of Tolstoy when he discovered that his own ideas had been formulated by Chelcicky four hundred years ago. Masaryk's idea of humanity and humanitarianism is different. He defines it as "a fight, everywhere, always and by every means, against evil." His is a religion of action. "Humanity is not sentimentalism—it is just work, and work again."

IV

That utmost tolerance is part of Masaryk's religion need not be pointed out. During the war, when he went about in the world exhorting to battle to the bitter end against German autocracy, he never failed to emphasize that he bears no rancour against the German people. He adopts Hus's saying, "I love a good German better than a bad Czech." In this, again, he is thoroughly Christian

—for true Christianity combines eternal hatred for sin with forgiveness for the sinner.

At a mass meeting in Cleveland he pronounced a terrible indictment of Magyar tyranny, in a flaming speech whose burden was *Delenda est Hungaria*. At the end of the meeting he said to a Magyar newspaperman: "Don't think that I hate your people. It is my hope and my conviction that we and the Magyars will be friends yet, and that before long." As President of the Republic he applied the Golden Rule to the complicated racial problems of the country. The result was that within three years he gained the complete confidence of the important German minority, and enabled his Prime Minister and beloved disciple, Dr. Benes, to conclude a treaty with Austria that amounts almost to an alliance. Yet anyone who three years ago would have predicted a Czech-Austrian *entente cordiale* as an impending development would have been denounced as a hopeless Utopian by both sides.

Masaryk carries this tolerance into minute details of everyday relationships. A lifelong total abstainer, he disbelieves in enforced prohibition. Once at a dinner party given in his honour somebody proposed, out of deference to his well-known views, that all those present should refrain from taking wine. Masaryk protested, not with the perfunctory politeness of one who does not want to spoil other people's fun, but with the religious-logical fervour of one who defends a principle. He took the stand

that for people who have no conscientious scruples
to drink wine it was right to do so. Needless to
say, a little insistence carried his point. This lati-
tudinarian attitude of his greatly shocks his wife.
Mrs. Masaryk is an American—a Brooklynite with
a New England conscience. One of her sorrows
is that her husband, as President of the Republic,
is obliged to keep a wine cellar for state functions.
She is also very much perturbed over the cigarette
ashes that remain after a cabinet council in the
sacred precincts of her husband's study.

Which reminds me of a story Masaryk once told
about Tolstoy. They were great friends, and many
years ago Masaryk visited him at Yasnaya Poly-
ana. It was in the early days of Tolstoy's resolution to live the life of a peasant. He was an
inveterate smoker. One day Masaryk said to him:
"You have undertaken to live as a peasant—it sur-
prises me that you indulge in an expensive habit
which peasants cannot afford." Tolstoy said he
had never thought of that before. He put away
his tobacco and never used it again.

Masaryk is extremely devoted to his American
wife whom he met when, back in the seventies, both
were students in Leipzig. Their romance began like
so many others—they read together. Once he was
asked what they had read. He thought for a moment and said: "Well, it was Buckle's 'History of
Civilization' "—he smiled, bashfully,—"you know
how those things are." Shades of Paolo and
Francesca!

One of the most liberal and humane of men, Masaryk has his blank spots, too. I remember with what amazement I heard him expound his views on monogamy. He considers monogamy as one of the basic institutions of our civilization. Good. But he carries his conviction to the length, not only to utterly repudiating divorce, but of maintaining that monogamy should not be merely "simultaneous," but also "consecutive"—that for a widower or widow to marry is immoral! This, I thought afterwards, was, of course, the view of a man who wooed his bride, not over sinful stories of the flesh like Launcelot and Guinevere, but over Buckle's chaste and pompous work.

V

Yet he would be gravely mistaken who concluded from this that Masaryk is altogether too good to be human, a mere doctrinaire puritan, a slightly overdrawn Hussite saint. There is nothing that visualizes for me the spirit of the man more adequately than the story told to me by the above-quoted American scholar. He visited Masaryk at Prague in the summer of 1920. One day they were sitting in the library of the Hradcany, the proud ancient castle of Roman emperors and Bohemian kings, now the presidential residence. Masaryk pointed to the side of the room lined with books on philosophy, and said: "When I was young and stupid I read those books to find out truth, but now I read novels which more exactly interpret the real things, the struggle of man for reality." One of his students tells me that in a course of Practical Philosophy they used for textbook Dostoevsky's "Brothers Karamazov."

JOHN BRATIANO, Jʀ.

JOHN BRATIANO, Jr.

I

THE overwhelming victory of John Bratiano in the Spring elections of 1922, won immediately on his reappointment to the Premiership of Roumania after two years' vacation, did not surprise those familiar with the drift of political events in that distant but interesting land of Latinity on the Black Sea. To be sure, his triumph was attributed by the Opposition press to "unprecedented governmental terrorism." Pressure in elections on the part of those *intra dominium* is never absent in any country. Now whatever may be said of political ethics, political manners have certainly not achieved, in the states of Southeastern Europe, the efficient smoothness which in the older countries of the West conceals political humbug and chicanery to all but the enlightened and articulate few. In other words, when in Southeastern Europe some one hits you on the head with a spade, the assault is not aggravated by the aggressor's polite insistence that the spade isn't a spade but a bouquet of violets, and that anyway the whole affair is staged exclusively for your own benefit. Such refinements are the mark of a higher civilization than that of which the primitive nations of the European Near East can boast.

So, whatever its exact amount, the terrorism that assisted in M. Bratiano's victory conformed strictly to precedent by being, in the language of anti-ministerial journalism, unprecedented. It is a fact that a considerable number of Roumanians had for some time looked forward to Bratiano for the execution of that economic programme which is destined to secure for Roumania, gatekeeper of the hardly tapped wealth of Euxine lands and of Caucasia, herself one of the richest countries, potentially, of Europe, a place of first importance in the continental hierarchy of States.

No Roumanian statesman has contributed more to the formulation of that programme than M. Bratiano. He is often denounced by personal enemies both at home and abroad as a reactionary. However, it should not be forgotten that it was he who conceived, long before the word Bolshevism was ever heard of in Western Europe, the idea of building a dyke against it by creating a strong and contented freehold peasantry in Roumania. The land reform, enacted after the war, and providing for distribution of the great estates among the peasants with compensation to the old owners, was originally championed by Bratiano.

But Bratiano's popularity among his people does not rest on the soundness of his ideas alone. Roumanians regard him as the typical Roumanian, the representative man of their nation.

JOHN BRATIANO, JR.

Now there are two senses in which the representative man of a nation may be defined. In one sense the representative man is the incarnation of the national genius, depository of the best racial traits raised to the nth power. It is in this sense that one calls Abraham Lincoln the representative American, Goethe the representative German, Tolstoy the representative Russian. But there is another, more humdrum and pedestrian meaning of the term "representative man." One that merely implies a blend of average racial traits, perhaps intensified in degree, yet typical,—that, plus the quality called personal magnetism. Using the word in this second sense, the representative man of a nation is one whom women of his own race adore, perhaps because some deep-lying instinct tells them that he is particularly fitted to perpetuate the species in its utmost purity.

Roumanians will tell you that John Bratiano, Jr., is a representative Roumanian; they will also tell you that he is the idol of Roumanian women. He certainly possesses qualities the value of which is evident to the objective observer: he has family and wealth, he is extremely clever and very well educated, he has a good physique, he is energetic and industrious; but all these advantages do not quite explain, to the foreigner at least, the peculiar, one almost would say, mysterious, power that he wields over the feminine half of his people. He is irresistible. He is a variant, coloured by his time and place, of that great eternal inexplicable type, Don Juan.

Before his marriage he was treated by his coun-
trywomen like an oriental Sultan.   After his marriage—well, he is an affectionate husband, and his
wife—one of the most charming ladies in Roumania, whose salon at Bucharest is a European institution—has no reason to complàin.

He is perhaps not handsome in the Anglo-Saxon
taste, but his appearance is striking.   With his olive
complexion, his long pointed black beard, he may
be described as a sort of Byzantine Christ in a
morning coat and spats.   But this Byzantine Christ
speaks French like a Paris clubman.   Only Roumanians can appreciate how thoroughly Roumanian he is even in his exquisite French culture—for
you cannot be a good Roumanian without being,
spiritually, at least three-quarters French.

Also, he is the consummate party leader,
equipped with all the infinitesimally refined tools
of Eastern intrigue and yet Western as a manipu-
lator of big finance for political ends.   For the
great banks of Roumania there exists one Roumanian statesman—Bratiano.   The rest are mere
parish politicians.   Again, how typically Roumanian he is in his blending of the political ideology
and methods of East and West!

II

His part in the Great War must not be under-
estimated.   It was a curious part, antedating not
only Roumania's entrance into the war, but the
outbreak of the war itself.   The uncertainty in

which he left the whole world of diplomacy as to
the side Roumania would eventually take was a
master-piece of political strategy. Vacillation as
a fine art had been brought to the highest pitch
of perfection by Roumanian rulers during centuries
of precarious existence wedged in between the deep
sea and a whole assortment of devils—Turkish,
Tartar, Polish, Hungarian, Imperial. Bratiano
proved a worthy successor. The Germans
thought that he would never fight against them, but
feared that he might not fight for them. The
Allies doubted if he ever would fight for them,
but hoped that he would not fight against them.
In the moment of decision he went in with the
Entente. The results were catastrophal for Roumania, but out of the catastrophe she emerged with
her population and her territory doubled, the sixth
largest country in all Europe, and the dominant
one in the Southeast. To be sure, neither the catastrophe nor the apotheosis were exactly due to Bratiano's efforts—but it is all the more typical of
his paradoxical personality that although he had
slipped the reins in the race he was there when
the goal was passed, and very much there when
the prizes were distributed. Moreover, every one
in his country thought that this was exactly as it
should be. Roumanians have come to acquiesce
in Bratiano as they acquiesce in the weather—they
may complain about it occasionally, but there is
nothing to be done.

At the peace conference in Paris he scored an-

other typical achievement. Of all the plenipoten-
tiaries he was probably, not even Mr. Wilson
excepted, the most thoroughly unpopular, He
succeeded in rousing against himself the enmity of
everybody that counted—above all, the enmity of
the Big Three. What was the cause of this peculiar
and emphatic isolation of his is not clear. With
Lloyd George and Wilson it was, perhaps, the good
old Anglo-Saxon distrust of a beard too black and
too pointed to be entirely honest. Also, there was
that subtle Jewish influence over these two arbiters
of the world—one of the most interesting aspects
of the Paris conference, often alluded to but never,
as yet, elucidated. This Jewish influence was *a
priori* anti-Roumanian, owing to the old grievances
of the Roumanian Jewry. Wilson's antipathy was
carried to such extent that it was only with the
greatest difficulty that Bratiano could obtain an
audience with him, and when the two left Paris
they were still almost total strangers to each
other. But no one was quite so rude to Bratiano
as Clemenceau, not even Wilson who was, God
knows, rude enough. Perhaps M. Mandel, Clemenceau's factotum, had something to do with
this rudeness. Perhaps Clemenceau had, in Bratiano's presence, a feeling which whispered into his
subconscious ears: "There, but for the grace of,
as it were, God who created me a Frenchman, go
I." The only one among the important persons
who was nice to Bratiano was Colonel House—but
then, Colonel House was nice to everybody; he

could not help it; he was, as they say in the States, born that way.

Here were indeed, the makings of a fatal failure for a statesman and a diplomatist. For Bratiano they netted a political capital on which he may live, the thrifty soul he is, till the end of his days. He held a brief for Roumania. He stood up for the sacred rights of Roumania. He was insulted—in his person the honour of the Roumanian nation was outraged. If he failed it was not because he was weak—it was because the others were wicked. Bratiano had come to Paris as the plenipotentiary of the King of Roumania, and was beaten. He returned home as a national hero.

Perhaps this strange fruition of success out of defeat was possible just because Bratiano was such a typical Roumanian. He had his country undivided with him as no other statesman had his; certainly not Wilson, not even Lloyd George. Whatever else Wilson may have been he was not a typical American. The English may permit a crafty Welshman to rule them, they may even condescend to admiring the crafty Welshman, but they cannot forget his being Welsh for a moment. Then there was Venizelos. He, too, stood up and fought the battle of his country, and fought it well; yet his country could never quite forget that it was not entirely his; that he, the Cretan, was after all a foreigner, subtle mercenary at the worst, clever proselyte at the best. Herbert Hoover could not become President of the United States because he had lived in England for several years. Wasn't the breakdown of Venizelos due to the fact that he had come to Greece at the age of forty-six?

Then Bratiano went home, in the triumph of his defeat. After a while he resigned, but in his country everybody felt that this was not so much a retirement as an absence of leave. They looked forward to a Bratiano ministry as something inevitable. But Bratiano remained in the background, well knowing that time was working for him. At the end of 1921 his shadow was already on the wall. In January, 1922, he was Prime Minister again, with his rivals scattered into nothingness, within and without Roumania—the one representative statesman of the Balkans. What has the future in store for him?

III

The past had certainly been gracious to Bratiano. He was not, as the French say, a son of his works. His father, scion of a prosperous Wallachian clan, played a part second to none in the making of the Roumania of to-day. He was one of the leaders of the revolution in 1848 which expelled the ruling Prince Stirbey, protégé of the Russians. Later he had to flee and took refuge in Paris. But, once acquired, the taste for revolutions is habit-forming. In Paris Bratiano was among the instigators of the Orsini bomb attempt which nearly cost Napoleon III. his life. Some revolutionists are hanged,

others are electrocuted, others, again, guillotined,
according to the form that national culture gives
to legally enforced murder. But there are revolutionists who fare better. In this snobbish world
of ours good family connections are essential
in every walk of life, even in that of the bomb-
thrower. If you are lucky enough to possess
them you get fined only where others get
finished. For his part in the Orsini conspiracy
young Bratiano the elder was fined £120 and then
sent on a vacation, in one of those lovely quiet
establishments where sons of millionaires are wont
to live down indiscretions, whether of a financial,
amorous or political nature.

The rest-cure house of Dr. Blanche at Paris was
justly famous, and its guests were amply compensated by comfort, quietude and an excellent cuisine
for the slight disadvantage that in plebeian parlance
the place was known as a lunatic asylum. In this
idyllic retreat young Bratiano spent some delight-
ful years in study and epicurean contemplation.
In the end he was freed, a wiser though not necessarily sadder man, and returned to Roumania. At
once he became leader of the Liberal party, the chief
political instrument in the forging of Roumanian
unity. It was Bratiano's party which imported
Prince Charles of Hohenzollern-Sigmaringen for
a ruler, which later made a King out of the Prince,
and which secured for the new Kingdom access to
the Black Sea.

Here I would remark, in passing, that party

names in Eastern Europe are not always inter-
pretable by their Western phonetic equivalents.
The Liberal party of Roumania, like the Liberal
party of Hungary between 1867 and 1900, would
have been more correctly called the Mercantile
party. It was the party favouring Western methods
of finance and industry as opposed to the patriarchal Oriental economy, and advocating a certain
enlightened administrative centralization as against
the traditional Oriental indolence. It had as little
to do with philosophic liberalism as the National
Democrats of Poland—originally the party of the
Czarophile and anti-Semitic magnates—have to do
with democracy.

During twenty years John Bratiano the elder
governed Roumania as if he were the real King.
He also became the father of a large family, and
accumulated a very considerable fortune. When
he, shortly before his death, fell from power, it
seemed that nobody would take up the sceptre
which he had dropped.

John Bratiano was his eldest son. He had
studied in Paris, was fond of engineering and none
too fond of politics. But in a small country the
scion of a great political family has no choice.
Some go in for politics, others are dragged into
politics; all are in politics. John Bratiano, Jr.
was dragged into politics—people said, on the
strength of his father's reputation. For years he
played a quiet, almost obscure part; but even then
he was busy forming those friendships with the

great financiers of his country which later became
his principal asset.

Then, little by little, he asserted himself. By
1907 he was the leader of the Liberal party which
presently engaged in the advocacy of land reform.
That advocacy culminated in the law providing for
the breaking up of big estates in 1920–21. The
idea of a land reform from above as the best safeguard of internal stability was Bratiano's one contribution to Roumanian politics; the other was the
realization, obvious enough to the foreign student,
but not quite so obvious to those engrossed in the
personal intrigues and parliamentary marches and
counter-marches of a small country, that Roumania's salvation lay in the development of her
colossal natural resources. Since 1907 Bratiano
was sometimes in power, at other times out of
power; but all the time he was, more or less, *the*
power; and his countrymen, including the King,
knew it.

Economically Roumania was, largely speaking,
tied up with Germany and Austria-Hungary, although the bond was the unwilling one of Isolde
with old King Mark, with the French Tristan in
the background receiving clandestine tokens of
affection. John Bratiano bided his time.

IV

From 1914 to 1916 Bratiano executed one of
the most notable performances of political rope-

dancing in history, across the vortex of the European war. He succeeded in keeping both the Entente and the Central Powers guessing as to Roumania's real designs. The doubts of friends, the trust of enemies were equally insulting, but Bratiano did not mind. "The double face of the weak is more powerful than the sword arm of the strong," says an Arabic proverb.

At last Roumania entered the war, at her own terms. The terms were good enough, but the Allies, who underwrote them, did nothing, or next to nothing, to keep them. Roumania was overrun and broken. She cannot be entirely blamed for the catastrophe. She did what Italy had done, only under much less favourable circumstances.

Assuredly, Bratiano had his share of the responsibility. There was always an Oriental element in him, which is a polite name for laziness; diffident by nature, he had occasional spells of trusting the wrong people; he now was guilty of an unscientific acceptance of unverified premises. Wherever the blame lay, Roumania paid a heavy price. Bratiano fell. The Peace of Bucharest was signed by the old pro-German politician, Marghiloman, as Premier. But just as Roumania owed her defeat to Allied delinquency, in the end she came out on the top because of Allied victory. The Peace of Bucharest was thrown aside. Before the armistice was signed Roumania, though badly maimed, was on her feet again, and her troops took possession of the liberated provinces, Transylvania, Bucovina and the Banat—Bessarabia had already been occupied.

The victory brought justification and power to Bratiano. He was again President of the Council. He went to Paris full of hope as his sovereign's plenipotentiary. He had every reason to be hopeful; for the secret treaty which he had concluded with the Entente assured to Roumania the frontiers that she desired; also, equal rights at the Conference.

What awaited him at Paris was the greatest disappointment of his life. La Rochefoucauld said, *"On promet selon ses espérances et on tient selon ses craintes."* The Allies did not fear Roumania. All the pledges of 1916 were forgotten. The Big Four, or rather the Big Three, or, still more exactly, the Big Two, dominated the scene with dictatorial power. The story need not to be retold. Everybody knows that the representatives of the minor Allies were treated iniquitously. The representatives of Roumania were treated like dogs.

They were not admitted to secret sessions. When the Treaty of Versailles was being drafted they were not consulted. Certain clauses of the treaty having a vital bearing on Roumanian interests, the Roumanian delegates were summoned to take cognizance of them. Bratiano found certain provisions objectionable and rose to lodge a verbal protest— the treaty was to be presented within a day or two to the Germans and there was no time for written exchanges. No sooner was he on his feet than

Clemenceau shouted at him: "M. Bratiano, you are here to listen, not to comment."

When the drafting of the Austrian treaty was completed Bratiano was shown the text only on the evening before the document was to be handed to the Austrian delegates. He entered objections to a number of clauses which he thought injurious to the interests of his country. The objections were recorded. When Bratiano and his colleague Misu were called upon to attach their signatures to the treaty they glanced at the text once more and discovered that the clauses which they had opposed were left unchanged.

The humiliations of the Roumanian delegates in Paris are told at length by Dr. Dillon in his book "The Inside Story of the Peace Conference." He suggests, among other things, that in the matter of the guarantees of minority rights * pressure was applied to Roumania not only by way of satisfying Jewish sensibilities, but also in order to extort important commercial concessions for a group of Jewish financiers. As he graphically puts it, "abundant petroleum might have washed away many of the tribulations which the Roumanians had afterward to endure." **

None the less insulting was the attitude of the

* The Roumanian attitude was, in effect, that what was sauce for the goose should also be sauce for the gander—that they were willing to undertake any obligation which the Great Powers also assumed.

** The reader is referred to Chapter VI of Dr. Dillon's book for a full account of the high-handed methods of the Big Three in dealing with the Roumanian delegation.

Big Two in the course of the crisis that arose in connection with the Bolshevist régime in Hungary. The Roumanian delegates had the impression that the British, in particular, were inclined to bolster up Béla Kun's power for the sake of an early restoration of trade with Hungary. Be that as it may, the Roumanians were justified in feeling that their pleas for safety did not receive adequate consideration. Tired of the constant snubbing, they at last decided to take matters into their own hands. They were unexpectedly assisted in this by Béla Kun himself, who on July 20, 1919, attacked the Roumanian army. He was defeated, and the Roumanians entered Budapest in triumph.

It is one of the ironies of history that while Messrs. Wilson and Lloyd George tried to ruin Bratiano, the dictator of Soviet Hungary should have rushed to his rescue. Bratiano scored a victory not only over Béla Kun, but also over the Big Two. The latter's revenge was not delayed long. In September the Supreme Council, yielding to White Hungarian influence, ordered the Roumanians to withdraw from Hungary. Whether the order was justified or not is a point I do not wish to discuss here. What is certain is that the line of procedure chosen by the Supreme Council stands unparalleled as an instance of diplomatic bad manners. Instead of communicating with the Roumanian Prime Minister next door, they sent their ultimatum to the Roumanian government in Bucharest by radio. There can be no doubt whatsoever that this was a calculated insult, a deliberate attempt to torpedo Bratiano. Indeed, the latter showed considerable restraint when he described the course of the Supreme Council as being of a "malicious and dangerous character." *

A generation earlier Bratiano's father, as representative of his country at the Congress of Berlin, was subjected by Bismarck to humiliations hardly less galling than those heaped upon his son at Paris. They did not prevent him from governing his country for another twelve years—indeed, they strengthened his position, for the Roumanian people felt that its own honour was involved. Curiously enough, that incident of the father's career was duplicated in the son's; and just as Bratiano the elder had survived politically his overbearing enemy the Iron Chancellor, Bratiano the younger survived Mr. Wilson, and for all I know may yet survive Mr. Lloyd George.** When after two years' retirement from active politics he was, in

* Cf. Dr. Dillon, op. cit. The attitude of the American representatives at Budapest toward the Roumanians was none the less provoking. In particular General Bandholtz, head of the American mission, took pains to display his antipathy against the Roumanians, while maintaining friendly relations with the unspeakable Stephen Friedrich and other leaders of the Hungarian White Terror. Not only were the charges, circulated by the Magyar Whites, of Roumanian atrocities unfounded, but there is authentic testimony that the presence of the Roumanian army alone prevented large scale massacres of Jews and Socialists by the Magyar Hooligans.

** In 1919, when Bratiano resigned from the premiership, Mr. Lloyd George asked the Roumanian representative in London to convey his felicitations to the successor, and then added: "I do hope that I shall not see M. Bratiano Premier again."

January, 1922, appointed Premier all Roumania heaved a sigh of relief—the inevitable had happened at last!

Today he is the one powerful personality in Roumania. His position is unique. What has the future in store for him? Will it be still more brilliant than his past? Characteristically, it is his enemies who hurry to answer that question in the affirmative. One Bratiano—his father—had overturned a throne; perhaps the streak lingers in the son.

One of the paradoxes about Bratiano the younger, son of the revolutionist of 1848, the Carbonaro of 1858, is his love of the aristocracy. Leader of the party that in Roumania stands for democratic progress and against the pretensions of the old oligarchy, he married a Princess Morouzi, daughter of an old Greco-Russian noble house. Divorcing her, he nearly got engaged to a Frenchwoman, the Marquise de Belloie. The affair did not come off, and he ended by marrying a Princess Stirbey, niece of the ruler whom his father had driven from Roumania. All his friends were shocked. "It is the ruin of his career." It was not. The marriage was a happy one; it did not hurt his political affiliations, and helped greatly his social ones.

In the study of the Carbonaro's son one could see, with dedications that dazzled his followers, the photographs of the Archduke Karl Franz Josef, of the Kaiser, of the King of England—but the place of honour was reserved to a huge oil portrait of Prince Stirbey, his father's defeated enemy. That was in the days before the war; today the pictures of the Kaiser and the Archduke are gone; their places are taken by King Albert of Belgium, Mr. Balfour, and Colonel House; but Prince Stirbey remains.

What is the significance of this portrait in Bratiano's study? There are people in Roumania who wonder. Napoleon married the Archduchess Marie-Louise, daughter of the Emperor Francis whose empire he had beaten to frazzles, in order to invest his own greatness with a halo of legitimacy. John Bratiano the younger has married the daughter of a former ruling house of Roumania. Even before that marriage Roumanians spoke, jokingly, of the Dynasty of Bratiano. Jokes have the funny habit of turning serious at times. Bratiano today is Prime Minister once more. He is by far the most powerful man in the country. King Ferdinand, a weak though not unintelligent ruler, cannot do without him. Those interested in the development of the European Near East might just as well keep an eye on John Bratiano, Jr.

COUNT MICHAEL KAROLYI

COUNT MICHAEL KAROLYI

I

No character of the recent world upheaval, with the exception of the Big Four of Entente exorcisers, the Kaiser, Constantine of Greece, Lenin and Trotzky, has been subjected to such vehement and protracted abuse as Count Michael Károlyi, first, and temporarily, it would seem, last, President of the Hungarian Republic. He is under attainder in the land of his ancestors for high treason —he has, so his persecutors tell the Magyar people, sold the country to the Allies. In Paris, London, Rome, Washington, that charge, of course, does not form the basis of an indictment; so it is twisted into the accusation that he sold out Hungary to the Bolsheviki.

He was hunted from his country at night like a common criminal; and the unrelenting spite of his enemies—foremost among whom are his own cousins, brothers-in-law, whatnot—drives him from one place of refuge to another. Once one of the dozen wealthiest men on the Continent, today he lives in the penury of a little flat of a small Dalmatian town; his wife, daughter of Count Julius

Andrássy, last Foreign Minister of the Austro-
Hungarian Empire, one of the most beautiful
women in Europe, hostess of resplendent salons at
Budapest and Paris, cooks his meals and mends
his linen; and their children are brought up like
those of a workingman.

Surely the outward contrasts of this extraordinary career present the outline of a monumental tragedy. But in Michael Károlyi's case
the external downfall envelops an inner flight upward, the attainment of peace with himself, a triumph over the mere accidentals of Destiny. His
fate is tragic; but his tragedy winds its way to the
final *kathcrsis,* the purifying bath of the soul. He
is a poor man today, a downed man, an outcast, if
you will—but defeated he is not; for his faith is
stronger than ever. He has won his battle—he has
proved himself true disciple of the Son of Man
who blessed the peacemakers and the pure of heart.

II

Michael Károlyi was born in purple—or, if you
prefer the homely figure of folk tale to the classic
metaphor, with a golden spoon in his mouth. His
family is one of the oldest in Hungary, with a
pedigree reaching back over nine hundred years.
His uncle, Count Alexander, held the family estate,
estimated at over $30,000,000, in entail—an estate
second only to that of the Prince Esterházy. When
he died the entail devolved to young Count Michael
who, still in his twenties, thus advanced from the

COUNT MICHAEL KAROLYI

comfortable and irresponsible state of a junior
member of his clan to a position of unique splendour and responsibility as the second temporal peer
of the Magyar realm.

The Károlyi estate contained, among other
things, the ancient palace at Budapest, covering,
with its park, a site of several acres in the most
fashionable section of the city, and harbouring
treasures of art second to no other private collection in Europe.   One of the inhabitants of the
palace was a ghost.   Count Louis Batthány, a rela-
ation of the Károlyi family, had been Premier of
the first parliamentary ministry of Hungary,
a patriot of the purest water, a statesman of
parts and of moderation.   In the revolution of
1848 Count Batthyány held out, at the jeopardy
of his own popularity, for reconciliation with the
dynasty.   It availed him nothing.   When the
Austrians retook Budapest after the flight of
Kossuth's government to Debreczen, Batthyány,
who saw no reason why he should flee, was imprisoned, courtmartialled and shot to death.   He
was arrested in the Károlyi Palace.   The Austrian
general who ordered his arrest was Prince Alfred
Windischgraetz.   These two details are not unimportant.

The Magyar nobility is noted for three qualities
above others—its extravagant splendour, its dash,
and its wonderful physique.   The splendour is an
oriental heritage.   The dash is reminiscent of the
aristocracy of Louis XIV., called by Macaulay—

hardly a favourably predisposed critic—the gallantest class in history; of the marquesses and chevaliers who, clothed in gorgeous silks and snowy laces, perfumed and periwigged, charged into the squares of Marlborough's infantry with the nonchalance of a cavalcade at Versailles. The physical beauty of the Magyar nobility is the mark of pure though not inbred stock, and the result of centuries of outdoor life, cultivated in Hungary very much in the English fashion. The Magyar aristocracy probably numbers more flawlessly handsome men than any save the English, and more devastatingly beautiful women than any other whatsoever.

In Michael Károlyi the type of Magyar aristocrat was somewhat modified. He was well-built, tall and lithe—good-looking withal, but not exactly handsome by the high standards of his race. If he inherited the oriental tendency for extravagant display, it was mitigated in him by his intimate contact with the West, where he not only travelled and amused himself—that his cousins did, too—but also saw and learned. But if he had less of these two qualities than his fellows, the lack was compensated for by an excess of the third—of dash. From his adolescence he was known for a recklessness verging almost on madness. His stunts on horseback and at the motor wheel were the talk of a society where physical prowess is taken for granted. And his feats as a gambler attracted notice in a milieu where forty-eight-hour baccarat or poker battles with "pots" running into a quarter million dollars were not infrequent.

But if he possessed this attribute of his class to an excess, he also possessed another quality which marked him off the rest.   Intellectual curiosity is not one of the virtues of the Magyar aristocracy. Had Matthew Arnold written of Hungary instead of England, he wouldn't have had to change much his description of the barbarians.

There were members of the Magyar nobility who won for themselves honourable places in the history of Magyar culture.   There was the Baron Valentine Balassa, singer and humanist of the sixteenth century; there was Count Nicholas Zrinyi, epic poet and military writer, in the seventeenth.   The most remarkable figure of the Magyar spiritual *risorgimento* in the first half of the nineteenth century was Count Stephen Széchenyi, publicist, economist, historian, called by his great enemy Kossuth "the greatest Magyar."   The most important of Magyar novelists is the sombre pupil of Balzac, the Transylvanian Baron Sigismund Kemény; the leading exponent of the English liberal school was Baron Joseph Eötvös, politician, humanitarian and writer of historic romances.   But herewith the list of names contributed by the Magyar nobility to Magyar culture is exhausted: and these men had to fight as their bitterest opponents their own class and kin.   With all their European manners, with their linguistic gifts, with their smatterings of the arts, with their polish of international

culture so markedly in contrast with the parochial
and patriarchal spirit of the gentry, the Magyar
aristocracy, in its innermost soul, has remained
savage and Asiatic, much more nakedly contemp-
tuous of things spiritual than the corresponding
class of other European countries.   They cared
for horses, cards, wine, women, shooting—above all,
for horses.   Their hippolatry exceeded, if possible,
even that of the English.   Their greatest representative, the Count Stephen Széchenyi, who founded
the Academy of Sciences, imported Western sys-
tems of banking, and started the first steamship
line on the Danube, also introduced horseracing on
the English model.

In this milieu Count Károlyi's bent toward serious study was not only noticed but also suspected.
He read, much and with discrimination—he was
discovered in the act of perusing works on history,
politics, even—*horribile dictu*—sociology.   It
wasn't natural.   It was affectation at the best—
sign of sinister proclivities at their worst.   It was
abnormal.   But then, of course, everybody knew
that Count Michael *was* abnormal.

There is a volume of memoirs by Prince Ludwig
Windischgraetz, the friend of the late Emperor
Charles, who during the latter part of the War
was Food Minister in Hungary.   His grandfather
was the Austrian Field Marshal who in January,
1849, had Michael Károlyi's relative, the "rebel"
Count Louis Batthyány, arrested at the Károlyi
Palace.   His father, also a General, settled in

Hungary and married a Countess Dessewffy, of old Magyar stock. Ludwig Windischgraetz, scion of an ancient Austrian house, was raised on a Hungarian estate as a Magyar of Magyars. He was a clever, restless youth with more than average courage and more than average imagination—with tremendous ambition and a whole assortment of amateurish abilities blending into an aura of vague brilliancy. He hunted lions in Africa, fought gangsters on the lower East Side of New York, was an attaché in the Russo-Japanese war, acted, in the disguise of first a mechanic, then a waiter, as a spy of the Austrian General Staff in Serbia. At the beginning of the war, he rode, at the head of a reconnoitring party of half a dozen dragoons, through the lines of a whole Serbian army. As Food Minister he displayed great industry and resourcefulness, and when all was over he calmly walked across the Swiss frontier with twelve million kronen of Hungarian state funds in his pocket. As this sum was originally intended for the purchase of potatoes, he is now familiarly known in the Danubian region as the Potato Prince.

His book is extremely interesting, though rambling and unven. It has two main themes, or *leit-motivs*. Showing what a political and military genius he was himself is one; showing what a black-hearted scoundrel his cousin Michael Károlyi was is the other. Its interminable loosely-written pages of self-praise and irrelevant detail are illuminated,

here and there, by the lightning of a first-rate epi-
gram, or the unforgettable flashlight picture of a
character or a scene.   It is an extremely unreliable
book—Windischgraetz must be taken with a grain
of salt whenever he speaks of matters impersonal,
and with tons of salt wherever he speaks of matters
personal.   He is never more personal than when
he speaks of Michael Károlyi.

Michael Károlyi was born with a serious defect of speech
[he writes.] It is well known that he has a silver palate, and
had, of course most unjustly, to put up with a good deal of
ridicule and many slights on account of this defect when he
left the hothouse atmosphere of his home in his youth. He
felt this all the more because he had been very much spoilt
by his parents, proud and haughty magnates, for whom no
one was good enough, and who thought themselves better than
any one else. . . . And now people were rude and cruel
enough to elbow him aside, ignore him and look down on him
as on an inferior being. This treatment by a pitiless world,
and the rebuffs he received from one or other young lady of his
own milieu whom he admired had already stung him deeply
and left an incurable wound.

This is a malicious sketch, introductory to a still
more malicious account of young Károlyi's eccentricities and dissipations. But like all accomplished
blagueurs, Windischgraetz fortifies his malice with
ingredients of truth. It was true that Károlyi had
a physical defect. But the consciousness of this
defect mobilized in him a compensation mechanism
that broke through to expression not only in an
inordinate ambition, but also—as Windischgraetz
himself, with a rather self-conscious gesture of fair

play, admits—in an extraordinary will to **and** capacity for work.

III

He was still in his twenties when he inherited his uncle's vast fortune. He also inherited, as it were, his uncle's position as chairman of the Agricultural Society, the most powerful economic organization in the country—the phalanx of junker interests, a second government, a state within the Hungarian state. It was not long before Michael Károlyi threw away his inherited career,—just as a few years later he threw away his inherited fortune.

The break did not occur without preliminaries. Young Károlyi had first hit on a path that led so many of his betters to their ruin. He discovered the most dangerous of drugs, at once a stimulant and a narcotic. He began to work.

He set to work [continues Windischgraetz] with extraordinary diligence to retrieve what he had left undone; he braced up his muscles, studied agriculture, history and social economy, learnt to ride and fence, showed marvellous tenacity in trying to master his defect of speech, threw himself into politics, and was successful in every direction. He could say with pride that he had given himself new birth at the age of thirty. He had acquired knowledge; an iron will impelled him to do what was beyond his strength; ambition, pride and love of power led him into extremes, eccentricities and absurdities. He was never a good motorist, but he drove with a foolhardiness that made one nervous and anxious; never a good rider, but he played polo with amazing courage; he could not speak, and made speeches which compelled respect and admiration. Michael Károlyi began to show who Michael Károlyi was.

An excellent, though chronologically over-condensed account of the Károlyi in this particular period. Also, a good instance of the way in which Windischgraetz, anything but a fool, disguises his individual dislike and class prejudice as begrudging admiration. For Károlyi's seriousness, his passionate quest for knowledge was looked upon askance by his fellow-aristocrats from the outset. His behaviour was highly unprofessional. He was a blackleg. He worked.

He worked on. He was member by hereditary right of the House of Magnates; but in Hungary nobles possessed of political ambition usually availed themselves of their privilege to renounce, temporarily, their seats in the Upper Chamber and sought election to the Lower. The reason was obvious. The Magyar Upper House resembled nothing so much as City Hall Square, New York, on a sunny May afternoon—a band of professional unemployed sleeping on benches, and in a corner a fakir reciting in a deadly drone something no one paid any attention to. What if the loafers in the gorgeous Gothic palace on the Danube wore frock coats, monocles and gardenias, and the benches were of wine-red velvet—the essence of the two scenes was the same.

Károlyi got himself elected to the House of Representatives, the real law-making body, and joined the Opposition without officially attaching himself to any party.

The name of the Prime Minister whom Károlyi

opposed was Count Stephen Tisza. One cannot
understand Károlyi without knowing something of
Tisza; one cannot understand Hungary without
knowing a good deal of Tisza. Stephen Tisza is
the summary of a period; he is a chapter of Central European history.

Was Tisza a great man? If indomitable courage,
an iron will and a contempt for petty personal advantage and comfort constitute greatness, he was.
If unswerving devotion to an ideal is greatness,
he was. If, however, in addition to these qualities,
imaginative sympathy, a constructive understanding of human needs, be required; if the value
of devotion be determined by the quality of the
object it serves, he was not great. For he lacked
imaginative sympathy and constructive understanding. Not that he was stupid—far from it. He had
keenness though without depth; he had a good deal
of legalistic shrewdness; he had mental dash, a
kind of dauntless intellectual horsemanship, which
also implied that he regarded difficulties more as
hurdles to clear than as problems to solve.

He was, unquestionably, a personality and more
than a personality. He was a statue, carven in
black marble, of the fate of his race—an outpost
of Central Asiatic horsemen thrown by some dark
remote upheaval into a strange clime and left there
to perish or be adapted—or rather to perish by
adaptation. In his heart of hearts Tisza knew that
his nation could survive only in measure with its
power to lose its identity. He hated Europe, the

West; he hated the twentieth century. At bottom this sternest and most ruthless of *Realpolitiker* was a dreamer and a sentimentalist.

But courage he had; and faith. His faith was in his own race, a race of tall, dark, lithe Turkish warriors turned Calvinist; and in himself. He believed that his race was sent to rule the land of its fathers and the riffraff of Slavs and Roumanians whose fathers had been indiscreet enough to be on the spot when the Magyar supermen arrived, or foolhardy enough to sneak in afterward. And he believed that he was sent to rule and save this race.

He was tall and gaunt, with a slight stoop, angular of figure and motion; his face was sallow, he had his hair cropped close, and wore dark ungainly clothes. He had large eyes ordinarily of a somewhat owlish expression, but occasionally contracting into the quick flash of an eagle's glance. He usually wore darkened glasses, and for a time he was threatened by loss of his eyesight. Through those grey glasses of his he saw this world as an unmovable gigantic pattern of good and evil—he derived his fatalism, his belief in predestination, both from the ancestral plains of the Oxus and from Geneva.

In his scheme of things Good was represented by the Magyar "historic classes," meaning the aristocracy and gentry, and by everything conducive to the power and safety of those classes: autocratic government, militarism in general and Prussian militarism in particular, property, especially landed property, still more entailed property; strict discipline in education for the children of the select few, and strict discipline without education for the children of the motley many. Evil was represented by whatever tended to oppose or endanger the supremacy of the Magyar historic classes: persons, things and principles like democracy, the non-Magyar races of Hungary, intellectuals, liberals, Jews other than the bankers who lent money to his government; Socialists; popular education; Serbia; Russia; the Archduke Francis Ferdinand; freedom of the press; and the effeminate French, the allies of Russia. Curiously enough, in the days before the war he used to speak well of England. He admired English legal tradition and the aristocratic features of the English constitution. He was a Conservative, but an eighteenth century Whig Conservative rather than a Tory, for what he feared more than anything else was a *rapprochement* and alliance between the Crown and the Masses as against the Classes. A fanatic Magyar and Calvinist, he did not like the Hapsburgs, but he was their faithful servant nevertheless. In his loyalty to his race-idol he swallowed even the Hapsburgs, for they were useful in keeping the dirty Slavs and unspeakable Roumanians in their place.

His physical prowess was admirable. He was a first-class horseman, a master swordsman, and before his eyes began to trouble him an excellent shot. His moral courage was that of his opinions. He did not conceal his manifold contempts and

prejudices—he boasted of them. They were the
scales of an armour behind which he defied the
twentieth century in terms of the fifteenth. He was
a junker, but not a hypocrite. He had no use for
the efficiency devices, the quasi-humanitarian allure-
ments of Prussian junkerdom. He did not believe
in the scientific method and in bribing people into
submission by social betterment as in Germany.
His fathers used the whip, and when the whip
ceased to work the sabre; and these means of political suasion seemed good enough for him, much
better than factory hygiene legislation and minimum wages and compulsory bathrooms for tene-
ments and other new-fangled Prussian nonsense.

If he ever was afraid of anything it was that the
King and the people—*plebs,* not *populus*—might
get together. That's why he hated the Heir to the
Throne with such unrelenting hatred—he knew that
Francis Ferdinand planned to establish and en-
trench autocracy by strictly democratic methods.
Something of the sort had already been attempted
in Austria where universal suffrage, introduced by
imperial decree, was used to break the back of German and Czech political cliques, although with
little success.

But if he was afraid of Francis Joseph plus the
people, Francis Joseph was afraid of *him,* without
bothering much about the people. It would be,
perhaps, an exaggeration to say that Francis
Joseph trembled before Tisza; he was too much of
a gentleman to tremble before any one. But it is

COUNT STEPHEN TISZA

a fact, testified to by the few who knew him well, that in his latter years the old Monarch could not confront an emergency without asking himself first—*"Was wird der Tisza dazu sagen?"*

Tisza's political strategy was simple. It could be visualised by that emblem of simplicity and of completeness—and hopelessness: a circle. It was based on the fact that the Crown—Francis Joseph, that is,—had one ideal: that of the Great Power. Now, to bring the thing down to its crudest terms, Tisza reasoned thus: "To maintain the status of a Great Power the King needs two things; recruits and taxes. If I supply him with these two, he will give me a free hand in Hungary to defend Magyar supremacy. Defending Magyar supremacy means oppressing Slavs and Roumanians; it also means fleecing the Magyar peasantry. But Slavs and Roumanians resent the oppression, and will foment conspiracies against the Magyar State with their kin across the frontier. In time the Magyar peasantry, too, will resent the fleecing, and will turn Socialist. Meanwhile, however, I can utilize the Slav and Roumanian resentment by telling the Magyar people that it must give me more soldiers and taxes—otherwise the Slavs and Roumanians will rise and devour them. I get my soldiers and taxes, and give them to the King, and he gives me a free hand in Hungary, and the whole begins *da capo.*"

In other words, oppression was convenient not only because it oppressed, but also because it was self-perpetuating; it produced its own machinery. The more there was of oppression, the more soldiers could be obtained; the more there was of soldiers, the easier it was to oppress.

It was one of the most vicious circles in modern history, and it was called "maintenance of Magyar hegemony."

Yet Tisza was no hypocrite. When he said "we, the Magyar nation" or even "we, the Magyar people" he meant to say, *gens Hungarica,* or *populus Hungaricus*—terms that in ancient Magyar usage excluded Magyar serfs and all non-Magyars, whether serfs or freemen. *Gens* and *populus* were the "historic classes"; the rest—Slavs, Vlachs, peasants, Jews and intellectuals, formed the *plebs.*

The old Liberal party, so-called because it had secured emancipation of the Jews, and founded by Tisza's father, returned to power after an interregnum of five years in 1910, rebaptized Party of National Work. Tisza soon resumed what he called the policy of the Strong Hand—his terminology was as forceful as his ideas were crude. He introduced a new Army Bill, providing for larger contingents of men and money than ever before. The opposition besieged the bill by what in Magyar parliamentary idiom was called technical obstruction. It consisted in utilizing the Standing Rules for stopping business. Every member was entitled to make a speech of unlimited length on each reading of a bill. He could take the floor any number of times as a matter of "personal privilege" when he felt himself attacked or slighted by any other member.   He could interpellate the Ministers, and rejoin to their replies.   At the end of a debate he was entitled to "closing remarks."   No doubt it was an awful nuisance, this technical obstruction, the methods of which were developed to utmost *finesse* by the Magyar parliamentarians, greatest sticklers in the world for legal niceties.

Tisza first tried to break the deadlock by manipulating the Standing Rules.   This was the reign of a figurative Strong Hand.   It did not work.   Then the Strong Hand grew physical—and effective.

One day Tisza instituted a parliamentary guard, in substance a detail of the regular army.   It was in flagrant violation of every parliamentary by-law and tradition.   It also turned the trick as desired. The guards—they had beautiful uniforms of the best Magyar historic pattern—invaded the floor of the House, dragged the recalcitrant Opposition leaders to the lobby, and kicked them down the stairs to the street.

By this *coup d'état* Tisza made himself the virtual dictator of the country.   Henceforth until the very end of the war—and of Austria-Hungary—parliamentarism was a farce in Hungary not only in substance, but also in form.

Prince Windischgraetz, an implacable though respectful enemy of Tisza in a later period, was prior to this coup an ardent partisan of the Premier. We are indebted to him for two snapshots.   One is from the eve of the electoral victory of 1910. Tisza asked some friends, Windischgraetz included, to dine with him in a private room of the Hotel Hungaria at Budapest. A gipsy band was playing.

When I arrived, [writes Windischgraetz] Tisza was standing in his shirtsleeves in front of the conductor, who was fiddling away with his orchestra for bare life, and dancing. Tisza was dancing. There were no women present, only myself and the two or three other men of the party, but Tisza, the grey-haired old man—he was past fifty at that time, the highest official in the land, Prime Minister—was dancing, lost in thought, speechless, bewitched, and fired by the rhythms which are the breath of life to Hungarians. We sat in a corner and ate and drank and talked interminably. Only Tisza danced. Alone, for four whole hours without intermission, engrossed in the thoughts the gipsy music set in his Hungarian brain. Now and again he looked at the conductor with his large eyes—the dark gipsy instantly divined what was wanted, changed the key, started another and yet another song, always a Hungarian song. . . .

The other picture is dated 1914. Early in the spring of that year the extreme political tension which followed the curbing of the opposition by the means described above was relieved, for the participants of the game at least, in a series of political duels fought by Count Tisza with various leaders of the Opposition. He fought Windischgraetz's father-in-law Count Széchenyi, the brothers-in-law Marquis Pallavicini and Michael Károlyi, and others.

But the most interesting duel [relates Windischgraetz] was

the one with the former President of the House of Deputies, Stephen Rakovszky, an old adversary with whom he had already crossed swords twice. It took place in a fencing saloon in the town. Baron Vojnits and Baron Uechtritz seconded Tisza, Pallavicini and I seconded Rakovszky. The pugnacious old fellows—both were already past sixty, this is what was so remarkable—attacked one another furiously. They fought one round after another. Blood poured down their bodies and over their brows and arms from cuts and slight wounds; but still they fell on one another again and again, and fought eleven rounds, puffing and blowing, till at last both laid down their arms, exhausted and disabled. (Old Rakovszky would not be dissuaded from going to the front, a few months later, as a Lieutenant. He rode meekly in the squadron of the 6th Dragoons commanded by his son, who was a Captain. It is well known that Tisza also spent some time in the trenches as a Colonel. Hungary. . . .)

IV

Károlyi's enemies, led by Windischgraetz, sneer at him because, as they say, he turned radical under the influence of the thrashing administered by Tisza's soldiers on the floor of Parliament. One does not see why drawing a lesson from a painful experience should be discreditable; as a matter of fact, however, the assertion isn't true. There is the testimony of Oscar Jászi,* the brilliant intellectual leader of Young Hungary, a close friend and yet

* Oscar Jászi was the founder of the Hungarian Society of Sociology and of the leading Hungarian monthly review, the *Twentieth Century*. Before and throughout the war he championed democratic reform and the full emancipation of the Subject Races. He was Minister of National Minorities in the Government of Count Károlyi, and went into exile after the Communist upheaval. At present he lives in Vienna. The following quotations are from his

an impartial analyst of Károlyi, to the effect that weeks prior to the coup Károlyi was already the soul and leader of the Opposition. It was he who frustrated every attempt at petty compromise, at hushing up and passing over things—baleful methods of Magyar politics. Not physical, but moral blows. says Jászi, swept Károlyi, the conservative aristocrat, into the camp of democracy. Jászi records a conversation Károlyi had with Mr. Julius Justh, ex-Speaker of the House, at the discussed period Chairman of the Independence Party.

Tisza has destroyed my entire political past [Károlyi had told Mr. Justh]. I can see now that the ancient, much-vaunted Hungarian Constitution is nothing but a mirage. There was no people behind it. You can put over anything on this constitution. If tomorrow they should want to establish Greater Austria, or a military dictatorship, all they have to do is to despatch another Tisza, and they will obtain anything from this Parliament. It is a body without a will, a decayed body. The only thing that can save us today is a Pariament of the people. The national cause must be linked with the cause of democracy.

"The national cause must be linked with the cause of democracy"—that was a new note in Hungarian politics, a note contributed by Count Michael Károlyi. Hitherto the national cause, championed by the Opposition, signified independence from

excellent book "Magyar Calvary—Magyar Resurrection," published in Hungarian at Vienna, 1921. It is the only reliable source dealing with the two Hungarian revolutions, those of October, 1918, and March, 1919.

Austria, or at least more through separation; it signified a Magyar court at Budapest—or at least one for six months of the year; Magyar language of command and Magyar emblems for the army; and Magyar diplomatic representatives abroad equalling in number those of Austrian birth. The most substantial of the national demands was for a separate customs frontier from Austria, and a separate Hungarian bank of issue.

Though its upholders spoke all the time of the "People" as against the "Court," this Opposition was oligarchic in its character none the less than the Governmental party. The two had each a numeral for a battle cry. That of the Opposition was 1848, the year of the revolution and separation from Austria. The Governmental party had 1867 on its banner—the year of the Compromise with Austria and the dynasty, ending the struggle that had begun in 1848. Roughly speaking, 1867 was the party of the large landowners, Jewish high finance, and the Budapest bourgeoisie, 1848 that of the middle and small landowners, the Calvinist clergy, the burgesses of smaller cities, and such peasants as had the property qualification for franchise.

Historically, the cleavage was the modern continuation of the four hundred year old division between the pro-Hapsburg, Imperialist, Catholic, *labancz* party, and the Nationalist and Calvinist party that looked for leadership to the independent Princes of Transylvania, the *Kuruczes* (cruciati) of Rákóczi's time.

Democracy had nothing to do with the programme of the Nationals except as an electioneering cry. Now, in Hungary the chief demand of democracy was for universal suffrage with secret ballot,—as governmental power rested on the high property qualification for the vote, a system of gerrymandering and of pocket boroughs, as well as on terrorism made easy by open polling. For some time past universal suffrage was a plank of the Opposition platform; but nobody took it very seriously. In 1905 the Crown tried to put over the Austrian experiment and establish universal suffrage by decree. The plan was wrecked by the autonomous municipal system of Hungary, whereby the County assemblies could withhold taxes and refuse to carry out ministerial measures. A general election followed, which gave an overwhelming victory to the Coalition of the Opposition parties, chief of which was the Independence Party. This was the first time since 1848 that the Nationals obtained a majority over the Court party, and everybody expected the immediate establishment of the Millennium. To that the first step was universal suffrage. However, the Coalition, once safely in the saddle, broke every pledge and sat down to such unmitigated revelry of corruption and reaction that by 1910 popular indignation returned with a landslide the old Liberal Party, led by Count Tisza and revamped as the Party of National Work.

For Tisza universal suffrage was a contrivance of

the Evil One himself. Throughout his career runs as a *leitmotiv* his bitter-ender antagonism to the enfranchisement of the masses. He perceived, rightly, that universal suffrage meant the end of Magyar supremacy in Hungary in the political sense, for it would give the Slav and Roumanian majority of the population adequate representation in Parliament.* It would also mean the end of Magyar supremacy in the economic sense—for in Tisza's mind Magyar supremacy was identical with the system of big landed estates held in entail; and he knew that the first thing a parliament elected on the basis of universal suffrage would enact would be a radical land reform law. Here, indeed, was the kernel of the whole problem. Stripped from its romantic trappings of race superiority and historic mission and all that sort of thing Magyar supremacy meant monopoly of land.

Now the same complex of reasons and considerations and sub-conscious currents of sentiment as prompted Tisza to oppose universal suffrage with a fervour recalling the atmosphere of religious controversy in seventeenth-century Scotland made his opponents sabotage the cause of suffrage by a half-hearted support and equivocal lipservice more damaging than open antagonism. Apart from a few true old-fashioned Radicals in the English sense like Mr. Justh, at heart the leaders of the In-

* The non-Magyar races formed a little over 50 per cent. of the population. They never gained more than three or four per cent. of the seats in the House of Representatives under the old suffrage and division of constituencies.

dependence party and the other Opposition factions were oligarchs, too; but unlike Tisza, they lacked the courage of their convictions.

The real support of universal suffrage came, up to the challenge sounded by Károlyi, from three groups. There were the intellectual radicals and Fabian Socialists of Budapest, organized in the Society of Sociology and the Galilei Club under the brilliant but somewhat, necessarily, academic leadership of Oscar Jászi. There were the trade unions of Budapest, weak but growing. And there were the oppressed nationalities, Slovaks, Serbo-Croats and Roumanians. Of these three groups only the last had representation in Parliament, and that was a diminutive one.

V

Károlyi's declaration, "The national cause must be linked with the demands of democracy" was a challenge not only to the Right, the party of Tisza, but also to the oligarchic elements of the Opposition. It was a declaration of war on tyranny and humbug alike. From that moment onward Károlyi had to face his former comrades-at-arms within the Independence Party, the moderates following Count Albert Apponyi and Francis Kossuth, a well-meaning nonentity, son of the great Kossuth, with the old programme of national salad-dressing: red, white, green *porte-épées* for officers instead

of gold and black, Magyar coat-of-arms for the
consulates at Port Said and Timbuctoo, and Magyar language of command for the army. Oh yes—
the programme also included the demand for extension of the suffrage. Of the senior leaders only
Mr. Justh went with Károlyi.

Agitation for democratic reform now began in
earnest. There were agricultural strikes in the
country, industrial strikes and demonstrations at
Budapest, dealt with by Tisza's well-known
methods. The Strong Hand was reinforced by the
machine gun. The general bitterness was enhanced
by the mobilization orders following upon one
another in the course of the Balkan wars of 1912-
1913. The spectre of a war with Russia loomed up
on the northern horizon.

VI

It was in the period of the anti-Serbian measures
of the government—opposition to the reasonable
Serbian demand for an Adriatic port, and the embargo on Serbia's most important export, pigs—
that Károlyi conceived a stratagem that was as
much of a new departure as his idea of linking the
national cause with the demands of democracy.
The stratagem consisted of extending the internal
battlefront to the field of international affairs.

Up to this time Magyar politics was fundamentally provincial. The joint Foreign Minister
of Austria-Hungary was not responsible directly to

either the Magyar Parliament or the Austrian
Reichsrat, but to the so-called Delegations, in effect
committees elected yearly by the two legislatures
for the discussion of appropriations of the Joint
Ministries—War, Foreign Affairs and Bosnia-
Herzegovina. Consequently foreign policy was
hardly ever discussed in the House of Representatives, so much the less as it was easy for the Prime
Minister to dodge interpellations by pleading "no
jurisdiction" and referring to the Delegations.

Moreover—and no more convincing proof of the
utter superficiality and gingerbread character of
Hungarian political life is needed—there was in
"respectable" political circles no real interest in
foreign affairs. The Triple Alliance (engineered
by a Magyar statesman, Count Julius Andrássy the
elder) was the unquestioned, God-ordained basis
of everything happening outside the boundaries of
the Dual Monarchy. A good Magyar was sup-
posed to admire Prussian efficiency and honesty
(as opposed to Austrian sloth and craftiness), to
hate Russia, to despise all other Slavs except Poles,
to detest Roumanians, to have a sort of sentimental
weakness for the Turks in their capacity of victims
of Slav imperialism, and for the rest, to give vent
to such *libido* as citizens of other countries are wont
to expend on international politics in endless
harangues against the Austrian partner of the business.

Magyar nationalists insisted that the Hungarian
coat-of-arms should adorn embassies together with

the double-headed eagle of Austria. Whatever
went on inside the embassies thus adorned was im-
material. Intelligent discussion of world affairs
was restricted to the radicals of the Jászi group; but
these were not represented in Parliament, and were
regarded by respectable God-fearing Magyars as
cranks at best, traitors at worst.

The Balkan wars brought a change. There was
shooting at the door, and a few people awoke and
rubbed their eyes. The realization dawned on
Hungarian public opinion that foreign politics may
be, after all, a vital matter. It was understood that
Turkey's defeat was a blow to German-Austro-
Hungarian interests: that the victory of the Balkan
alliance was a Russian victory. Tisza's Army
Bills, and the expense, inconvenience and uneasi-
ness of mobilization suggested the possibility of a
subtle connection between the stakes of high
diplomacy and the everyday routine of the man in
the street.

For the average Hungarian M. P. the intellectual
adventure did not proceed beyond this point. But
Michael Károlyi was not an average M. P. Of
course he had known before this what was going on
in the world; but now, all of a sudden, he drew the
obvious inference of his knowledge. It was a
revelation—a twofold one. German policy was
making for war: Hungary needed peace—therefore
the German alliance was a bad thing for Hungary.
But the German alliance depended on Tisza and the
oligarchy—and Tisza depended on the German

alliance. Tisza's Army Bill and strong hand
methods, the withholding of democratic reform, the
suppression of Slavs and Roumanians, the embargo
on Serbian pigs—all the things that had hitherto
completely filled the Magyar political horizon, now
shrank to a mere sector of the gigantic curve Berlin-
Bagdad.

So far it was all reasoning. The next step was
action. If "Tisza—militarism—oligarchy" meant
Germany, the natural allies of Magyar democracy
were the enemies of Germany. Károlyi conceived
the idea of seeking moral support against Tisza at
Paris and Petrograd.

The idea was novel only in its application.
Historically the co-operation of the Magyar anti-
court party with the enemies of the Hapsburgs was
an obvious and frequently invoked policy. In the
first half of the seventeenth century Gabriel Bethlen
and George Rákóczi, Princes of Transylvania, were
the allies of the Porte and of Sweden. During the
war of the Spanish Succession Prince Francis
Rákóczi II was the ally of Louis XIV. In
the nineteenth century, Kossuth sought contact
first with the German liberals, then with Napoleon
III and Piedmont. Magyar legions fought in the
army of Italia Unita.

Nevertheless Károlyi's risk was tremendous. One
of the few things in which Hungarians, most
factious of peoples, agreed was their hatred of
Russia. A politician caught in having relations
with Petrograd exposed himself to moral death and

even to criminal prosecution. Trials for high treason were to be had cheaply in Hungary. But Károlyi was not the man to shirk the right course because it involved personal danger.

Once landing on the shores of Western democracy, [writes Professor Jászi] for a personality like Károlyi there was no hesitancy, no turning back. He drew the conclusions of his new standpoint with a passionate logic—yes, if you will, with the *élan* and ruthlessness of the sportsman and gambler. For Philistinedom was right in its instinctive recognition that the core of Károlyi's character was the sportsman and the gambler in him. Philistinedom was wrong only in condemning him on that score. There is a fundamental energy, there are a few dominant traits in every real personality that remain the same whatever their channel of manifestation be, just as the wild torrent of the hills remains the same whether it rushes unbridled from cataract to cataract or is hitched to a sawmill or electric power station. Károlyi, the Magyar aristocrat, put all his imagination, his intuition, his unswerving courage, his chivalry, his romanticism to the service of democracy. It is just this adventurous element in him which Philistines of all kind hate so unrelentingly, the same Philistines who creep in adoration before any successful adventurer. Yet the great pioneers of today were the adventurers of yesterday—or were not Cromwell, Napoleon, Bismarck, adventurers?

In the spring of 1914 the first advances were made toward the Entente. At the same time Károlyi made a trip to the United States, to preach the cause of democratic reform to the million Hungarians in America. His trip was a success, of

13

a kind. He raised some funds and started for home. The outbreak of the World War found him mid-ocean.

On landing in France he was detained, but shortly afterward released and allowed to proceed to Hungary.

From the moment of his arrival at Budapest Károlyi conducted a passionate anti-war and anti-German campaign. He opposed war credits, demanded definition of peace terms and repudiation of plans of conquest, denounced atrocities, attacked German policies on land and sea. He pointed out that Allied victory would mean dismemberment, German victory absorption by Prussia.

In the time of the great German triumphs his attitude had merely the moral value of a demonstration, of going on record. From 1917 on, when the clearer-minded in Hungary began to realize that the Central Powers could not win the war, his influence gained; by the summer of 1918 he was the rising star. All the while the authorities, egged on by powerful personal enemies like Prince Windischgraetz and his own cousin, Count Emery Károlyi, did what they could to "get" him, or at least to discredit his policies. The German High Command detailed an intelligence officer (*vulgo,* spy) of proved ability, Major Consten, to ambush Károlyi. Consten offered a bribe to Károlyi's secretary, who took it and hurried to his master to report. The frame-up was exposed, there was a row in Parliament, and Major Consten had to vanish from

Budapest.   The incident only served to enhance
Károlyi's prestige.

In October, 1918, Austria-Hungary collapsed.
In the course of September, and especially after the
Bulgarian surrender, it had become plain that in
Hungary only Károlyi could save the situation, and
King Charles, well-meaning as always, utterly weak
as always, was restrained with difficulty by Windischgraetz and the Jewish pseudo-democrat and
reactionary demagogue Vázsonyi from appointing
Károlyi Premier.   At last the appointment came;
but it came, like the decree federalizing Austria,
too late.   When Oscar Jászi announced from the
balcony of the Hotel Astoria that the King had
appointed Károlyi Prime Minister, he was interrupted by shouts from the crowd: "The King?"
"Who is King now?"   "We have no King!"   "The
Revolution appointed Károlyi!"   "Long live the
Hungarian Republic!"

The bloodless revolution of October 30-31 swept
King Charles aside and lifted the National Council,
the Károlyist organization formed on the Czech and
Jugoslav model, into power.   By a single stroke the
dreams of Hungary were achieved—the dreams
both of independence and of democracy.   Budapest
swam in a sea of pro-Entente exultation; Wilson
was the national hero.   The *Marseillaise* was sung
on the streets, in restaurants, in theatres; British
and French officers interned in the city were cheered
and kissed by the crowd.   On those two days, had
the Allies an army corps available at the gates of

Budapest, it wouldn't have been able to march into
the city—the population would have carried it
through the streets on its shoulders. Never had a
nation a more glorious dream of the millennium
descended on earth than Hungary on the last day
of October, 1918.

VII

Alas! the dream was to remain a dream. In his
book Professor Jászi presents a convincing analysis
of the failure of the Károlyi Republic.* There were
wonderful potentialities in theory; in practice, there
was not half a chance. First of all, it was too late.
Disorganization had begun at the front; streams of
soldiers pouring homeward, not even awaiting
orders, brought with them the breakdown of discipline, the sense that everything was possible and
nothing mattered much.

But Károlyi was too late in another respect, still
more fatal. He wanted to preserve the old
boundaries, the old unity of Hungary. The Magyar people would not have tolerated him for a moment had he not promised to do so. There was in
Károlyi and in most of his associates an honest
desire to satisfy the oppressed nationalities by a
liberal scheme of federal autonomy. But the
clearest-sighted, Jászi, for instance, knew that that
could not be done any more. The subject races

* See also the chapter on Admiral Horthy.

would have accepted federalism a year earlier; now they would not stop short of secession and independence. Jászi, on whom devolved the thankless task of attempting the impossible, offered a cantonal solution, well knowing that it would be rejected. It was. He then suggested a plebiscite in every country where over 50 per cent of the population was other than Magyar. This, too, was rejected. The Slovaks and Roumanians were engaged in the delectable pastime of turning the tables, and they were not to be cheated out of their pleasure.

The impossibility of forestalling dismemberment alone would have predetermined Károlyi's failure; but he was pushed downhill from behind by the very Allies to whom he had rendered such important services, on whom he had staked all his hopes. We know today that it was not the Allies who changed suddenly; it was Károlyi who had been deceived all the while, together with liberals in all lands. He had taken Mr. Wilson seriously. Now he was to pay the penalty of his gullibility. There was a whole queue waiting with him in front of the cashier's window; but no one paid a heavier price than he.

The powder magazine of hunger, disappointment, humiliation, general decay was there. On March 20, 1919, the lightning struck. On that day Lieutenant-Colonel Vyx, the Allied representative, handed to Károlyi a note establishing a new line of demarcation, slashing territories of pure Magyar population off the Hungarian state.

Colonel Vyx added orally that the new line was to
be regarded, not as a mere armistice arrangement,
but as the final political boundary.

Next day the red flag was hoisted at Budapest,
and the dictatorship of the proletariat was proclaimed.

VIII

It is in connection with this event that the
bitterest charges are raised against Károlyi.   His
enemies assert that he deliberately turned the
supreme power over to Béla Kun, that he betrayed
Hungary to the Bolshevists.   Supposing this assertion were true—it would not, before the tribunal
of history, constitute a crime in itself; for the sup-
plementary question would have to be asked: Had
he adequate reasons to believe that by hoisting the
Communists into power he was doing the best possible thing for Hungary?   If the answer be in the
affirmative, Károlyi must be acquitted.   But, as a
matter of fact, the question need not, can not, be
asked; for it is based on a wrong premise.   Károlyi
did not turn the country over to the Communists.
He was not a traitor—if anything, he was betrayed.
Whether the affair was a tragedy or a melodrama,
Károlyi was the victim, not the villain.

Károlyi's indictment has been spread broadcast
before the public opinion of the world—above all,
by Prince Windischgraetz, and the unspeakable

French calumniators, the Brothers Tharaud. His
defence, published in a single article by the
Arbeiter-Zeitung of Vienna on July 25, 1919, has
been ignored so far. Its main features are presented
below.*

Károlyi begins by relating the events that led up
to the fatal Cabinet Council late in the afternoon on
March 20, 1919, and describes the presentation of
the Allied note by Lieutenant-Colonel Vyx. He
then proceeds:

Lieutenant-Colonel Vyx wound up his verbal represen-
tations by saying that unless he received an absolute acceptance by 6 p. m. on the following day, March 21st, the
Allied missions would leave Budapest at once. This last
statement could only be interpreted as the threat of a new
state of war.

I at once replied to Lieut.-Col. Vyx to the effect that his
demands were unfulfillable as they implied further grave
mutilations of Magyar territory, mutilations gravely infring-
ing on both the letter and spirit of the Belgrade armistice
agreement;** they rob us of territories of ancient Magyar
settlement, and render the economic reconstruction of the
country totally impossible. The conditions, I said, were so
much less acceptable as the short term of the French ultimatum (twenty-four hours) and the immediate dismemberment of the country precluded consultation of the people.

Then I continued my address to the Cabinet Council. I
realized, I said, that the position of the Coalition government had become untenable, as the bourgeois parties had
forfeited all moral support of the country, so terribly humili-

* These extracts are translated, not from the original article
written by Count Károlyi in German, but from a Hungarian translation included in Professor Jászi's book.
** Concluded with General Franchet d'Espérey.

ated nationally. Only a purely Socialist government could maintain law and order under these circumstances. The fact was that for months the actual power had been in the hands of the trade unions. If we were to refuse the murderous demands of the Entente, we needed a disciplined army. Such disciplined army could be formed, in this period of economic crisis and class warfare to the knife (Communist risings were the order of the day) by the Social Democratic Party alone. . . . In any event, only a purely Socialist government could maintain itself in the face of the constant attacks of the Communists, attacks growing keener and more ruthless every day; for under the present Coalition the Communists were in the position to accuse the Social Democrats of being the mercenaries of the bourgeoisie.

Such a Socialist government, I continued, would be supported even by the bourgeoisie in its defence of the country against imperialistic raids, and in the maintenance of law and order. At the same time the Socialist government would enjoy the support of the International as well.

I suggested that this new Social Democratic government should conclude a pact with the Communists to the effect that while the life-and-death struggle against the imperialistic invaders is carried on there would be no disturbance within the country. . . .

I concluded my *exposé* by saying that I would not resign the Presidency of the Republic, but would insist on retaining the rudder of the State in my hands in this difficult situation. If the Cabinet, I said, approved of my stand, I would on the morrow communicate with Lieut.-Colonel Vyx and would appoint the new Premier, who, in accordance with the desires of his Party, would then submit the list of the new Social Democratic Ministry. The rest was up to the new Socialist Government.

Károlyi adds that his proposals were unanimously endorsed by all Ministers present. They accepted not only his conclusions, but also expressly identified themselves with his reasoning. Immediately Premier Berinkey announced the resignation of the Coalition Cabinet. The Socialist Ministers of the retiring government, says Károlyi, emphasized as a *conditio sine qua non* of the formation of a Social Democratic cabinet that he, Károlyi, must remain President of the Republic.

Next day was the 21st. In the morning Károlyi was advised that 30,000 metal workers, the best organized and hitherto most conservative trade union, went over to the Communists as a protest against the Vyx note. In the afternoon the Executive Committee of the Social Democratic Party had a conference. This was followed by a Council of the retiring Ministry. The Socialist members of the Cabinet did not refer with a single word to the proceedings of the Party Executive meeting. They had an interesting reason for this reticence.

That afternoon at three o'clock, [continues Károlyi] the Executives of the Social Democrats concluded a pact with the Communists, proclaiming the fusion of the two parties and the formation of a Soviet government instead of the Social Democratic Ministry agreed upon in last night's Cabinet Council. Of this pact the Socialist Ministers of my Government said nothing, either to me or to their bourgeois colleagues. . . .

The whole situation was thus settled in a sense entirely different from that of the Cabinet Council of the day before. Early in the afternoon the Council of Soldiers decided, on motion of its Chairman, Pogány, to support the Communists, and at 5 p. m. they requisitioned all available motorcars, including those of the Ministers.   The whole garrison turned Communist, and when at 7 p. m. Garbai announced in the Workers' Council the formation of the Soviet Government, the power was already in the hands of the soldiers and sailors. *Of all this I and the bourgeois members of the Cabinet* (we were still in session) *knew nothing.* It was only afterward that Béla Kun told me that they had set up four pieces of artillery on Mount St. Gerald, with the idea of shelling the Government buildings in case of resistance.

Of all this I, the President of the Republic, was not informed.   Instead, after seven o'clock, when the news of the establishment of the Soviet was already spreading over the city, the chief journalistic adviser of the Communists, Paul Kéri, confronted me with the demand that I should, in disregard of my previous attitude and of the Cabinet resolution of the day before, draw the conclusions of the new situation.

After what had happened there was nothing for me to do but to resign.   In order to avoid absolutely futile bloodshed—the only organized force in the land was that of the Socialists, and the entire armed establishment: the garrison, the People's Guard, the police, the army, were under Communistic command—I signed the proclamation announcing my resignation and turning over the power to the proletariat —the power which the proletariat had not only seized previously, but had also proclaimed.   I preferred this sacrifice to assuming the cheap martyrdom of letting them arrest me, because I wanted to avoid bloodshed and mass murder in the streets of Budapest, to spare the country from the worst horrors of civil war.

This is, in brief, the true story of the proclamation of the Soviet Republic. I did not turn the power over to the Proletariat—the Proletariat itself had acquired the power by the systematic building up of a Socialist army. I had no choice. The alternatives were bloodshed and civil war, or bowing be-

COUNT MICHAEL KAROLYI   203

*fore a fait accompli. I might have chosen the cheap rôle
of the martyr of the bourgeoisie—it would not have cost me
anything beyond getting arrested—but it might have cost
Budapest hundreds of lives.*

Károlyi's narrative is endorsed by Professor
Jászi, himself a member of the Coalition government. He arrived late at the Cabinet Council on
March 20, and on being told of what had happened
acceded without reservation to the decision of the
Council. He was one of the bourgeois Ministers
who were left unenlightened by their Socialist colleagues of the Communist *coup* until after the event.

Never have I felt more clearly [he writes] the power of
the magnetic fields of the mass soul than on the fatal night
of March 21. I beheld Károlyists, Radicals, Social Democrats, even Communists, all agreeing in those hours that it
was *impossible* to submit to the brutal violence of the Vyx
note. We knew what we had at stake. But all the misery,
despair, humiliation of the past six months, all the baseness
and perfidy of it, strained to the snapping point the bow of
our bitterness. Yes, it was at a tragic conflict between the
pacifism and political realism of our conscious mind, and the
nationalism and instinctive sense of justice of our sub-
conscious.

IX

Károlyi was downed—forgotten, for the moment,
by the people for which he had sacrificed his all,
betrayed by the Entente whose supporter he had
been throughout the ordeal of five years, tricked by

his friends and cooperators. He retired to his villa on the Schwabenberg, a suburb of Budapest. But his cup was not filled yet.

It happened during his American trip in the spring of 1914 that, while addressing a mass meeting of Hungarians, he was asked by a heckler why he did not live up to his principles and turn over his vast estates to the Hungarian people.

I will not give my estates to the Magyar people, [he answered] because I want the people to come and take them away. I won't give alms to my people and I won't bribe them. The land belongs to them by right—when they awake to this they'll go and seize it, and as far as I am concerned they are entirely welcome.

His government never had a chance to carry out its project of breaking up the landed estates, the most important step toward the democratization of the country. But after he was elected President he offered, as a preliminary to the wholesale reform, his estates to the people. The establishment of the Soviet government found him already a poor man.

Soon after the Communist *coup* his friends got wind of a conspiracy hatched by noble officers of the army for his assassination. Jászi called on him in the garden of his Schwabenberg villa and tried to persuade him to leave the country. Károlyi listened sadly. An emaciated cow, purveyor of milk for the children of the ex-President, was grazing on the lawn. Jászi looked at the cow. Károlyi must have suddenly realized the symbolism of the scene, for he pointed at the poor beast with a bitter smile. "Voilà," he said, "les dernières restes d'une fortune jadis presque princière."

But even that miserable cow did not last forever. The Allied blockade was winding tighter and tighter around Soviet Hungary. Budapest was put on starvation rations. There was no milk in the city. There was no milk for the children of Count Michael Károlyi, ex-President of the Republic, but yesterday one of the greatest feudal lords of Europe, recipient of a yearly income of a million dollars.

Professor Philip Marshall Brown of Princeton University, late American *chargé d'affaires* at Constantinople, was at this time attached to one of the American missions at Budapest. He liked Károlyi —he admired his unselfish devotion, his idealism, his courage under the ordeal. One day Károlyi came to him and asked for a tin or two of condensed milk—for his new-born baby. Professor Brown gave him a dozen tins, all he had at the time. He had tears in his eyes when he told me this story after his return to America.

The first week of August, 1919, brought the *débâcle* of the Soviet, and Károlyi, who had lived in utter seclusion ever since March, was now hunted out by the victorious Whites. He, his wife and his children had to flee on foot, at night, pushing their belongings on a little cart, in constant danger of being caught, until they reached the Czechoslovak frontier and safety. The ex-President settled down in a little town, Gablonz, living with his family in two rooms of a garret. He made friends with the townspeople—everybody loved him and his wife, and when news came that the Horthy government had dispatched officers in disguise to murder him, the burghers and artisans of Gablonz organized an armed guard to protect their guest.

Nevertheless Gablonz was too near the Hungarian border to be a safe place for Károlyi. He went to Italy. But the hands of Horthy, like those of Ali Pasha of Ianina, are long. The services of a female *agent provocateur,* one Miss Türr—(she had a personal grudge against Károlyi: she had asked for an appointment as publicity representative of his government in Italy, and was refused) —were enlisted to implicate Károlyi in conversations with Bolshevik refugees. One day Károlyi was ordered by Premier Giolitti to leave Italy. The Jugoslav government now offered him asylum. He accepted. Since the spring of 1921 Károlyi is living with his wife and children at Spalato, in Dalmatia, in utter poverty. The National Assembly of White Hungary passed a bill of attainder—his estates have been confiscated, and he is too proud to accept help from his friends.

But his spirit is undaunted. He and his wife— one of the most beautiful women in Europe, who adores him—have broken with their past completely. In their souls, writes their friend Jászi, has blossomed forth a new solidarity that links them with suffering, struggling humankind. "The terrible crisis which nearly killed him swung upward into a magnificent *katharsis,* out of which he passed, more spirited, better prepared to battle for the right, than ever. He believes in the cause of which he was the protagonist, even though he sometimes despairs of his personal fortunes. . . . He has made arrangements that should he ever be restored into his ancestral wealth his wife and children shall receive only a sum sufficient to insure a modest living, that of the average brain worker—the rest of the estates shall be turned into a foundation to promote social betterment and popular culture."

Michael Károlyi and his wife, Catherine Andrássy, have lost all they had possessed in this world, but they have found a treasure that compensates them for their loss. They have found their souls. There are in Europe today no more ardent Socialists than Count and Countess Michael Károlyi. That they are naïve dogmatists? That they expect the impossible? True. The early Christians were naïve dogmatists. They expected the impossible. *We* know that Socialism is not a panacea—that there are no panaceas. Are we, in our sober wisdom, happier than the Count and Countess Károlyi in their dream? After all, for the individual it is not the contents of religion that matters—it is religion. "Blessed are they which do hunger and thirst after righteousness; for they shall be filled."

X

Károlyi's greatest fault—one which contributed much to his downfall—is that he is a bad judge of character. He trusts people beyond the limits of reason. "He has something in him," writes Jászi, "of Dostoevsky's *Idiot,* so called because he takes principles and men seriously with the *naïveté* of a child. . . . Democracy, socialism, pacifism were for him, not political theories, but moral realities, tremendous live beings, as it were, persons with whom he maintained some sort of mystic communion. . . ."

One of the men who accompanied him on his trip to America was a small hardware manufacturer of Budapest, one Stephen Friedrich, an aggressive young man whose vociferous professions of undying enthusiasm for the cause of democracy could not be suppressed. This same Friedrich elbowed himself, after the revolution of October, 1918, into the berth of Under-Secretary of War. At the time he was leader of the Jacobin wing of the Károlyi party. This same Friedrich became, in August, 1919, the henchman of the Archduke Joseph, organizer of pogroms and patron saint of the White Terror.

When Károlyi returned from the United States he met a friend of mine, a Hungarian priest who was, and still is, one of his most ardent followers and who has rendered him important services. They discussed the personalities Károlyi had met among American Hungarians, and among others the Count spoke with the greatest enthusiasm of a certain journalist.

"Oh, X. is a marvel" said Károlyi. "If I ever should want to erect a statue to Loyalty, I would use his likeness."

Even then Mr. X. was known to every novice of Hungarian politics as a most dangerous turncoat— a man of undeniable gifts but one with whom treason was a livelihood as well as an avocation, who not only joined old causes but also invented new ones so he could betray them—a man, moreover, in whose family treachery was an inherited passion.

"That is Károlyi, all over" adds my friend sadly.

From the moment when he first entered politics whole hosts of retainers—journalists, politicians, nondescript quasi-intellectuals, lived on him, and lived well.

Some of his friends wishing to damn him with faint praise called him the Pure Fool of Hungary. If he be that—the accent is on the pure.

14

IGNACE JAN PADEREWSKI

IGNACE JAN PADEREWSKI

I

THERE are two ways of assaying individual success in life. One, the more customary, is to set it against the failure of other individuals, to measure its height from the sea level of human mediocrity. The other, the more true, is to compare it with individual aspiration. The thing that really counts is not what a man has become, but how far that which he has become falls short of that which he had set out to be. From the point of view of the adoring flapper in a concert audience, or the nameless young pianist squirming in a callous impresario's antechamber, the life of Ignace Jan Paderewski must appear as an unbroken flight upward, a pyramid of triumphant genius. In his heart of hearts Paderewski knows that his was a life of failure, a life whose external brilliancy merely deepens the shadow of the internal tragedy. For the supreme failure is not the man who failed—for him there is still the solace of misjudged genius, the indictment of an uncomprehending and therefore undeserving world. The supreme failure is the man who set himself a fine aim and achieved something else, less fine; for he lost out with **Fate** not against him, but on his side.

Ignace Jan Paderewski started out in life with two great visions. He saw himself as a great composer. But, being a Pole, he also saw himself as the saviour of Poland—every young Pole of his century did. In his case the two visions united in the dream of saving Poland by his music. He ended as a virtuoso and an unsuccessful prime minister.

Mythology, tireless pursuer of the great and the almost great, did not overlook him. When an infant—so the story goes—he clambered on the piano of his father's drawing room and "produced beautiful tones." There is probably an old teacher alive somewhere, or an old peasant from his father's Podolian estate, who predicted that the little flaxen-haired boy with the clever dark eyes would some day become the liberator of Poland. Such prophecies occur in every bright boy's life. Other infants have clambered upon pianos and produced tones, more or less beautiful; but the prediction is not recalled unless borne out by the event.

At seventeen Paderewski was touring Poland and Russia as a pianist. Once he was asked to play at the house of a Grand Duke. He refused—he would not play for a kinsman of that Czar whose gendarmes had dragged his father away from him to Siberia when he was only three years old. He was a recognized artist, at least within the parochial limits set by the broad gauge of the Imperial Rail-

IGNACE JAN PADEREWSKI

ways, when he in 1884 came to Vienna for postgraduate instruction under Leschetitzky, that great
miller whose mill poured forth an incessant stream
of virtuosi. But Paderewski disdained virtuosity.
He wanted to express himself in creation—even
more he wanted to express Poland, her greatness
and her sorrow, her hopes and her ultimate, inevitable triumph. He wanted to be a Chopin who was
not half French in his antecedents and three-quarters French in his life.

But he was poor. For a while he taught for starvation wages in various German conservatories.
And he wanted money—a good deal, and he set out
to earn it.

Now one of the popular fallacies is the laboured
contrast between an artist's and a philistine's outlook on money. It is assumed that the artist *ipso
facto* despises money and chooses to do without it,
while the philistine craves it and works for it shame-
lessly. To be sure, there are artists and philistines
who live up to this generalization. Yet the real difference between the two is not in the importance
that each attributes to money, but in the use to
which each puts money once he has acquired it. The
artist has a clear-cut notion of money's value, and,
unless he be an ascetic or a sentimentalist, he sets
out frankly in its pursuit, because for him money
means a road to higher ends—it means independence. The philistine, having no higher ends, apolo-
gizes for his own lust for money, all the while
accumulating it. As a compensation or penance he

delights in sob stories, invented by underpaid hire-
lings, about the purity and bliss of poverty.
"Blessed are the poor"—that saying affords a great
comfort to the bourgeoisie. It rocks its conscience
to sleep.

Young Paderewski's difficulty was the old difficulty of the slave with the divine spark in him. In
Renaissance times, in the eighteenth century, his
case would have been taken care of by the institution of the aristocratic patron. In the nineteenth
century he could only depend on himself.

The dilemma confronting, under our order of
society, the young writer was defined by John
Stuart Mill in his autobiography. When he was
eighteen he had made up his mind that he was going to devote his life to philosophy and literature;
but he had to earn a living. He could solve his
problem either by becoming a journalist—which
meant making a livelihood out of the things he was
interested in—or else by entering a government office at a fixed and secure, though small, salary, with
short hours and more or less routine work—a livelihood very far removed, indeed, from his real life's
work, but one which would leave him plenty of time
and energy for his avocation. With characteristic
maturity of judgment young Mill chose the second
alternative, realizing that by trying to combine the
pursuit of his higher aims with the winning of his
daily bread he would only compromise the former.
The event, as everybody knows, amply justified his
choice. His case affords an object-lesson to the

young intellectual who chooses journalism as a
jumping-off board only to realize, in most instances
when it's too late, that he chose a *cul-de-sac*.

Even more difficult is the case of the young
musician; because for him that technical prowess
which is indispensable to his success depends entirely on constant tireless practice. A writer may
earn his bread and butter by sitting six or eight
hours a day at an office desk and then may forget
about it and create a masterpiece in the evening—
the thing can be done, though it is not easy.
But a musician, working in the most abstract,
least easily tractable medium, one which postulates a tremendous physical pliancy and exacti-
tude, becomes a slave to his technique. Many
a musician has been lost between the Scylla
of technical inadequacy and the Charybdis of
virtuosity.

Young Paderewski's craving for money was not
only respectable in the bourgeois sense—it was
creditable from the artistic point of view. It showed,
not that he was less of an artist, but that he was no
fool. He had an intelligent artist's clear and honest
conception of the importance of money. Money
meant independence. Independence meant possibility of creative work.

With a healthy contempt for mere virtuosity,
Paderewski set out to be a virtuoso in order to earn
money and independence, and then to turn to creation. His success was overwhelming—no one was
more overwhelmed than himself. He was called the

greatest pianist of his generation; he certainly became the richest.

II

He had to wait for his turn, but at last it came.
In 1888 he gave his first concert at Paris. The hall
was not quite filled, and the affair came near to being a failure. At least so Paderewski thought when
he left the platform that evening. But his fate was
present among the rows of that scant audience. Its
messengers were two great conductors, Colonne and
Lamoureux. They heard the young Pole with the
oriflamme around his head, and they exchanged
glances. "Chopin has arisen" said one to the other.
"A genius." That evening the great change came,
the great event which is the dream of every young
artist. Paderewski was discovered. His success
on the platform was doubled and supported by his
success in society. He was very handsome, and,
unlike many of his colleagues, he had flawless manners. More than that: he had the grand manner,
and he had an exquisite and broad culture. He became the idol of Paris, and not only of Paris. From
that evening back in 1888 up to the Great War his
artist's career was an unbroken line of successes.
He became rich, famous, beloved, envied.

All this was as he had planned and dreamed. He
had wanted success as a pianist in order to attain
independence and to become a composer. Success
now was assuredly here; but where was the com-

poser? He had composed things—a concerto for
the pianoforte, a symphony,—they were performed,
politely reviewed and politely forgotten. As a composer he never even achieved the third-rate glory of
a Rachmaninoff. He wrote an opera, "Manru"—
to the libretto of Alfred Nossig, a Teutonic melodrama with gipsies, mountain lakes, sorcerers, pine
forests, curses and philters and murders—the sort
of thing that does not go in the movies any more.
It was produced for the first time in 1901 at Dres-
den and then at Paris; the reviewers said it was
a fine piece of work, and then hurried to assure that
Mr. Paderewski was a very great pianist indeed.
"Manru" was forgotten, just as the symphony and
the concerto had been forgotten. Not long ago I
asked for the book of "Manru" at the New York
Public Library. "Manru—Manru" said the kindly
old music librarian who makes a point of knowing
every item of his collection by heart. "It's Paderewski's opera," I explained. "Goodness, you are
the first person ever to ask for it," said the librarian,
shaking his head doubtfully.

His opera was performed, more or less, by courtesy, but his Minuet is, as one musical review put it,
one of the five most popular pieces ever written.
It took him twenty minutes to do it, and it is a
charming little piece, no doubt. Ask anybody about
Paderewski the composer, and the reaction will be,
instantaneously: The Minuet. Fancy Beethoven
being remembered as the man who composed *An
Elise!*

III

Some one ought to write a book on nationality as it affects the character and the fortunes of an author or artist. The terrible limitation that nationality can be is not at all evident to a Frenchman, Englishman, German or even Italian, whose national cultures are little self-sufficient universes and who find within those universes their material, method, emotional satisfaction and external reward.

A young American of the self-conscious, aware variety will understand better what I mean—he will realize the burden of his own Puritan, frontiersman and utilitarian antecedents. The idea must be still clearer to a Dane or Dutchman who has to forget his own language the moment the train crosses the frontier of his country. But the classic cases of nationality as a handicap are those of the oppressed and persecuted races—above all, those of the Irishman, the Jew and the Pole. These three can never live down their nationality. It stares at them from every nook, shouts at them from every housetop, mocks them from behind every turning. The Irishman, the Jew and the Pole, each lives his whole life confined to a closet that has nationality as a skeleton in it.

Of the three the Pole is the most tragic; for the Irishman is saved by his wit and humour and rationalistic type of mind, and, not the least, by his English language; the Jew is saved by his adaptability, his self-criticism and his internationalism; but there is nothing to save the Pole, archetype of pathological nationalism. Moreover, he does not want to be saved; like many neurotics, he seeks refuge in his affliction. He is an incurable romanticist. He is willing to face death for his country; but he is not willing to face a fact for his country. Self-delusion is the great national vice of the Pole; it is also the cement of his nationality—the moment he gets disabused from his dreams he is apt to become an alien in his own country.

Somebody has said that the Poles, as a nation, suffer from a redeemer-complex. Intensely Catholic, the Pole merges in his adoration of his country the legend of the crucifixion with the worship of the Holy Virgin. Poland is the Virgin, the Dolorous Mother; but she, crucified, is also to redeem the world in her blood. But this national redeemer-fantasy is duplicated in the individual Pole by a personal dream of salvation. The Pole believes that Poland, of all nations, is marked off to save Humanity, and that he himself, of all men, is marked off to save Poland.

During the century of his bondage, from 1815 to 1915, the Pole throve on the legend of his country's martyrdom. Poland, pure, innocent, magnanimous, the land of the free and the brave, the sanctuary of all liberty and virtue, was wantonly attacked, raped, outraged, torn to pieces, and oppressed by her rapacious, wicked neighbours. The story of Poland and her enemies was part of the eternal struggle of good and evil, of light and darkness, of right and might. But "Poland was not yet lost": in the end she was to rise from her dead and triumph over her enemies, as sure as the powers of Heaven were to prevail over the hosts of Hell.

Alas!—the findings of history tear this myth of Poland to shreds. For centuries her annals recorded nothing but incessant fratricidal warfare of her kings with rival kings, of king against nobility, confederation against confederation, noble against noble, nobility against gentry. In no country were burgesses subjected to worse oppression or had serfs to suffer worse exploitation and maltreatment; in no country led the nobility a more wanton life of private luxury and held the purse-strings more tightly where public needs were concerned. Though outwardly still great and powerful, Poland was in the first half of the seventeenth century already a moribund state; the terrible rising of serfs under Chmielnicki, in 1648, provoked by the unspeakable cruelties of the nobles and avenged by them with horrors still worse, was the beginning of an end that lasted another hundred and fifty years. From a great and glorious past, says Bain, the greatest English authority on Poland, the Polish republic decayed, by the end of the eighteenth century, into "a nuisance to her neighbours and an obstacle to the development of her own people." The Polish nation "had fallen by the justest retribution that was ever meted out to a foreign policy of incessant aggression and an oppressive and barbarous domestic rule," said Lord Salisbury.

The Poles are a baffling race [writes Ralph Butler, another English student of Polish affairs]. In all Europe there is no people, with the possible exception of the French, which is naturally so gifted. No one can study Eastern Europe without feeling that they are infinitely the most attractive of the peoples with which he has to do. . . . Their culture is not borrowed; it is original and creative, the true expression of their national genius and their historic tradition. Yet in the political sphere their genius is unfruitful. They are of those artists who produce nothing. Their conceptions are brilliant, but they have no technique, and do not see the need of it; and they never finish their work. Their political capacity is, as it were, negative. . . . Lack of positive qualities, of discipline on the one hand and of moderation on the other, brought them to their fate in the eighteenth century. . . . Faction ruined Poland. Faction was the case of the partitions. Faction made a failure of the two insurrections in the nineteenth century.

In 1914 Paderewski, wealthy, successful, and, for all the world knew, happy, was living in his idyllic retreat near Morges, in Switzerland, on Lake Leman. He had a large, comfortable dwelling for a home (he had originally wanted to purchase some picturesque medieval château, but his wife preferred plumbing to romance, and her counsel prevailed). He had an orchard; he kept bees; he was interested in fancy poultry. There were seven pianos in the house, and among other objects of art several canvases by Fragonard, his favourite old master. He had exquisite wines in his cellar, and visitors carried the fame of his cuisine to the farthest corner of that world in which such things as cuisine are discussed.

When the war broke out Poles all over the world were gripped by a feverish hope: the hour for whose advent they had prayed for a century struck at last! They did not exactly know in what way and by what means the war was to bring about the deliverance of Poland; the tendency toward a clear definition of ways and means was never a Polish quality. But a certain confused tenacity of purpose was ever since 1815 a very Polish quality, and from August 1, 1914, Polish patriots held themselves ready for the long-awaited emergency.

In 1915 Paderewski started at Geneva, with Sienkiewicz, the novelist, the Polish Relief Fund. It was a great success, and in that success the lion's share was due to Paderewski, his tireless, self-sacrificing industry, his organizing ability, his tremendous prestige. He contributed his money, his time, his art, his sleep, his health to the cause. Then he came to America.

The four million American Poles were the greatest single asset in the struggle for Polish restoration that had now definitely begun. They had numbers; they had money; they had an excellent framework of organization. But the ancient curse had pursued them across the ocean: they were torn by factions. "Two Poles and a sofa make a political party" says the malicious but truthful proverb. Among American Poles the pro-Ally orientation which saw in Prussia the most dangerous obstacle to Polish independence fought tooth and nail the pro-Austrian orientation which, while far from loving the

Germans, regarded Russia as the arch enemy. The latter school was, all things told, justified by the past; the former was to be borne out by the future.

In the meantime both great parties were rent asunder by a multiplicity of petty factions, personal rivalries, parochial jealousies; their often uncoordinated, clashing efforts neutralized one another. There was one man, and one only, who could bring order and unity into this chaos: the greatest living Pole, Paderewski. He crossed the Atlantic, and although he failed to restore complete unity (after all, Poles were Poles), his tremendous prestige and his tireless work secured ascendency to the pro-Ally group, managed from Paris by an extremely able politician, Roman Dmowski, former member of the Russian Duma, a junker of junkers and diplomat of diplomats.

IV

Paderewski's arrival in America virtually marked the end of his career as an artist, and the beginning of his career as a statesman. He gave several concerts for the benefit of his relief fund; but his art was now a mere subsidiary of his political aims, until he gave up the piano altogether. But his prestige as an artist, while his principal asset, implied also a grave handicap. Americans may worship an artist—a successful one, that is, as measured by standards of external success—but it is very difficult for them to take an artist seriously.

In any country the pianist turned, overnight,

politician would have met with a kind of polite diffidence, amused expectancy. In America, where a pioneer community attached a slighting connotation to the very word "artist" as something effeminate and being *per se* in the way of a joke, Paderewski's position would have been untenable but for the general fermentation of minds, the popular acquiescence in new unheard-of makeshifts brought about by the war. In an age of portents Paderewski's metamorphosis slipped by the established notions of Main Street. But it did not slip by altogether unobserved. We have an excellent record of a more or less general view of Paderewski's transformation in a chapter of Mr. Robert Lansing's book "The Big Four and Others at the Peace Conference." The document is important both because it furnishes a vivid picture of Paderewski the fighter and diplomat and because it sheds a ray of light on the mind of America's Foreign Minister in the most fateful period of her history.

Mr. Lansing tells us that his first impression of Paderewski the statesman, gained when the latter visited him repeatedly at Washington during the war, was rather unfavourable, because Paderewski was a great pianist, "the greatest, indeed, of his generation," Mr. Lansing believed, and yet this pianist engaged in politics, which was none of his damned business.

"I felt that his artistic temperament, his passionate devotion to music, his intense emotions, and his reputed eccentricities indicated a lack of the qualities of mind which made it [Mr. Lansing means to say, 'would have made it'] possible for him to deal with the intricate political problems"

on whose solution hinged the fate of independent Poland. Mr. Lansing could not avoid "the thought that his emotions were leading him into a path which he was wholly unsuited to follow."

To be sure, no such misgivings worried Mr. Lansing, at that moment, as to the emotional fitness of Mr. Wilson for the part he had assumed. But then, Paderewski's exterior was against him.

"With his long flaxen hair, sprinkled with gray and brushed back like a mane from his broad white forehead, with his extremely low collar and dangling black necktie accentuating the length of his neck, with his peculiarly narrow eyes and his small moustache and goatee that looked so foreign"

Paderewski appeared to this statesman of Main Street everything that a politician should not be, a man "absorbed in the æsthetic things of life rather than in practical world politics."

Later developments showed that gentlemen who wore no goatees and who had nothing to do whatsoever with the "æsthetic things of life" were quite capable of making a frightful mess of practical world politics; but at this particular juncture Mr. Lansing could still afford that pleasant sense of superiority which made him feel that in dealing with Paderewski he had to deal with "one given over to extravagant ideals, to the visions and fantasies of a person controlled by his emotional impulses rather than by his reason and the actualities of life." He could not help thinking that Paderewski lived "in a realm of musical harmonies and that he could not come down to material things and grapple with the hard facts of life."

All of which, of course, was the typical Anglo-Saxon prejudice against a man who wore an extremely low collar with dangling black necktie and was interested in "the æsthetic things of life." It did not occur to Mr. Lansing, as yet, that it was quite as dangerous for a statesman to live in a realm of legal abstractions as in one of musical harmonies. However, don't let us digress.

This first impression that Mr. Lansing had conceived of Paderewski was superseded by an entirely different one at Paris. His second impression, indeed, Mr. Lansing avers, was rather in the nature of a conviction, and a conviction that he still holds —or held, at any rate, at the time of writing his book. It was to the effect that Paderewski was "a greater statesman than he was a musician," and that his emotional temperament never controlled the soundness of his reasoning power. Mr. Lansing at Paris extols just those qualities in Paderewski whose lack alarmed him so at Washington: his poise of character, his conservative judgment, his calm and unexcitable manner at the table of discussion.

This change of opinion is an excellent illustration of the typical American unfitness to deal with intricate European character and background. What Mr. Lansing distrusted in Washington were the external attributes of the artist and foreigner. In Paris the amenities of intimate contact prompted him to improve his opinion, and he rushed to the opposite extreme with a characteristic inelasticity that admits of no gradations, with that American colour-blindness which knows of no greys and yellows and purples and greens, but which conceives this world as a neatly designed pattern of blacks and whites. In all fairness I ought to add that if this mental stiffness is American, so are the generosity and grace which hurry to acknowledge a former mistake.

But, alas!—such was Mr. Lansing's luck—no sooner did he amend his first impression of Paderewski than it became true. It was his first impression that had been realistic, even though its motivation was sentimental; it was the second impression that was sentimental, even though it was disguised by matter-of-factness. At Paris Mr. Lansing thought that Paderewski was a statesman and not a mere artist because he refrained from playing sonatas in the council room. But observe: the qualities that Mr. Lansing praises at Paris are the same as he despises at Washington: they are but different aspects and names of Paderewski's extraordinary suavity of temper and manner, a suavity that, like his goatee, was so foreign to the American philistine. It was this suavity that Mr. Lansing at last came to mistake for statesmanship.

What wrought the change? Mr. Lansing made the strange discovery that Paderewski was honest; that he told the truth. An unexpected quality, indeed, in a man who wears long hair and a goatee! What Mr. Lansing ignored was that Paderewski was a Pole, and that the truth-telling of a Pole is more unreal than the lie of, say, a Frenchman. Mr. Lansing knew nothing of Polish history; he knew nothing of Polish character.

Even Mr. Lansing must have suspected that there was something wrong with some of Paderewski's assertions, for he took occasion to emphasize that if the latter misstated a fact he did so not by deliberate purpose but owing to incomplete knowledge of or erroneous information upon the subject. I am inclined to disagree with this diagnosis, not as though I wanted to impugn in the slightest Mr. Paderewski's good faith—he is one of the sincerest and most honest of men—but because I know that his factual knowledge of Polish history and politics was remarkable. No, where Mr. Paderewski failed was not on the point of knowing facts, but of interpreting them and setting them in their proper perspective.

Once in the mythical age before the Great War Mr. Paderewski spoke of what he called a constitutional defect common to all Poles—arrhythmia, or uneven heartbeat, which, he said, causes his countrymen to live in a perpetual state of *tempo rubato*. It is this physiological fact, he asserted, which explains Polish moodiness, Polish unrest,

Polish incapacity of steady effort.   That sounds convincing—one may discover that chronic *tempo rubato* in Chopin's music, in Paderewski's playing, in the prose of the greatest Polish novelist, Joseph Conrad—as well as in the minutes of any Polish political organization.   But arrhythmia is not the only Polish national disease.   There is another that affects the eyesight—a peculiar Polish brand of astigmatism that gives Poles a pitifully distorted view of themselves and their history.

In 1916 Paderewski made a speech at Chicago in behalf of his Polish relief campaign.   He dwelt on the historic glory of Poland, painted in glowing colours her greatness and her suffering, and then spoke of the liberal reforms of Stanislaus Ponia-towski, the last Polish king, enacted by the diet of 1791.   He enumerated the measures alleviating serfdom and preparing for its final abolition; the enfranchisement of burgesses, compulsory popular education under a system of state schools, the equal-ity of all Polish citizens before the law, the introduc-tion of hereditary monarchy—a most necessary and essentially democratic reform, as most of Poland's woes had been due to the oligarchic rivalries center-ing around the election of kings; and the abolition of the greatest curse of all, the *liberum veto*.   Then he referred to the calumnies spread by Poland's enemies, and wound up: "All these momentous re-forms were accomplished without revolution, with-out bloodshed, by unanimous vote, in a quiet, most dignified way.   Does it prove our dissensions? does it prove our anarchy? does it prove our inability to govern ourselves?"

Alas! It does prove all that, and worse. For there were just three trifling details concerning the reforms of 1791 that Paderewski failed to mention. First, that the reforms were "put over" by the king—an intelligent and well-meaning though weak ruler, far exceeding in statesmanship the oligarchy which fought him—through a *coup d'état* in the face of a fatuous and confused opposition. Second, that at the very moment when the reform was enacted Prussian, Russian and Austrian armies were poised to jump at Poland's throat, and that the reform itself was an eleventh-hour attempt to remedy the evils which had brought about the partition. Third, that within a year of its adoption the new constitution was abolished by a *coup* of a handful of Polish magnates who invoked the aid of Russia to deal this death blow to Polish freedom.

I have analyzed this sample of Paderewski's patriotic eloquence because it is so typically Polish and because it illuminates the ideology which he and with him so many of his compatriots brought into play in their attempt to solve the problems of their country. Like the Bourbons, the Poles had learned nothing and forgotten nothing. But this time they could not thwart their good luck; they could not arrest a drift of events which, by destroying both the Prussian and the Russian empires, automatically restored Poland to independent statehood.

V

The end of the war came, and Bismarck's prophecy was fulfilled. The White Eagle of Poland was soaring high again on the day when the Black Eagle of Prussia was smitten dead. Once more there was a government at Warsaw; once more there was a Polish army. Paderewski went to England; there he boarded a British cruiser which was to take him to Danzig. When he went on board the sun was just setting; against the dark red waters the body of the cruiser, covered with seagulls, stood out in glaring whiteness—the national colours of Poland! Paderewski's eye caught the name of the ship, glittering in gilt letters on her bow: "Concord." A good omen, said Paderewski.

He arrived at Warsaw, and found twenty parties in the Diet, an Armageddon of factionalism, of petty personal and local rivalries—in a word, a truly Polish foregathering. He also found General Pilsudski in the seat of supreme power—a man at least as remarkable as himself, with a career typically Polish and reminiscent of the old national heroes. He had been a revolutionist by profession, had been sent to Siberia, escaped, lived in exile, formed conspiracies. At the outbreak of the war he organized a Polish legion to fight on the Austrian side against Russia—was then arrested and imprisoned for refusing obedience by the Germans. He was a fine romantic type of soldier; he was an astute politician; he was the idol of the army. His

rivalry with Paderewski ended by a compromise:
he was made, not President, but merely Chief of
State, a provisional dignitary; Paderewski became
his first Premier.

It cannot be my aim to enter here on a detailed
account of the hopeless muddle of Polish politics
which for the next year was the scene of Paderewski's activities. He endured it for a year—he sacrificed the last remnants of his wealth, his nervous
energy, his hopes. In December, 1919, he resigned
—every word of his uttered since breathes disillu-
sionment. He had sold his piano. He returned to
America just before the Polish politicians launched
on their mad adventure against Russia that ended
when the French General Weygand stopped the
armies of Trotzky within a few miles of Warsaw's
gates.

VI

Paderewski the composer gave up his career for
Paderewski the pianist; Paderewski the pianist sacrificed his art for Paderewski the politician; Paderewski the politician gave his everything for his
beloved Poland, including his dreams. When
the politician finished Paderewski had nothing
left.

There are those who suspect him of secret selfish
ambitions and who regard his ultimate downfall as
just retribution for pride. This feeling may be a
reaction to the cult of Paderewski, the sentimental

hero-worship which was fashionable during the war
in certain American circles; it may be a reaction to
some of his political views, which in their lack of
moderation and historic sense were not at all individual, just typically Polish. It is an unfair and
unfounded suspicion. People who sit in judgment
over him in that manner miss altogether the essential fineness of his character, his real devotion to the
cause, his very palpable sacrifices. Again, it has
been suggested that the motive power for his political career was furnished by his wife. His second
wife, rather, for Paderewski had been married at
eighteen and lost his girl-wife at nineteen—she was
survived by a son born paralyzed, who lived only a
few years. Much later Paderewski married for a
second time, a Russian woman by the name of
Baronne de Rosen and who had been the wife of a
violinist, the Count Ladislas Gorski. The second
Mme. Paderewska contributed to his career as a
business manager and publicity expert. She was
shrewd and ambitious. Though (or because) she
did not know much about Poland she sensed unlimited possibilities. Once in the agitated days of
1918 an American friend of mine dined in their
apartment in New York. They were a party of
four, with Paderewski's young Polish girl secretary.
A salad was served: Mme. Paderewska, drawn out
by general approbation, avowed authorship. The
secretary grew eloquent. "This salad is fit to be
eaten by a King—by the King of England" she
said. Whereupon Mme. Paderewska, with the quiet

seriousness of a matured conviction: "But it is being eaten by a King—the King of Poland."

No, Paderewski did not become King of Poland. At the age of sixty-two he lives the quiet life of a retired man of affairs on his California property at Paso Robles; his flaming hair has turned grey, and so have his glowing dreams. He has but one hope left: that some day oil will be struck on his estate, and then he will become rich once more—he still wants to be rich, but today, as in the gone-by days of his youth, he wants to be rich only in order to serve an ideal—he wants to aid his beloved Poland.

For Paderewski is, first and last, in what he achieved and in what he fell short, a Pole, son of the most brilliant and most futile race in Christendom. By hitting a mark his life missed its aim; his success proved more barren than the failure of others; for a moment his art conquered the world, and when he dies he will be remembered by a minuet.

EDWARD BENES

EDWARD BENES

I

ONE of these days somebody will sit down and write a history of the "ifs" of the great war. Some of the larger "ifs," to be sure, have been threshed out as, for instance, "if the British had persevered at Gallipoli for another day or two"; "if the tank had been adopted on the western front in 1916"; "if Germany had refrained from suicide by submarine," etc. But there was a number of less obvious and spectacular, yet in their smaller way no less important, "ifs" which have hitherto escaped public notice. For the encouragement of enterprising young historians, the following "minor if" is herewith submitted: "If on a certain night in August, 1915, a dog had barked at a certain spot on the Czech-Bavarian frontier, what difference would it make today for the prospects of Central European consolidation?"

That, to say the least, sounds rather mysterious. But it is not the purpose of the writer to build up an international detective story around the fateful omission of an unsuspecting Austrian dog which, to tell the truth, may never have existed at all. The

239

suspense of the reader will be cut short instantly. Had the supposititious canine barked on that particular August night in the locality in question, the suspicions of the Austrian sentry guarding the frontier might have been aroused; he might have investigated and alarmed his colleagues. But the dog—if there was one—failed to bark; the sentry remained undisturbed as he stood there, leaning on his rifle and dreaming of a bowl of Szegediner goulash or spareribs with sauerkraut, as the case might be, and a young and slender professor of sociology could continue the uncomfortable and undignified but highly timely process of crawling on his knees through the thick underbrush across the Bavarian frontier. Presently he was on German soil—not yet in safety, but the worst was over—the road to Switzerland was open.

Today the young and slender professor of sociology who had the good fortune of not being observed in the course of his somewhat constrained progress is one of the leading statesmen of Europe and the world. He is Dr. Edward Benes, Prime Minister of the Czechoslovak Republic, and in all likelihood its next President, master mind of the Little Entente, one of the engineers of the Genoa Conference and, above all, one of the four or five foremost exponents of international common sense. By many authorities, with whom the writer finds himself in accord, he is regarded as the greatest and most promising practical statesman on the European Continent today.

EDWARD BENEŠ

In August, 1915, the young professor of sociology had very excellent reasons to choose the rather unusual method, above described, of travelling from Austria to Germany. The Austrian Empire had made up its mind, such as it was, to destroy him. There was some justification for this decision, as Dr. Benes, on his part, had made up his mind to destroy the Austrian Empire. It was a sort of race, with the odds heavily against the young professor. From August, 1914, to August, 1915, only an extremely innocent life insurance company would have underwritten his policy. But he eluded his enemies just in the nick of time: the warrant for his arrest had been signed. Once in Bavaria, where nobody knew him, he used a forged passport. Everything is fair in war, and young Dr. Benes was at war with the Austrian Empire. He got safely into Switzerland, where he joined another professor, also a refugee—Thomas Garrigue Masaryk. It proved to be a very good combination. In the end the two between them destroyed the Austrian Empire which had sought to destroy them and their people.

II

The eminent American historian, the late George Louis Beer, called Edward Benes, in the days of the Paris conference, the greatest of the younger statesmen of Europe. The antecedents of the man who earned this emphatic epithet from such a conservative authority had been anything but brilliant.

Edward Benes, like his beloved master Masaryk, rose to a leading place in the affairs of this world from and through the darkest poverty. He was born in 1884, one of five children of a Czech peasant. Young Benes had to starve his way through college. Incidentally, he was, unlike many great Europeans, not of the bookwormish, pampered kind of teacher's pet. He was a star football player—association football is the great national game in Bohemia—a confirmed fighter, on the whole, the sort of chap who squeamish European pedagogues usually predict will not end well. At the same time he was a passionate reader of serious literature. Under the influence of his brother he became a Socialist. His chief interest was philology. His linguistic achievements were useful to him later, when, as Foreign Minister of Czechoslovakia, he could discourse at the Paris Conference with equal ease in French and English. He could have added half a dozen languages had there been a call for them.

It was in Prague University that he, like many hundreds of his contemporaries, came under the spell of Professor Masaryk. The latter's influence turned him from philology to philosophy and sociology. In 1905 Benes went to France to study in the Sorbonne at Paris and in the University of Dijon. His stay in France was a continuous struggle for a miserable living. He wrote for Czech newspapers and magazines for a pittance, and felt bitterly the soul-crushing handicap which poverty imposes on a man bent on study and thought.

His sojourn in France had an extremely important bearing on his future. He became imbued with the Western spirit, with Western political, economic and cultural ideals. He was, of course, an ardent Czech nationalist; but his Westernism meant breaking away from the orthodox school of Bohemian patriots who looked for the spiritual salvation and political deliverance of their country toward Holy Russia. The Westernist school, of which Masaryk was leader and Benes now became a faithful follower, professed, on the other hand, that a thousand years of close contact with Western Christianity and with Latin and German civilization had made the Czechs a Western nation. Writes Professor Robert J. Kerner:

Benes became a believer in the West, in France, in the fact that Western Europe and America, not Russia, represented progress. He became filled with the idea that his own nation must learn from the West and not from the East; that like the West it must depend on realism—it must know how to do things, it must learn to observe, to analyze, to contemplate, sanely. It must not remain romantic as the other Slavs.*

Europeanism instead of Pan-Slavism became the watchword of the Realist school.

* "Two Architects of New Europe: Masaryk and Benes." By Robert J. Kerner, Ph.D. The Journal of International Relations, Vol. 12, No. 1.

In 1908 Benes returned home and became instructor in sociology, first in a college and later in the university. For the next five years he led the quiet life of a scholar and author. But a few days after the outbreak of the war he called on Masaryk with a memorandum outlining a complete plan of a Czechoslovak war for liberation—first, passive resistance at home and co-operation with the Allies abroad, culminating in revolution.

Masaryk went abroad. Benes stayed at home and organized the so-called Czech mafia, an underground society which furnished detailed and accurate information to the Allies on what was going on in Austria-Hungary and sabotaged the war efforts of the Dual Empire. He directed this work until August, 1915, when he got wind of his impending arrest by the Austrian police and escaped to Switzerland under the thrilling conditions referred to above.

III

Once safely abroad, Benes hurried to join Masaryk and became the latter's chief of staff. They organized, first at Paris and then in London, in Russia and in the United States, the Czechoslovak National Council, which became the principal organ of the struggle against the Hapsburgs.

The importance of the anti-Austrian political offensive conducted during the war by Masaryk, Benes and their English and French associates is not sufficiently realized. Of that campaign the English weekly review, *The New Europe,* was the chief mouthpiece; Professor Masaryk was the spirit and the soul, and Professor Benes the directing brain. It was perhaps the most brilliantly conceived and executed political movement in modern history. Its ultimate idea was this: that there could be no peace and uninterrupted progress in Europe as long as the political map was not brought in accord with the natural map—in other words, as long as eighty million people, from the Baltic to the Aegean, lived under alien domination fastened upon them by the Congresses of Vienna and Berlin.

Masaryk and his followers realized that satisfied nationalism was the means and the stepping stone toward achieving that economic and cultural, though not in the narrow sense political, internationalism which alone could put an end to war. Some of their followers, as was only natural in the heat of the struggle, elevated the means into an end, the stepping stone into an ideal. These extremists contended that once the aspirations of nationality were fulfilled people could sit down and clip the coupons of the millennium. This idle dream benefited only those who for one reason or another deplored the passing of the Hapsburgs and all that they were the symbols of. These reactionaries exploited the after-war chaos as an argument to show that Austria-Hungary was, all things considered, a European necessity. Even many liberals, fright-

ened by the drastic first effects of the remedy, joined
in shedding tears for the Hapsburgs.

Men like Masaryk and Benes knew better. They
knew that the destruction of Austria-Hungary was
not a solution, merely the indispensable preliminary
to a solution. They acted on the simple common
sense proposition that if you have one site, and one
only, to build upon, you have to raze the old ram-
shackle firetrap of a house standing there before you
can erect your up-to-date structure. They had a
fully articulate program of construction in their
pockets all the while they were going about demol-
ishing the old nuisance. It was the program of a
Europe reformed on the basis of national equilibrium, political democracy, reorganization of pro-
duction and interstate co-operation. It was the
programme, largely, put forward by *The New
Europe,* and some other British and American
periodicals.

The story of how Masaryk, Benes and their
French and English friends organized this campaign; how they won over, gradually, the Western
Governments and public opinion to their plan; how
they worked for a united military command and for
a rear attack on Austria from the Balkans; how they
conducted the process of sabotage and "boring from
within" in Austria itself; how they organized out
of refugees and exiles three armies, one each in
Russia, France and Italy; how they lined up the
financial and moral power of American Czechoslovaks; how, finally, they achieved recognition of

the Czechoslovak people as one of the allied belligerent nations, and of the Czechoslovak National Council as a belligerent Government; all this has been told and retold many times. Benes's part in these transactions was second only to that of Masaryk himself. Masaryk travelled—went to Italy and England, later to Russia and the United States, enlisting with the marvellous power of his personality the aid of Governments and peoples; while Benes remained in Paris in charge of the headquarters of the National Council, directing the tremendous technical work of the organization.

One of the first victories won by Benes at Paris was when he announced to the Allied governments that within twenty-four hours the Skoda plant in Bohemia, the most important cannon and ammunition works of the Austro-Hungarian Empire, would be blown up. He was met with polite doubts. Next day brought the news of the explosion. Thenceforth the Allied leaders treated Benes with courtesy unqualified by scepticism.

But more important triumphs were to follow.

Through Colonel Stefanik's friendship with Berthelot of the French Foreign Office, [writes Professor Kerner,] Benes negotiated the specific mention of the Czechoslovaks in the famous Allied Note of January, 1917, in which the Entente replied to President Wilson that, among other war-aims, they counted as one "the liberation of Italians, Slavs, Roumanians and Czechoslovaks from foreign rule." This was the first great international success in diplomacy for the Czechoslovaks. They had obtained international recognition.

The incident of the Emperor Charles's letter, conveyed to President Poincaré of France by Prince Sixtus of Bourbon-Parma, and the subsequent strivings of certain Allied statesmen to detach Austria-Hungary from the German alliance threatened, for a while, to thwart the Czechoslovak campaign of liberation. But the negotiations led to nothing.

It was Benes's task, [continues Dr. Kerner] to point out the illusion under which the "separate-peace" negotiations suffered. Backed by the achievements of the Czechoslovak armies in France and in Russia, and confident of the inevitable failure of the "separate-peace" plans, Dr. Benes negotiated in the spring and summer of 1918 perhaps the most notable diplomatic victory of the whole war. He obtained first the consent of Balfour, British Minister of Foreign Affairs, and Clemenceau, Premier of France, to complete the break-up of Austria by having them recognize the Czechoslovaks an allied and belligerent nation. It was for that reason that the French publicist, Fournol, declared: "Benes has destroyed Austria-Hungary."

In carrying out their programme and obtaining Allied sanction for its various *étapes* Masaryk and Benes had to combat a powerful pro-Austrian clique both at London and Paris. Most formidable, however, among the opponents of the Czechoslovak leaders was the Italian government, which, under the direction of its Foreign Minister, Baron Sonnino, worked with all its might against the plans of the Austrian Slavs—both Czechs and Jugoslavs. But at the decisive moment Benes, the young professor, defeated Sonnino, the veteran diplomatist, and the Czechoslovak National Council was recognized as a *de facto* belligerent.

IV

The Austrian *débâcle* in October, 1918, found Benes fully prepared for the emergency. Masaryk, elected President of the Republic while still in New York, hurried to Prague. Benes was appointed Foreign Minister in the first Czechoslovak Cabinet, and in that quality he accompanied Premier Kramar to the Paris Conference.

One of the most remarkable debaters in this singular parliament, [writes Dr. Dillon*] where self-satisfied ignorance and dullness of apprehension were so hard to pierce, was the youthful envoy of the Czechoslovaks, M. Benes. . . . He would begin his exposé by detaching himself from all national interests and starting from general assumptions recognized by the Olympians, and would lead his hearers by easy stages to the conclusions which he wished them to draw from their own premises. And two of them, who had no great sympathy with his thesis, assure me that they could detect no logical flaw in his argument. Moderation and sincerity were the virtues which he was most eager to exhibit, and they were unquestionably the best trump cards he could play.

Once his task at the Peace Conference was completed, Benes returned home to assist the President in the arduous work of internal organization. They worked out the domestic application of

* "The Inside Story of the Peace Conference."

their programme so well that today Czechoslovakia is a compact little island of culture and prosperity amid a topsy-turvy Central Europe.

But important as his contribution to the remaking of the European structure had been, it was to be surpassed by the *rôle* he now assumed in securing and developing all that which was sound in the fruit of victory and in pruning away its excrescences. From the beginning, Benes, like his chief, Masaryk, set his shoulder against the spirit of vindictive nationalism, which would merely reproduce the old conditions with the tables turned on the old oppressors. Master and disciple alike were and are for reconciliation with the Germans.

The chief danger that threatened Czechoslovakia was on the part of the anachronistic military autocracy that fastened its stranglehold upon Hungary. It was against this crazy Magyar revanche and irredentist ideology that Benes devised and carried out the plan of the Little Entente, aligning Czechoslovakia, Roumania and Jugoslavia in a series of commercial and military agreements. To a more limited extent Poland and Italy also have entered this arrangement as the best safeguard of peace. Although the principal aim of the combination was to prevent Magyar aggression and Hapsburg restoration, Benes always took pains to emphasize that the Little Entente is directed against no nation or people, and that the Magyars were welcome to join as soon as they adjusted themselves to the situation. The former enemy, Austria, had already been

included in the scheme through the negotiations at
Lana Castle.

Of course, aggressive intentions are always dis-
claimed by any alliance of States, and such pro-
testations need not be taken at their face value.
But in the case of the Little Entente, as conceived
by Masaryk and Benes, the disclaimer happens to
be true. Their idea is to develop the present formation into a system of general European co-operation—a League of Europe, as it were, imposed not
from above and without, but developed from within.
Some well-meaning people in America scorn the
Little Entente as a mere tool of French militarism
and an insurance scheme to protect territorial loot.
They forget that but for the Little Entente the
military terror of Horthy's Hungary would have
overrun Central Europe long ago, and the Hapsburgs, and even the Wittelsbachs of Bavaria, would
be restored by Magyar armies. They also forget
that the influence of Benes has always been cast
into the scales in favor of the sane reconstructionism
of British and Italian liberals, and not of the sabre-
rattling bitter-enders. They forget, finally, that
Benes was the first Foreign Minister in Europe
to advocate a dispassionate, soberly realistic treatment of the Russian question.

As a first measure of such treatment Benes
means resumption of trade with Russia. He concluded a commercial treaty with the Soviet Government, and is prepared to back up Czech merchants
who want to do business with credit guarantees.

He defined his attitude toward Russia in conversations with Mr. H. N. Brailsford, the British publicist, early in the summer of 1922.

Dr. Benes [writes Mr. Brailsford] told me that he regards the Bolsheviks as much the most capable among the Russian parties. None the less, he refuses to believe that an essentially aggressive doctrine can be combined with steady reconstructive work, and he bases his calculations on the belief that this logical incompatibility (as he sees it) will bring about their fall, it may be in 1 or 2 or 5 or 10 years. In the interval he is ready to move with a view to gaining positions for the remoter future.

But in no circumstances, he said emphatically, would he grant *de iure* recognition. His reason for that refusal is based on internal politics. It would be, he said frankly, too much of a triumph for the Czech Communists. He did not say it, but it may also be in his mind, that it would strain the rather close relations which bind the present leaders of the Czech state to the Russian Social Revolutionary party. The attitude, in its shrewd realism, is typical of Czech policy.

Among the most notable achievements of Benes, the diplomat, was the settlement of the Czech-Polish controversy over Teschen, which not only averted armed conflict between the two Slavonic sister nations, but actually linked Poland as a semi-official member of the Little Entente. Benes's share in bringing about the Genoa conference is also remembered: it was he who smoothed out the apparently irreconcilable disagreements between Messrs. Lloyd George and Poincaré. That in the end the Genoa foregathering was relegated to the limbo of missed opportunities is not Benes's fault.

Today Edward Benes is barely 38 years of age, the youngest Prime Minister of Europe, and prospective President of his country. His possibilities are practically unlimited; his determination to exploit them for the common European weal is doubted by none. One does not have to exaggerate the importance of personality as a directive force in history in order to maintain that it was Europe's good luck that nothing interrupted the doze of an Austrian sentry on a dark August night seven years ago, somewhere on the western frontier of Bohemia.

ADMIRAL HORTHY

ADMIRAL HORTHY

I

HE is a handsome man, this Hungarian admiral, and he knows it. He is also a practical person, and he knows how to exploit his impressive appearance as a political asset. British and American correspondents who have interviewed him since his accession to power in November, 1919, rarely fail to note the resemblance he bears to Admiral Beatty. To be sure, that resemblance increases in reverse ratio with the square of the correspondent's familiarity with the Hero of Heligoland; it is more apparent to Americans than to Englishmen; it is more apparent after dinner than before. The cuisine of the royal castle at Budapest is excellent, and its wine cellar is famous. But, whether or not the likeness be real, the myth that has grown up around it is a very real item on the credit side of Horthy's balance sheet. In strange lands, after all, anything that reminds of home, however slightly, is a source of comfort; and to bewildered Anglo-Saxon reporters, thrown by fate into a country whose psychology they understand as little as its language, the tilt of Admiral Horthy's cap affords one of the few links with known reality. The cap is the cap of Beatty; whose head the head be is of less importance to reporters, overworked priests of the great modern cult of the obvious. They accept Horthy at the face value of Admiral Beatty's cap.

At a conservative estimate, thirty-three per cent of Admiral Horthy's prestige in England and America is accounted for by his cap. Fifty per cent, say, of it is due to the belief, assiduously fostered by a well-organized propaganda, that it was he who put an end to the Hungarian commune. The remaining seventeen per cent is derived from his reputation as Hungary's saviour from the Hapsburgs.

Now, it is true that Horthy is responsible for the killing of a great many Bolsheviki, and, as will be seen, of a great many non-Bolsheviki as well; and laudable though that achievement may appear to some, to the unprejudiced mind it is not the equivalent of his having defeated Bolshevism. And as to Horthy being the man who kept the Hapsburgs out of Hungary—well, it is a fact that he was present when the sun of Charles's hopes set for the last time. Even so was Chantecler present at sunrise. But Chantecler, with his sense of humour stirred to life at the wrong moment, went down in tragedy; whereas Horthy, who has no sense of humour at all, but, instead, a very keen sense of business, proceeded to present the bill. "For one Hapsburg sunset, a blank cheque, drawn by the

ADMIRAL NICHOLAS HORTHY

Entente on the people of Hungary to the order of Nicholas Horthy, Regent."

The bill was approved, the voucher issued. It was not the first instance in Horthy's career that he cashed in on a coincidence.

He is nothing if not unoriginal. He takes the patterns for his actions and gestures, like his successes, wherever he finds them. By the way, it is not only his cap that reminds of Lord Beatty. It's his chin, too. Once he explained to the correspondent of a New York newspaper that he was determined to maintain law and order at all cost. (Of Admiral Horthy's conception of law and order, more anon.) He quoted a pronunciamento he had made to a deputation of workers. " 'Remember,' he had said, 'that I am here to keep order, and' — here the Admiral's jaws squared like Beatty's, and his fist crashed down on his desk— 'I am going to keep order.' " Was that squaring of the jaw spontaneous, or was it aimed consciously at effect? We don't pretend to know. What we know is that it scored a full hit. British heroes ought to copyright their features.

Another historic character to whom he paid the tribute of flattery's sincerest form is Henry of Navarre. To that great Huguenot Paris was worth a mass. Budapest was worth another to Horthy, descendant of stiff-necked Calvinists. Rumour has it that in 1920, on his elevation to the Regency, he embraced Roman Catholicism—not unmindful, add the malignant, of the provision of Hungarian basic

law limiting succession to the throne to Roman
Catholics. Be that as it may, it is certain that
Horthy the Calvinist attends mass regularly, and
he has been photographed kissing the banner of the
Virgin Mary, ancient emblem of Catholic Hun-
gary. An emblem not unknown to some, perhaps,
of Horthy's own Calvinist ancestors, chained by a
Hapsburg king to Neapolitan galley benches.

Nor does his patent connection with the Roman
Church end with this act of homage. Terrible to
heretics, that Church can be most gracious to the
returned prodigal. To Horthy belongs the distinction, not divulged ere this in English print, of
being the first Calvinist canonized, albeit infor-
mally, by Rome.

That same Catholic renaissance, reigning in
Hungary since the overthrow of the Soviet, which
revived the long-abandoned Banner of the Holy
Virgin, postulated that the Hungarian army be
provided with a special patron saint. In the bad
old days of the Austro-Hungarian empire when
the Hungarian army was less Hungarian than it
is now, but a great deal more of an army, it could
get along without such patron saint. But then
Prussian generals were available for command.
Today the supply of Prussian generals—and of
Prussian auxiliary divisions—is shut off as far as
Hungary is concerned; is there any wonder that
she seeks support from the powers beyond? Application for a patron saint was officially made to the
Holy See, which in due time announced the ap-

pointment to the post of St. John of Capistrano, a Neapolitan monk whose fiery eloquence helped the recruiting campaigns of John Hunyadi, scourge of the Turks in the fifteenth century.

Now the appointment of the heavenly captain-general pleased the Catholic element of the country, but it displeased the Calvinists whose power in Hungary, though far less articulate and at present rather dormant, is potentially quite considerable. For once these Protestants lived up to their name and protested against pasting a sectarian label over the National Army. This protest did not embarrass the Chaplain-General, the Roman Catholic Bishop Zadravecz. If, he said, the Calvinists resented that the army should have a Catholic patron saint—why, it was perfectly simple: there ought to be a Calvinist patron saint, too. Would the High Presbytery kindly suggest one of its own saints for the office of co-patron? The amazed Calvinists replied that they were obliged for the kindness, but that they had no saints. And now Bishop Zadravecz had an inspiration. He ordered a large panel painted for the church of the Budapest garrison—a panel representing in friendly company St. John of Capistrano, the fighting Franciscan of Naples, with Nicholas Horthy, the Calvinist Admiral. Between the two the likeness of Bishop Zadravecz himself was portrayed, evidently a sort of heavenly liaison officer. Everybody was happy, except, perhaps, the spirit of John Calvin—but then he was left out of the consultation.

In this triptych Admiral Horthy appears mounted on his white horse. That white horse, like Beatty's cap, has become a fixture of the Horthy myth; like Beatty's cap, it is a plagiarism—its spiritual ancestor, as it were, was the celebrated black horse of the French royalist General Boulanger. He rode this white horse when, in November, 1919, he entered Budapest as a conqueror, at the head of his National Army, with the Banner of the Virgin waving above his (alas! heretical) head. That ride was one of the climaxes of Admiral Horthy's career. Official Hungary celebrated the event as a great victory over the Roumanians who had evacuated the city on the day before. Official Hungary disregarded the trifling detail that there was no causal connection between the Roumanian withdrawal and Horthy's entry. The National Army had never had a chance to fire a shot at King Ferdinand's troops. They left because the Allies at Paris ordered them to. Had the Hungarian Government desired to commemorate the event by a special coin, in all honesty the inscription should have been: *"Afflavit Concilium Supremum et Dissipati Sunt."* But no special coin was struck, and even had there been one, the chances are that the inscription would have contained more poetry than truth. Servility to humdrum fact is none of the vices of the new chivalry that rules Hungary in the person of Admiral Horthy.

There are people, in Hungary and out, to whom the idea of a mounted Admiral appears irresistibly funny. Such exaggerated sense of humor is classified by the Hungarian penal code, as amended under Horthy's reign, as a kind of *lèse-majesté*—the technical term is "violation of the governor," *crimen læsi gubernatoris*. But in the music halls of Vienna and Prague, cities outside the jurisdiction of Hungarian courts, allusions are often heard to the mounted Admiral at Budapest, and the tone of these references is, I am afraid, rather Offenbachian. There are, moreover, iconoclasts who question the necessity, and even good taste, of wearing an Admiral's uniform in a country that has as much of a seaboard and as much of a navy as Switzerland. These ill-mannered people sneer at Horthy's promotion lists which usually include a few naval appointments—Captain of Corvet So-and-So to be Captain of Frigate; Lieutenant This-or-That to be Captain of Corvet, and so on. But making fun of this sort of thing is a sign of bad breeding in Budapest; usually only Bolsheviki are guilty of it.

II

There is one point on which both Horthy's enemies and his friends emphatically agree: that he is the prototype of his class, and the symbol of that class returned to power. Hungarians call this class, with a word borrowed from English, gentry; squirearchy would probably describe it better.

Up to 1848 this class, together with the aristocracy, was the sole possessor of the land and of political and civil rights. The serfs—*glebæ adscripti* since 1514—paid their tithes and their taxes, worshipped God and the landlord, and bred and died like cattle. The aristocrats were absentees, mostly at the Vienna court, in whose atmosphere they were slowly denationalized. In the seventeenth century most of the great noble houses were reclaimed from Protestantism by Hapsburg counter-reformation. This fact accentuated the cleavage between them and the gentry, which remained Calvinist to a large extent. In contrast to the Austrianized nobles, the squirearchy preserved intact the old national customs and traditions, including a thorough contempt for the national language; up to the nineteenth century, a sort of pidgin-Latin was the official and the polite idiom. These gentry lived in their manors a life of idleness tempered by a little husbandry, a good deal of hunting, eating and drinking, and peppered by occasional outbursts of rhetoric which they called politics. Upon culture they looked down as something alien and therefore detestable. They seduced pretty peasant girls and administered corporeal punishment to indignant peasant fathers.

Originally their *levées-en-masse,* called "noble insurrections," provided defense for the country against external enemies. But gradually these *lévées* ceased, and the country was protected by professional armies of royal mercenaries and impressed serfs, the expenses being, conveniently, borne by the serfs who escaped impressment. The gentry were in eternal opposition to the central government, which they denounced as alien oppression. This also was a convenient arrangement, as it afforded an excuse for dodging public service and for glorifying passive resistance and political ca'canny as patriotism. Even their "stiff-necked" Calvinism became by and by not so much a matter of religious fervour as a political tradition, a mode of teasing the Catholic court. It was the gentry who frustrated the enlightened reforms of Joseph II, disciple of Frederick the Great and noblest of Hapsburg rulers. When Metternich's brilliant friend, Friedrich von Gentz said that Asia began at the gates of Vienna, he had in mind this Hungarian squirearchy, retrograde, narrow and cruel.

The reform laws of 1848 abolished serfdom and the nobility's privileges, including exemption from taxes, and enfranchised the burghers and propertied peasants. That was a terrible blow to the squirearchy. Deprived from the fruits of the tithe and *corvée,* they actually had to get up and work for a living. But worse things were yet to come. In 1868 the Jews of Hungary, mostly old settlers whose lot had been on the whole fairly good, were emancipated. That was the *coup de grâce* to the patriarchial economy. Western methods of commerce, industry and credit were introduced, with free competition safeguarded by law. The great noble houses with their immense wealth weathered

the storm; some of the more intellectually mobile
aristocrats even rode the crest of the wave; but the
gentry went down rapidly. Unwilling to surrender
old standards of life, unwilling to learn the new
profitable pursuits, they sold or mortgaged their
estates and their emancipation bonds, and squan-
dered the remnants of their patrimony in wild
revels, frequently followed by suicide, more often
by the slow death of genteel poverty in some county,
sinecure. On the other hand, the power of the
Jews, thrifty, provident, quick to learn the new
Western ways, increased in proportion. At the
outbreak of the World War Hungary was ruled
by the alliance of great aristocratic families and
the new class of industrial and financial magnates.
The country was still an oligarchy; but the type
changed from a semi-oriental patriarchal rule of
the squirearchy to a more Westernized system of
large scale exploitation.

The collapse of the Hapsburg empire in October, 1919, ended this chapter of Hungarian evolution. The revolution of October, headed by a
radical aristocrat, Count Michael Károlyi, was the
work of two elements which gathered strength in
the preceding decades of gradual Westernization
—the bourgeois intellectuals, mostly Jewish, and
the industrial workers of Budapest. It was a very
mild affair, indeed, this Revolution of the White
Aster; its leaders were middle class theorists or
Fabian socialists; its aim was to establish peace
with the Allies, friendship with the non-Magyar

races, and to reorganize the State on lines of Western democracy. The aspirations and the intellectual level of the movement were high; but it had no root in the politically undeveloped masses; it was topheavy.

Had Károlyi succeeded in dividing the great estates, with compensation to the old owners, among the peasantry, he would have won the support of the latter, and would probably have endured. But the blows of a short-sighted allied policy (*Les vainqueurs sont toujours Boches,* wrote Oscar Jászi, the brilliant leader of intellectual radicals), and of a Russian-financed Bolshevik propaganda of returned war prisoners from within, undermined his authority. Károlyi fell; the Soviet came into power. But the Soviet had even less vital strength behind it than the liberal revolution; it was born of despair, a makeshift run by a group of stupid, ill-educated adventurers and narrow-minded, if honest, dogmatists. Instead of trying to win over the peasants, the one real if inarticulate power in the country, they did everything to antagonize them. The Hungarian Commune was on the point of collapse from inner rottenness when the Roumanian attack, at the end of July, 1919, dealt it the deathblow.

The Roumanians entered Budapest, and disarmed not only the Communists, who at this time were throwing away their arms voluntarily, but also the anti-Communist Trade Unionists. They did not disarm the White Guards, formed either

beyond the frontiers of Soviet power or at Budapest, in the moment of the overturn. Three months
later the Roumanians left, on orders from Paris. At
that moment the only organized power in the
country was the army of White Guard detachments; and these White Guards represented an
armed class—the Gentry. After a lapse of almost
eighty years suddenly the Magyar gentry was back
in the seat of supreme power, unchallenged. It
was a return with a vengeance—only too literally
so. Their leader and standard bearer was Admiral
Nicholas Horthy.

III

It was in the days of the Soviet régime at
Budapest that a few hundred officers of the old
Austro-Hungarian army formed at Szegedin a
counter-revolutionary government. Szegedin was
beyond the reach of Béla Kun's power, in the zone
assigned by the terms of the armistice to the Jugo-
Slavs, and was garrisoned by French colonial
troops. A cabinet was appointed, or rather appointed itself, but this cabinet had no real attribute
of power except a small volunteer army consisting
exclusively of officers, on the Russian counter-revolutionary pattern. It had no constructive policy,
no programme, no working plan beyond the engineering of anti-Communist intrigue at Budapest.
It was financed by French subsidies and by "volun-
tary" contributions of wealthy Szegedin Jews,

whose patriotic zeal was stimulated by visits of grim-looking officers carrying, rather obviously, big Mauser pistols in their holsters. The one thing that forged these men into a potential political instrument was their hatred of Béla Kun and his gang. They might have adopted as their motto, "Hang the Bolsheviki—after that the deluge."

But this hatred, this lust of revenge sought out the Communists at Budapest only as the nearest target at hand, as the scapegoat conveniently substituted for a much more dangerous but much less palpable enemy. Almost without exception these officers belonged to the Gentry, the class dispossessed from its privileges during the last half century. They were victims of the evolution that wound its way through industrialisation toward modern Western democracy and reached a premature pinnacle in the brief period of the Károlyi Republic. In this evolution Soviet rule was a mere interlude, a diversion and delay rather than a realized aim. The more sophisticated among the officers and bureaucrats perceived that their real enemy was not violent revolution which, after all, could be countered by more violence, but democratic evolution with its subtle and irresistible processes. Now the carriers, the agents of that evolution were the intellectual and commercial bourgeoisie, consisting mostly of Jews. But most of the Communist leaders were Jews, too. Here was a coincidence, and in a sense something more substantial than a coincidence, that the leaders of the counter-Revolutionists realized afforded a great simplification, that could be exploited for purposes of propaganda.

To the great majority of the officers, of course, these considerations never occurred. All they could understand was that an intangible something, some sort of a human earthquake, had swept away the foundations of the old Hungarian State with its comfortable class privileges, had destroyed the Austro-Hungarian army, and with the army their own livelihood. All they knew was that if they could not be officers and gentlemen, they would have to starve. That intangible hostile Something now resulted in putting a bunch of "dirty Jews" into power. But even before the revolution, it was Jews to whom their fathers had mortgaged or sold their estates, who had the best lawyers' and physicians' practices, owned the factories, bought and sold the produce of the land, ran the newspapers, introduced all kinds of alien notions, French, English, German, into the country.

In a word, the Jews were at the bottom of all the misery that befell the "historical" class, the chief pillar of Magyar nationhood, the Gentry. The Jews had to go. The mood of the officers was symbolized by one Captain Prónay, head of one of the Szegedin detachments,—as the officers' units were called—who swore that he would not rest until he killed one thousand Jews with his own hands. The officers drilled at day—at night they

drank to the Day that was to end for ever the rule
of Communists, Liberals, intellectuals and other
Jews.

The commander-in-chief of this officers' army
was Nicholas Horthy de Nagybánya, Vice-Admiral of the old Austro-Hungarian navy. He was
the son of a fairly prosperous Calvinist squire of
County Szolnok, in the heart of the great Hungarian plain. Young Horthy went in for a naval
career, a very unusual thing among members
of his class, who commonly regarded the cavalry
as the only arm worthy of their choice. The navy
was a purely Imperial, un-Magyar institution;
naval officers had to be educated at Pola; they had
to speak German; they had nothing to do with
horses; and thus were apt to become denationalized.
To this very day Nicholas Horthy speaks Hungarian with a German accent. His advancement in
the navy was good. He was assigned to the
general staff, and later appointed aid to the old
Emperor Francis Joseph, a rare honour for a
Magyar and a Calvinist.

In the war Captain Horthy commanded the
cruiser "Novara," ominously named after Radetzky's victory over the Piedmontese in 1848. He
displayed considerable physical courage, the kind
of dash which is the mark of cavalry officers of his
class. It was his squadron that shelled, repeatedly,
Italian coast cities. He was wounded in the battle
of Otranto. But his supreme exploit, the one that
brought him the rank of Admiral was the quelling

of the naval mutiny at Cattaro. It was a most characteristic exploit in more than one sense.

The men who rebelled at Cattaro were, like the majority of the Austro-Hungarian naval personnel, Jugo-Slavs, Croat-speaking Dalmatians—since Roman days among the best sailors in Europe. What caused the mutiny is not quite clear—some say it was too much Jugo-Slav national feeling, others, too much sauerkraut. One day the red flag was hoisted on several destroyers and light cruisers in the harbor, and officers on board were disarmed. A loyal somebody in the land fortress flashed out a radio call for help. There was a fleet of German submarines in the Straits of Otranto. A squadron was dispatched at full speed to deal with the mutineers. The submarines entered the harbour. A few shots were fired. The mutineers surrendered unconditionally. When all was over Horthy appeared on the scene. His cruiser hoisted the Imperial ensign; the ship's band struck up the Imperial anthem; and henceforth Horthy was known as the Hero of Cattaro. He court-martialled the rebels and had a number of them shot. Soon he was promoted to the rank of vice-admiral.

When the end came, a particularly odious and humiliating task fell to Horthy's lot: he was instructed to turn over the entire Austro-Hungarian fleet to the Jugo-Slavs. From that moment the Austro-Hungarian navy was a mere memory, and Horthy was an admiral only *in partibus infidelium,* having no more to do with a fleet than the Roman

Archbishop of Trebizond has to do with his diocese. A prouder soul might have discarded the admiral's uniform, now the token of defeat and disgrace; a more realistic spirit would have sought new fields of patriotic endeavour, would have adapted itself to the exigencies of a situation where Hungary's interests lay in forgetting as quickly about armies and navies as possible. Not so Horthy. He wore his naval uniform when he retired into the steppes of his paternal estate in County Szolnok, and did not re-emerge until the formation of the counter-revolutionary government at Szegedin.

IV

When Béla Kun fell Horthy asked the French command for permission to enter Budapest with his troops. But they were not wanted there by the Roumanians, and the French, none too loath to be rid of the boisterous and rather useless auxiliaries, allowed them to cross into the Trans-Danubian country. Horthy now established headquarters at the popular bathing resort Siófok, on Lake Balaton. The detachments were turned loose on the countryside.

What followed now is comparable only to the record of the Turks in Armenia—nothing in recent European history furnishes a parallel. Before leaving Szegedin Horthy issued to the detachment chiefs blanket warrants "to pronounce and execute sentence on the guilty." Under the pretext of

18

searching for and punishing Communists, the officers raided and plundered villages, outraged
women, maltreated and killed Jews and whomever
else incurred their displeasure.   The brutality of
the acts committed and the flimsiness of the excuses
proffered surpasses belief.   Old grudges were
settled in a summary fashion.   Years ago a dis-
tressed squire may have sold his harvest to a Jew
for what he thought was a bad price.   Now the
squire came back, chief of a Communist-hunting
squad; he seized the Jew, hanged him and took his
property.   Or else an officer would see a Jew wearing a new suit of clothes.   He would shoot the Jew
and expropriate the suit.   In several places the
Catholic priests themselves tried to protect innocent
Jews; they were hanged on the spot.   It should be
remembered that well-to-do Jews had suffered just
as much under Communism as Christians; but that
did not make any difference; they were arrested,
tortured and murdered.   The number of victims
who perished in these atrocities can be put between
five and six thousand.   I have no space to relate
these horrors in detail; reliable accounts may be
found in the files of the *Manchester Guardian,* of
Vienna, Prague and Italian newspapers.   But I
have to tell of two incidents which help in rounding
out the portrait of the Hero of Cattaro.

One of the terror detachments was headed by a
Count Salm, a Hungarian officer of Austrian
descent.   He had achieved unenviable fame by an
exploit at Dunaföldvár, where he murdered a

wealthy Jewish merchant, not without having previously exacted a ransom for safe-conduct. After the murder the Count not only took all cash and valuables from the victim's house, but also pulled a pair of brand new shoes off his feet, remarking that dead Jews needed no new shoes. But Count Salm's most substantial claim to a reputation rests on the case of the Jewish millionaire Albert Freund de Tószeg, member of one of the greatest industrial families of Hungary. Count Salm's party raided Freund's château, near Lake Balaton. Without further ado, without even a pretext, the millionaire was condemned to be hanged in the presence of his wife. The peasants of the village witnessed the proceedings in dumb horror; Freund was a kindly man, and they all liked him. Count Salm asked an onlooker for a piece of rope. The peasant said he had none. Infuriated, the Count sent off the villagers to search for a rope; after a while they returned and said that no rope was to be found in the place. Thereupon Salm tore a piece of wire from a fence and hanged the unfortunate with his own hands. Mrs. Freund fainted; the peasants wept; the gypsy band which accompanied the officers played ribald songs.

Now hundreds of other Jews had been murdered before this in a similar way, and nothing further happened. But this was different. Freund was a millionaire and belonged to a very influential family. The case was reported to the Allied representatives at Budapest, and an inquiry was ordered.

Under this pressure Commander-in-Chief Horthy issued a warrant for Salm's arrest. A search was made. A few days later Horthy reported to the Allied Missions that he was very sorry, but Salm had disappeared. All the while Count Salm stayed right at headquarters, and dined and wined with Horthy every night.

Some officers captured a batch of Communists and took them to the encampment at Siófok. They were surrounded by soldiers, terribly beaten and ordered to dig their own graves. In the midst of this scene Admiral Horthy appeared, mounted on his white horse. He rode into the group of prisoners and exclaimed: "You dirty swine, you are getting what's due to you." Thereupon he spat on them, and rode away. The graves were dug, and a firing squad closed the incident.

These two stories were related by one of Horthy's own officers, who, unable to endure the horrors any longer, deserted the Siófok headquarters, and escaped to Vienna.

I had a friend, a young Hungarian, member of one of the oldest families of the untitled nobility. He had been educated in England and France, and became entirely Westernized, a sincere Liberal. During the worst days of the White Terror, I met him accidentally in New York. I expressed amazement at the behaviour of the noble officers. I said that this particular class had always impressed me with its handsome exterior, its good manners, its high sense of honour. I thought that the

Hungarian gentry was composed of gentlemen
in the English sense, and now these same men
perpetrated horrors that cannot be mentioned in
print, horrors from which Red Indians would have
shrunk.

He smiled, sadly. "You were wrong," he said.
"Whatever is going on in Hungary today does not
surprise me a bit. The dissolution of old bonds,
the *tabula rasa* of revolution and counter-revolution, have provided at last the Hungarian gentry
with an environment in which it can unfold its
latent character without hindrance. If they are
running amuck, they are only running true to form.
We have never learned to do anything useful. All
we can do is to drink, to cheat, to bully the weak and
to torment and rob the helpless. That's our tradition; today is our Golden Age. Scratch the thin
enamel of the European gentleman, tear off the
camouflage of the cavalry officer's code of honour,
and you will find the Tartar savage in us. We are
the true successors of Huns and Petchenegs. I
have a right to talk like that—my family tree is nine
hundred years old, and three of my cousins are
serving in Horthy's army. I assure you that
Horthy is our true representative."

V

In November, 1919, the Supreme Council ordered the Roumanian army out of Budapest. On
the day following the evacuation, Admiral Horthy
led his troops into the capital. Two of his declara-

tions on this occasion deserve notice. "I come as the lieutenant of my lawful ruler and sovereign, King Charles," he said. Admiral Kolchak gave way to General Monk. A delegation of Trade Unionists and Social Democrats waited on him. He declared: "I do not negotiate with workers. I command and they obey." Horthy is nothing if not unoriginal. Budapest had heard those words before. In 1849, during the revolution, Field-Marshal Prince Windischgraetz seized Budapest in the name of the Emperor, as Kossuth's Government fled to Debreczen. A group of Magyar notables called on him, seeking a compromise. The Prince was adamant. *"Mit Rebellen unterhandle ich nicht."* "I do not negotiate with rebels." Those words—and Windischgraetz's demand for *"unbedingte Unterwerfung,"* unconditional surrender—have burnt themselves into Hungarian history. Like at Cattaro, at Budapest Horthy, Emperor Charles's lieutenant, stepped into a ready-made pose and annexed a ready-made phrase.

And now came another victory, even more important. Sir George Clerk arrived at Budapest as Allied High Commissioner and peace-maker among the warring Magyar factions. He came and saw, and Horthy conquered. He wore a cap like Beatty's; he had good table manners; the atmosphere at the castle was pleasant. Sir George trusted Horthy. A compromise, insuring two places in the Cabinet for Social Democrats and free and impartial elections for a National Assembly,

was effected. Some Liberals demanded guarantees. Sir George did not see why guarantees were
necessary. He had not heard of Count Salm. He
had not spoken to the men who dug their own
graves at Siófok. Sir George said: "Horthy is
a gentleman."

Sir George left Budapest. The two Socialist
ministers were dismissed. The "free and impartial" elections were held under the auspices of
machine gun detachments. Forty thousand opposition voters were interned, over a score of opposition
candidates were imprisoned, two opposition editors
were murdered. The National Assembly convened,
and elected Horthy Regent. Unanimously. The
officers of the Ostenburg detachment, who with
drawn revolvers invaded the floor and the galleries
of the Assembly just before the session was called
to order, did not vote. They just furnished the
setting for the unanimity.

Once more the Regent emphasized that he was
a mere lieutenant of the King. "I shall cede the
supreme power to the lawful King as soon as
external circumstances permit," he said. Just the
same—safety first, one never can tell what may
happen—he made the army swear an oath of
allegiance to himself. Some elder officers refused
to swear—they protested that their oath to Charles
was good enough and accused the Regent of secret
ambitions to the crown.

He had betrayed the political traditions of his
class when he entered the Imperial Navy and

joined the Imperial Household. He now proceeded to betray his betrayal. He was, professedly, the lieutenant of the exiled King, and nothing else. At Easter, 1921, the exiled King returned. Only four days before Charles's arrival Regent Horthy declared in the *Petit Parisien;* "Hungary is a kingdom. In the absence of the King I am the Regent. Emperor Charles is our only lawful King."

Four days later King and Regent faced each other in the Castle at Budapest. The Little Entente had delivered its ultimatum: Hapsburg restoration was to be regarded as a case for war. Once more somebody volunteered to pick Horthy's chestnut out of the fire. Horthy ordered his "only lawful King" to leave the country. Charles obeyed. Horthy, who doubtless during the proceedings was congratulating himself for having had the foresight to exact an oath of allegiance from the troops, chuckled to himself. He chuckled even more, half a year later, when Charles tried his luck again. The airplane excursion ended in near-tragedy. Czechoslovakia, . Jugoslavia mobilized. Horthy, at the head of his troops, shelled the royal train. Charles was taken prisoner, and was soon on his way to Madeira. Europe and America applauded Horthy for saving Hungary from Hapsburgism. In reality, he only saved his own chance to the throne of Hungary.

In the spring of 1920 a delegation of British Labour, headed by Colonel J. C. Wedgwood, M.

P., arrived in Hungary to investigate charges of the White Terror. Their report, fully documented, tells of horrors unspeakable and unprintable. Two officers, especially, Captain Prónay (above mentioned) and Lieutenant Héjjas, were found guilty of atrocities beside which the worst German deeds in Belgium pale. Colonel Wedgwood asked Mr. Hohler, British High Commissioner, what he knew about these officers. Mr. Hohler said he had been informed by the Hungarian Government that Prónay and Héjjas had been "demobilized." Colonel Wedgwood went to the Ministry of War, and found that the two officers were still on the army payroll. Colonel Wedgwood then inquired from Regent Horthy. "They are my best officers," said the Regent.

But then, these officers are very powerful. A Pretorian Guard is a most useful instrument, but one has to pay the price. Once a delegation of Budapest Jews waited on Regent Horthy, who received them in state, attended by two officers. The Regent was most gracious. He assured the delegates that although he disliked bad Jews, he liked good Jews, that he knew the delegates belonged to the latter category, and that everything would come out all right. At this point one of the officers whispered something into his ear. The Regent retired to an adjoining room, followed by the two officers. A few minutes later they all returned. But the Regent was a changed man. He told, in the harshest tones, the astounded delegates that he expected them to do their duty, that he would stand for no foolishness, and that his hand would fall heavily on the disloyal. Thereupon he clicked his heels and turned his back on the visitors, a gesture copied from the old Emperor, to signify that the audience was over. God only knows what passed between the Regent and his officers—God only knows, but anybody can guess.

Hungary today is the most chauvinistic country in Europe. The Pan-Turanian movement, which aims at a spiritual and eventually political union of Magyars, Bulgars, Turks and Tartars against the effete nations of the West, is very popular, and Regent Horthy is its patron. He travels around in a special train named "Turan." But then, Horthy had an Austrian education; he speaks Hungarian with a strong German accent, and his grammar is bad. *"Le style, c'est l'homme."* When he opened an exhibition of the Hungarian steel industries at Budapest, he made a speech, and this speech was recorded in shorthand by a Magyar journalist who later fled to Vienna. Said Horthy: "It's with pleasure I came here to open this here industry—er—hm—to open this here exhibition, which, so to speak, lost more during the war than any other—or rather, er, suffered, yes, more. It is very nice that you could accomplish so much in such short time—it shows only that if we Hungarians want something, we go and get it, yes." He stepped to a group of exhibits, and read the label aloud. "Exhibit of Debreczen Machine

Works." He beamed. "Is this in Debreczen? How interesting! Debreczen Machine Works— is in Debreczen, yes. I didn't know." Even the detectives, his bodyguard, grinned.

VI

The German submarines quelled the Cattaro mutiny and Horthy was named Admiral. The Roumanians destroyed Béla Kun, and Horthy entered Budapest in triumph. The Little Entente eliminated Charles, and Horthy was hailed as the bane of the Hapsburgs. He wears his cap like Lord Beatty, has beautiful table manners, and Sir George Clerk called him a gentleman. What more do you want—in Hungary? Friedrich von Gentz said that Asia began at the gates of Vienna. He was right a hundred years ago. He is much more right today. In 1914 Budapest was twenty hours from London. In 1921 Budapest was twenty minutes from Bokhara. The Magyar people today is groaning under the yoke of Uzbeg chieftains who created themselves a ruler in their own image. That ruler is Nicholas Horthy, Turanian Khan who speaks with a German accent, Count Salm's friend and protector, Calvinist who renounced his faith, Admiral who abandoned his ships, Regent who betrayed his King.

JAMES RAMSAY MACDONALD

JAMES RAMSAY MACDONALD

I

THAT the first Labour Prime Minister of Britain should be a Scotsman is no accident. It was, if not in the stars, at any rate in the law of averages. Out of the eleven Premiers of the last half century no less than six were Scottish; one was a Jew, one a Welshman, and only three were English. No greater contrast between nations can be conceived than that of the English and the Poles. One might pardonably say that the Englishman is the opposite Pole. But at least one trait the two have in common. Both love to be ruled by a foreigner. The history of Poland is the history of Hungarian, Lithuanian, Swedish and Saxon kings. England imported hers from Wales, Scotland, Holland, Germany.

Every true Scot feels in his heart that the Union with England is merely a euphemism to make the grim fact of Scottish conquest palatable to the effete and gullible Southron. To Henri of Navarre

Paris was worth a mass. To King James London was worth calling himself the First instead of the Sixth. Ever since the name of the United Kingdom covered an arrangement under which England was every Scotsman's potential oyster.

The Scots are a strange race. Like the English, they are built of paradoxes. But the English paradoxes are like the English landscape: soft, undulating, amiable. The contrasting qualities blend like the ingredients in a high grade smoking mixture. The paradoxes of the Scot are rugged and sharp like the outline of the northern Highlands. His mentality (and this should not be taken as an allusion to a now proscribed brand of Scottish refreshment) is black-and-white. The Scots are the most practical and also the most romantic of races; Don Quixote and Sancho Panza rolled into one. They understand fully well, as Mr. Macdonald has said of the distinguished Scot Sir Robert Horne, both the power of cash and the power of spirit. They are the most bigoted and the clearest-headed; they are Jacobites and Jacobins; they are the most aristocratic and the most democratic people in the world.

Perhaps this last antithesis might be resolved into the term equalitarian. Their passion for equality forms the greatest difference between them and the English, who not only worship but also adore class. But then, English history is feudal; throughout that of Scotland runs the *leitmotiv* of clan. The clan system is one under which everybody is a noble-

PREMIER MACDONALD

man. Every Campbell in the world regards the
Duke of Argyll as the head of the family. The
swarms of Russells and Howards inhabitating the
London post office directory would no sooner think
of claiming kinship with the houses of Bedford and
Norfolk than of tracing their descent from the
Sun and Moon.

The Scottish tradition that everybody is not only
as good as anybody else, but better, comes out
clearly in Scottish history, Scottish manners, Scottish religion. That formidable institution called
the Kirk may be autocratic in its theology, but it is
certainly democratic in its politics. When the
other day King George appointed Mr. Jamie
Brown, Lanarkshire coal miner and M. P., Lord
High Commissioner of the Assembly of the Kirk
of Scotland, a post that may best be described as
that of His Britannic Majesty's understudy, some
Americans I met in London declared it was plain
Bolshevism and the beginning of the end. But
then, Americans are the last upholders in the world
of the purity of monarchical institutions. To
Scotsmen the appointment seemed perfectly natural—for was not Jamie Brown an Elder?

In a study of Mr. Lloyd George, which was as
amusing as it was penetrating, Professor Alfred E.
Zimmern said that the clue to the Protean personality of the Wizard of Criccieth was his Welsh
inferiority complex. The Welshman in England
can never forget that he is the son of a defeated race
among its conquerors. His virtues and his defects,

like those of the Jews, are those of the downtrodden. Like the Jew, the Welshman wants to show to those whom he at once despises and regards as his betters, what a fine fellow he is.

According to Dr. Zimmern, for a Welshman in England it is as difficult to forget his sense of inferiority as it is for a Scotsman in England to hide his consciousness of superiority.

II

The most striking thing about the first Socialist Prime Minister is his aristocratic appearance. He does not look like the descendant of Highland peasants—rather like the scion of a great Scottish house.

As a matter of fact he comes from a line of village blacksmiths at Lossiemouth in Morayshire. It so happens that Mussolini's father, too, was a blacksmith. There the parallel between the head of the first British Labour Government and the founder of Fascism ends. Mr. Macdonald's career —from barefooted boy in a Scottish fishing village to virtual ruler of the greatest empire the world has ever seen—has been told many times, and shall not be repeated here. It is a career which with that of Trotsky is probably the most phenomenal since the great Napoleon. But unlike that of Trotsky, Macdonald's way did not shoot skyward in a sudden flight after long years of trudging along the level of common humanity. He achieved his victory rising deliberately from step to step by hard,

conscientious work—a victory of self-help and self-
education in the best manner of Samuel Smiles's
chosen heroes.

If personal culture means a multiplicity of intelligent contacts with contemporary life rather than
the storing of mere knowledge Ramsay Macdonald
is one of the most cultured men in the world to-day.
It is probably no exaggeration to say that he
tackled the immense problems of governing the
British Empire with a better all-around equipment
than any of his predecessors, and that he knows
everything, or almost everything, that a Prime
Minister ought to know.   That equipment is
founded on his education at the village school of
Lossiemouth.   Not as bad a foundation as it
sounds; for village education in Scotland is quite
a different affair from the corresponding thing
in England or the United States.   Education
is the Scottish national passion much in the
same sense as business is the American passion and
sport the English.   The boy Macdonald was fortunate in having a teacher who must have been far
above the ordinary level, which in Scotland is not
a low one.   There is a curious similarity of this
particular phase of Mr. Macdonald's beginnings
with those of President Masaryk.   At fifteen the
future founder of the Czechoslovak Republic was a
total failure.   He was not up to the standard as a
locksmith's apprentice, and was sent home by an
angry master.   A kindly priest got interested in
the forlorn boy and taught him Greek and Latin

without compensation. Young Macdonald was salvaged from submersion in the ranks of agricultural labour by the Lossiemouth dominie who thought that the bright lad was born for better things, and gave him private lessons free. The dominie was interested in science, and imparted that interest to his protégé. The cue was followed up; and when Macdonald at nineteen came to London to earn twelve shillings and sixpence a week by addressing envelopes he dreamed of a scientific career. He actually studied science at South Kensington; but ill health intervened and he was shunted to other tracks. The kind schoolmaster of Lossiemouth knew no more at the time than did the nice old cleric in the Moravian village that his charitable act was making world history.

Many years later Mr. James Ramsay Macdonald, M.P., was dining in fashionable company one evening at London. Somebody asked what had been his university.

"Cassell's 'Popular Educator and Science for All,' " came Mr. Macdonald's answer.

He might have added: and the novels of Sir Walter Scott. For Mr. Macdonald would not be what he is without the influence of the author of "Waverley." Natural science and the glamour of the Scottish past are the two deepest sources of his inspiration, corresponding to that dualism of matter-of-factness and romance which runs through every true Scottish character.

III

It has been said of Mr. Macdonald that he is the best-read and most widely travelled of British Premiers. The former of these distinctions at least is not an unmitigated asset in the public life of a nation that instinctively distrusts theorists. A Prime Minister of Great Britain may be, like Gladstone, a profound classical scholar without arousing misgivings—for classical scholarship, like the pig-breeding of Mr. Baldwin, is at the worst an avocation and has no direct bearing on government. Mr. Macdonald is unprofessional enough to know a lot about modern history and political theory and economics. A nice old English gentleman with a vast store of anecdotes about Oxford life, fox-hunting, and colonial administration in Africa, who, though a thoroughbred Tory, said that he was "quite willing to give these new Labour fellows a fair chance," told me the other day that he sincerely hoped Mr. Macdonald would soon, in the business of running the Empire, forget most of the things he has written and at least some of the things he has read about "economics and such stuff." My friend admitted, however, that he had given up all hope in regard to "the President of the Board of Trade, Mr. and Mrs. Beatrice Webb."

On the other hand, the advantages of having a Prime Minister who has visited practically every dominion of the British Crown and almost all countries of Europe, are generally recognized in England. The mentality which denied to Mr. Hoover the presidential nomination on the ground that he had spent part of his life abroad is incomprehensible to the imperially-minded Englishman.   Having travelled a good deal is an essential requirement everywhere in English life except, perhaps, at the Travellers' Club, that august institution in Pall Mall whose hundred-year-old rules exact from members a travelling record of five hundred miles, —almost a weekend-trip distance as distances go to-day.

Mr. Macdonald's travelling methods are not those of the average British gentleman. The dreadful thing must be said—those methods have just a slight Germanic flavour.   Mr. Macdonald makes a point of reading everything there is to be read about a place before he visits it.   In all fairness it should be said that in this he is matched, if not outdone, by his predecessor at the Foreign Office, Lord Curzon.   The latter one day inspected, with a party of sightseers, Napoleon's quarters at St. Helena.   The French consul, who acted as guide, said: "This was the billiard-room."   "Oh no," remarked Lord Curzon, "*that* was the billiard-room." And he proved it.

But Mr. Macdonald not only reads up, but also talks up on his travels.   He interviews everybody— he tries to get the story from as many angles as possible.   When he, as a mere M.P., was in India he shocked Anglo-Indian susceptibilities by the catholicity of his contacts.   Again in all fairness: no such indiscretions can be laid to the door of the Marquis Curzon of Kedleston.

IV

Another distinction of Mr. Macdonald's has been noted, but not sufficiently emphasized. He is one of the best-looking Prime Ministers Britain ever has had, and probably the handsomest major statesman in the world to-day. There can be no doubt that his good looks were one of his most important assets. He shares a quality with some beautiful women—when he enters a room others present become invisible, as it were. This is not a matter of mere handsomeness. That may be even a handicap. In certain cases his own physical beauty overshadows a man—he is shoved into the background by it as by a too famous father. He is not expected to possess spiritual and mental accomplishments, and when he does possess any, he is apt to be patronized on their score. Such was the fate, for instance, of George Wyndham, quite a gifted person, who, however, could never live down the reputation of being the handsomest young man in the House of Commons.

Handsomeness in a man becomes a formidable weapon when it is coupled with that mysterious undefinable thing called personality. But even at the lowest rate of exchange good looks in public life are the equivalent of an introduction to a powerful editor. Your stuff will be judged on its merit, but the recommendation secures you a hearing out of your turn.

Quiet, unaggressive, unpretentious self-assurance has been one of Ramsay Macdonald's strongest points in the struggle for success. That self-assurance is the aristocratic heritage of the Highland clansman. It is the attribute of the true Calvinist with whom a sense of righteousness is the reflex of any chosen line of action. It is, finally, the happy privilege of an exceptionally handsome man —a tall man.

Those shrewd and sensitive psychologists the Polish Jews, turned into connoisseurs of men by centuries of blows and kicks, have devised a universal classification of mankind as good as Lamb's lenders and borrowers, James's toughminded and tenderminded, or Madison Grant's Nordics and steerage passengers. It is a very simple classification. There are big men and there are small men. The big man looks down on his fellows, expects homage and attendance, and gets it. He takes whatever comes his way as his due, and does not stop to worry. The small man is a constant apology for his own existence. But sometimes the small man turns—or, as that tall Jew Professor Freud would say, is inverted. He camouflages the apology as challenge. Lest he appear cowed he becomes cocky. He wants to show the world.

A tall man need not show the world. The world believes him. Had Napoleon not been undersized history might have taken a different course. And perhaps a Mr. Goliath Lloyd George would have thought a little less of himself and a little more of England and Europe.

Perhaps it is the good fortune of England and Europe that James Ramsay Macdonald is a tall man.

V

Mr. Chesterton says somewhere that the greatest fact of the nineteenth century is the English revolution which omitted taking place between 1832 and 1839. This sounds well, but, like so many of Mr. Chesterton's bright sayings, the less it is analyzed the better. The truth is that revolution, which was thwarted and sidetracked in most European countries, in England alone rose in a steady curve to victory. So revolutionary are the English that they have even discarded the traditional technique of revolution and managed theirs without barricades, tribunals and guillotines. They did not care, as long as they got what they wanted, if the thing looked like a Sunday school picnic from the distance of Moscow.

It was in 1894 that Benjamin Kidd recognized as the portent of the age the desiccation of Liberalism and the advent of Labour as *the* party of progress in Britain. It took thirty years from that prophecy for Labour to achieve supreme power in the State. Those thirty years are spanned by the growth of the Independent Labour Party, one of whose founders was James Ramsay Macdonald.

The Independent Labour Party was born out of the realization that the economic action of trades unions, aimed at bettering wages and working conditions, was merely curing the symptoms, instead of eliminating the causes, of the social unrest, and that the real need was for revising and reconstructing the moral fundaments of society. The Party thus signifies the combination of the ethical and political programme of Socialism with the industrial programme of the trades unions. But this Socialism was of a characteristic British brand. Its distinguishing features are insistence on parliamentary action, on historic continuity and on the necessity of winning over the majority of the nation; rejection of the idea of class struggle; and focussing attention on a concept of the good life instead of mere material betterment.

The right to live, the right to a full life, the right to sit in a library among the best books, the right to a well-equipped mind, the right to a sensitive soul . . . these are the rights a wise democracy will cling to and guard as precious possessions.

Thus writes Ramsay Macdonald in his tract "Character and Democracy"; and it is worth recalling in the face of this Socialist bill of rights that one of the principal reproaches levelled against Socialism is that it is grossly materialistic, a quality extremely repellent to sensitive idealists with incomes running into five figures.

The Socialism of James Ramsay Macdonald and

of the Independent Labour Party is a method, not a system—something dynamic and adaptable, not static and rigid—not a goal, but a road: a road to "the community organized to secure the good life for all."

The belief in parliamentary action and in the necessity of winning over the majority of the nation is, in the Socialism of British Labour, not an *a priori* postulate, but the distilled quintessence of centuries of British history. The supreme justification of that belief is the existence of Mr. Macdonald's Government.

VI

To the average American the most astonishing feature of the British revolution of 1924 was the cheerful acquiescence of the British ex-ruling classes. On the eve of the upheaval the Conservative press painted in lurid colours the terrible fate that would befall England if Labour succeeded to power. Mr. Asquith, who was giving Labour a lift, was denounced as a traitor to a God-ordained universe. Then Mr. Macdonald went to Buckingham Palace, announced his list of Ministers (including three authentic peers and a live General), and made his first speech from the Treasury Bench. With a lack of transition worthy of the modernest of German composers Jeremiad and philippic turned into a pæan. Indeed, the unison of Conservative and Liberal praise almost became embarrassing for the Government, for it aroused the suspicions of "the wild men from the Clyde," the extreme Socialist Glasgow contingent. That at Moscow Mr. Macdonald was immediately promoted to the rank of Arch Fiend Extraordinary goes without saying.

A few days after the formation of the Labour Government I met one of the leaders of German Social Democracy, a Left Winger who had been a member of the republican Government of the Reich. I asked him what he thought of the friendliness with which Mr. Macdonald was received by all classes. He said it was too much of a good thing.

"After all," he added, "the chief duty of a Labour Government doesn't consist in convincing the bourgeoisie that it is perfectly nice."

Even the *Morning Post,* the organ of the Baldwinite Diehards, suddenly discovered that there are more points of agreement between Labour and the Conservatives than between the Liberals and either. And the *National Review,* mouthpiece of last-ditch, bitter-ender, eat-'em-alive Toryism, after straining its imagination until the true-blue veins stood out on its titlepage, to conjure up some terrific vision of the Day of Wrath, suddenly collapsed to the anti-climax of Mr. William Randolph Hearst congratulating himself over England's misfortune.

But the most astonishing portent came from the direction of the Stock Exchange. On the morrow of Mr. Macdonald's appointment all securities rose several points. The Conservative newspapers in-

vented ingenious explanations to show that this was
in spite, and not because, of Labour's accession.
However, the man in the street forgot the explanations, and remembered the fact.

VII

In order to appreciate Mr. Macdonald's victory
in all its bearings it should be borne in mind that in
a sense he is his own ghost. He has been not only
dead once, but buried. It was in the early years of
the war, when his ultra-pacifistic attitude split the
Labour Party in two and made him the most hated
man in Britain. His opposition to the war, needless
to say, was not based on any love of Germany. But
unlike those unsophisticated liberals, Mr. Wells
and Mr. Wilson, he knew that the war could only
end in either of two ways: in a draw, in which case
bloodshed and sacrifice were futile, or in a Peace
of Versailles, whether dictated by France or by
Germany, in which case bloodshed and sacrifice
were worse than futile. It was, he realized, naïve
to expect that once Foch and Clemenceau had won
the war they would quietly bow to Mr. Wilson's
"Thank you, don't come again," and leave the stage
to mildly idealistic professors.

Ramsay Macdonald had foreseen Versailles.
To-day he is earning the reward of what was once
considered as suicidal madness and now stands revealed as prophetic insight. In a sense it was not
nice of him to contribute even indirectly to the
downfall of M. Poincaré; for no single individual

has done more to assist British Labour into power than the bitter-ender Premier of France.

VIII

One of the paradoxes about Mr. Macdonald is that he is more popular with the rank and file of Labour than with its general staff. To the former he is "Mac"; to the latter he is the Prime Minister. There is in him a certain aloofness, a shyness that, as his anonymous biographer shrewdly points out, he finds less difficult to overcome when facing an impersonal crowd than in his contact with individuals. One of the members of his Cabinet once said to a journalist: "I walk into Mr. Lloyd George's room with a much easier step than into the Prime Minister's. Ramsay freezes me."

In "The Man of To-morrow" the gentleman hiding behind the pen-name of Iconoclast connects Mr. Macdonald's exaggerated reserve with his lack of psychological curiosity.

In no writing of his own is there any sign of interest in character pushed beyond the Scot limit. Perhaps you can only know other people well if you are prepared to allow them to know you well; perhaps you can only want them to know you well if you have a longing to communicate, to escape from a spiritual and moral isolation. Whether or no, shyness and lack of psychological curiosity in the given case go together. The combination accounts for much misunderstanding, and perhaps for the failure to create and inspire lieutenants. Certainly it accounts, in large degree, for his overwhelmingly strong sense of decorum and exaggerated respect for some unimportant conventions.

Mr. Macdonald, like President Wilson, is a Presbyterian. A Presbyterian is just as much of a ritualist as a Roman Catholic; only his is an invisible ritual. He is also, as some one has well said, essentially a man alone with his God.

IX

Mr. Frank Simonds tells us about an Englishman with whom he discussed Labour's triumph in its early days. The Englishman remarked that he had expected a lively time. "But then," he added, "I read in the newspaper that Mr. Macdonald went to see the King at Buckingham Palace in a top hat, and I knew it was all over."

It was. Once they had a revolution in France, and they celebrated it by cutting off the heads of a considerable number of marquesses. In Britain Mr. Jamie Brown, coal miner and Lord High Commissioner of the Assembly of the Kirk of Scotland, celebrated the revolution by appointing a couple of marquesses his aides-de-camp.

When Mr. Thomas, the Labour Colonial Secretary, appeared at his office for the first time, he had some difficulty in getting in, for the ushers did not know him and he did not look like the average Colonial Secretary. At last he satisfied those staid officials that he was not an intruding Bolshevik, and entered. He was received by his predecessor, the Duke of Devonshire, who said to him: "Mr. Thomas, we have been enemies, and you have defeated us in a fair fight. Can I do anything for you? I am at your disposal."

If you want to realize, as poignantly as possible, the difference between America and England, I recommend the following experiment: Sit down in your favourite easy chair, light your favourite brand of cigar, and try to imagine Mr. Mitchell Palmer turning over the seals of the Department of Justice to Comrade Morris Hillquit with the words of the Duke of Devonshire. While doing so don't forget that Mr. Mitchell Palmer is not a Cavendish.

X

When the Russian Soviet delegation made its début in Downing Street they were lined up against a wall. Much to the regret of Mr. Winston Churchill they were not shot, but merely photographed. Mr. Macdonald has never been on the staff of a newspaper, but he has been a journalist all his life, and on this occasion he did as the other journalists present. He hung about. A reporter perceived a rare chance. He stepped forward and began: "Mr. Macdonald——"

He got no further. The Prime Minister turned sharply on his heels and walked away.

Mr. Macdonald is a kind-hearted man. He did not mean to hurt the reporter's feelings.

He only forgot, for a moment, who he had been, and remembered who he was.

If such heaping of Pelion upon Ossa be permissible: that moment crowned the top hat in which he had gone to see the King at Buckingham Palace. The revolution was over. The British Constitution was saved. The Labour Prime Minister's treatment of the forward reporter was a gesture worthy of the snubconscious mind of a Duke.

BIBLIOGRAPHY

The Man of To-Morrow. J. Ramsay Macdonald. By Iconoclast. London, 1923.

By James Ramsay Macdonald:

The Socialist Movement. Home University Library.

Character and Democracy. 1906.

The Awakening of India. 1910.

Margaret Ethel Macdonald. 1912.

Parliament and Revolution. 1919.

Parliament and Democracy. 1920.

The History of the I.L.P. 1922.

The Foreign Policy of the Labour Party. 1923.

Claud W. Mullins. The Patriotism of Ramsay Macdonald. 1916.

Louis M. Lerous. J. Ramsay Macdonald. Paris, 1919.

RAYMOND POINCARÉ

RAYMOND POINCARÉ

I

In his "Makers of the New France" Mr. Charles Dawbarn says that the former President of the French Republic has a face like Socrates. Mr. H. G. Wells finds that M. Poincaré reminds him of a wirehaired fox terrier. "He even barks." Here are two extremes declining, most unprofessionally, to meet. Nor can they be averaged down. There is no happy medium between the hero of Plato's dialogues and a rough-coated little dog.

It is well known that compromises have no luck with M. Poincaré.

In the war years of 1914-'18 it was the good fortune of France that she had an unbending President. In the peace years, so called, of 1922-'24 it was the tragedy of Europe that France had an unbending Premier.

Several years ago Mr. John Maynard Keynes demonstrated that the reparation clauses of the Treaty of Versailles could not be carried out. M. Poincaré's reparation policy amounted, in practice, to making France pay heavily, in the rising cost of living, in ever-rising taxes, in dropping credit and dropping prestige, to demonstrate that Mr. Keynes was right. At last France found the process a bit too expensive.

M. Poincaré is, first and last, a lawyer. Now, there is a passage in Mr. E. Bowen-Rowlands's memoir of the great English barrister, Sir Harry Poland, which not only presents a classic picture of the legalistic mind, but also shows why and how that type of mind may become, under circumstances, a public danger. The author is discussing the tests of insanity as defined by the English court in a certain case. We are told that Sir Harry

accepted them (the tests) with finality; it was idle to speculate whether they were proper tests or not. If he had to pronounce upon their propriety he would compare them with the facts of law. If the opinions of the alienists prevailed, and the proper basis of comparison was medicine and not law, then there was an end of Judge and Jury, and the beginning of a chaotic dispensation by fanciful decrees of theorists. That would never do. The law was the law. It might be composite in detail, but in essentials any tampering with the rule of law was a *pro tanto* weakening of the supports of the State. And the law was not a thing of subjective idea. It was subjective fact; intention, will, mind, all such terms have any number of meanings; but they had only one for lawyers—and that had been established by the wisdom of their fathers. He knew what it was. That was enough.

Substituting a few terms, that is a perfect portrait of M. Poincaré's mentality.

He accepted the obligations of Germany under the treaty with finality; it was idle to speculate whether they were ful-

PREMIER POINCARÉ

fillable obligations or not. If he had to pronounce upon their propriety he would compare them with the facts of the treaty. If the opinions of the experts prevailed, and the proper basis of comparison was economics and not law, then there was an end of government, and the beginning of a chaotic dispensation by fanciful decrees of theorists. That would never do. The treaty was the treaty. It might be composite in detail, but in essentials any tampering with the rule of the treaty was a *pro tanto* weakening of the European settlement. And the treaty was not a thing of subjective idea. It was objective fact; intention and capacity to pay, all such terms have any number of meanings; but they had only one for lawyers, and that had been established by the wisdom of the treaty makers. He knew what it was. That was enough.

The maker of the Treaty of Versailles was Georges Clemenceau. Now Clemenceau is no lawyer. He is a statesman; and he judged his own treaty by the standards of policy, not law. He said:

The treaty is not something fixed and final which settles the affairs of Europe for ever. It is an instrument to be used. And on the manner in which it is used depends its value.

Poincaré had been a bitter opponent of the treaty. With Marshal Foch he held that it had not secured enough for France, and had not secured France enough. But when he, after M. Briand's fatal game of golf at Cannes, became Premier, he changed his attitude, and this very change was an act of consistency. The treaty was not the best possible treaty, but it was the Treaty. M. Poincaré became its most uncompromising champion. The treaty was the law; he knew what it was, and that was enough.

The fact that Poincaré suffered the greatest defeat of his life in the aggressive defence of a law which was not of his making, which he had originally regarded as bad law, tells the story of Poincaré in a nutshell.

II

From whatever angle you approach the life and character of Raymond Poincaré, you will, sooner or later, run up against a fact like a steel wall. The name of that fact is Georges Clemenceau.

The two men have only one thing in common— their love for France, their determination to serve her power and glory. Beyond that agreement begins their enmity—an enmity determined not by accidents of politics or personal history, but by human fundamentals.

To say that their antagonism is a matter of temperament is true but not enough. Both men possess indomitable courage. But the courage of Clemenceau is the courage of a tiger—or of an avalanche, if you will. The courage of Poincaré is the courage of his convictions. One of those convictions is that not to be courageous is both dishonourable and impractical. Mr. Sisley Huddleston, who admires and even likes M. Poincaré and has written a book about him that may be described as objectively eulogistic, explains M. Poincaré's courage by the fact that he is in reality a very timid man. He has,

Mr. Huddleston says in effect, shouted himself into the Ruhr adventure. Sometimes advance demands much less pluck than retreat. Like most timid but honourable men he is stubborn once he has made up his mind. A hero can afford to waver on occasion; a timid man cannot afford to be anything but a hero.

Perhaps the thing might be expressed this way: If Clemenceau had not possessed his courage he would not have been Clemenceau. If Poincaré had not possessed *his* courage he would not have been President and twice Premier of France, but only a highly successful and respectable attorney.

The contrast goes further and deeper. It has been said that Poincaré is not a sincere Republican; that he flirts with the Royalists. Mr. Huddleston rightly points out that this is nonsense. Poincaré is as good a Republican as can be. So is Clemenceau. Yet their particular types of republicanism are worlds apart. One might say that Clemenceau is Republican by temperament and as a reaction against the fanatical Royalism of his native Vendée. Poincaré is Republican by lack of temperament, and because there is no royalist tradition in his native Lorraine, which had not belonged to France when the old monarchy was at the height of its glory.

It has been said that Poincaré is a typical man of the Right and Clemenceau a typical man of the Left. This is not quite accurate. For had not Clemenceau been born the revolutionary freethinking son of a revolutionary freethinking father, he might have been the greatest of Royalist leaders France ever had. He was born in a château in the most reactionary province of France. One can easily fancy him leading a charge under the white banner of the House of Bourbon. Poincaré was born in a typical bourgeois family residence on the Main Street of a typical Eastern French small town. To think of him leading a charge under any kind of a banner would be preposterous—almost blasphemous. He would never in this world charge anything more dangerous than a jury.

The truth is that Poincaré is a typical Conservative of the Middle—a Moderate, if there ever was one. Clemenceau is a Radical—he happens to be a Radical of the Left, but he might have been a Radical of the Right with no less propriety. He is an Extremist. A Roman Catholic Clemenceau would be a Dominican and an inquisitor. A Roman Catholic Poincaré would go to mass every Sunday.

One of the tests of French public men of the last thirty years is their attitude in the Dreyfus affair. Now, not all the pro-Dreyfus men were pure angels. Many of them were men with axes to grind —anti-militarist, anti-Catholic, anti-Nationalist little axes. And not all anti-Dreyfus men were sinister conspirators and forgers of evidence. Some of them were sincere patriots. But the fundamental issue was simple and clear. The defenders of Dreyfus defended truth and justice against bigotry goaded on and stage-managed by dishonesty.

Clemenceau flung himself into the battle with the Swiftian passion of a cynic and despiser of humanity fighting for an abstract idea. With Zola, Reinach, Anatole France, and Jaurès he formed the intellectual vanguard of the Dreyfusards. And Poincaré? Well, he was, as Mr. Huddleston, who means to be friendly, says, not an adversary of the Dreyfusards, but he was not their supporter either. He was "non-committal"; he was "exceedingly cautious." The fact is he was tripped up by too much balance. He is no trimmer. He is thoroughly honourable. But perhaps he insists too much on the philosophic value of suspended judgment to be exactly a hero.

III

The ultimate difference between Clemenceau and Poincaré can be summed up in a few words. M. Clemenceau is erratic, unsteady, incurably romantic, full of malice, quick of temper. He is also a genius. M. Poincaré is substantial, respectable, reliable, of prodigious industry, kindhearted, tremendously clever. His is the most brilliant career of the Third Republic.

IV

When at the end of August, 1914, the Germans arrived within a few miles of Paris, the French Government decided to transfer its seat to Bordeaux. Poincaré was not responsible for this step; indeed, he had opposed it. Besides, it is difficult

to see what else under the circumstances the French
Government could have done. The loss of the
capital would have meant the loss of the war. Then
the miracle of the Marne turned the tide, and the
Government was restored to Paris. For months
afterward Poincaré could not appear in public without some one shouting at him, "Go to Bordeaux."
A cruel wit stabbed him with the pun, *Tournedos
à la bordelaise.* Poincaré's popularity was at a
low ebb in the first year of the war.

In March, 1918, the emergency of August, 1914,
seemed to return. Ludendorff's great offensive
was on. Those were the darkest days of the whole
war for the Allies. Ministers and generals agreed
that Paris must be abandoned. Clemenceau himself suggested to Poincaré the removal to Bordeaux. To his surprise Poincaré would not hear
of it. Clemenceau pressed the matter, and one
evening, while talking to the President over the
telephone, the latter hung up the receiver. A few
days later the fateful conference took place at
Doullens. Evacuation was advised by the generals.
Poincaré was adamant—and he was supported by
Marshal Foch. It was at Doullens that Foch was
appointed Commander-in-Chief of all the Allied
forces. The Government remained at Paris.

V

Still, caution is the better part of Poincaré's
courage. It was Briand, whose Red past was of a

particularly vivid hue, who as Premier introduced the bill to re-establish diplomatic relations with the Vatican. French Catholics rejoiced. The Parisian breeze wafted malicious whispers about poachers turning gamekeepers, and about the popularity of a certain ex-Socialist leader, of an interesting paleness and violoncello voice, with certain Duchesses. Perhaps M. Briand, who is not an aggressive disbeliever like Clemenceau, but simply indifferent, sponsored the measure because he thought it was good for France. In French politics nothing is impossible.

Poincaré, like the good Republican he is, is at heart anti-clerical. True enough, he has cherished friendly relations with the Right. But still.

On the day when the Senate voted on the reconciliation with the Vatican he stayed at home. The anonymous author of *Ceux qui nous mènent* puts down his abstention to his hostility to a pro-church measure. Another way of proving that hostility would have been to go to the Senate and vote against the bill. Doubtless M. Poincaré had excellent reasons for choosing the less conspicuous course. The most telling of these reasons was that he was M. Poincaré.

VI

A French wit once said that Paris belongs to him who can rise early. He might as well have said the world instead of Paris. M. Poincaré owes the most brilliant career of the Third Republic to the fact that his mother habitually rose at five A.M., winter or summer.

The son kept the habit. It was, one might say, his *faculté maîtresse*. With it went the ability of utilizing odd scraps of time. Punctuality may be the courtesy of princes; it certainly is the fountain-head of all bourgeois virtues. From it flow orderliness, efficiency, success.

M. Poincaré's days are mapped out to the smallest detail. His chauffeur gets an elaborate schedule every day. Mr. Huddleston records that when Poincaré stays at his country house at Sampigny he prefers to go to Paris by train, because he can't work in a motor-car. In this respect our Mr. Brisbane, who composes many of his articles into a specially fitted dictaphone while motoring downtown from Long Island, might suggest to him an improvement.

M. Poincaré's virtues are those of the typical successful business man. Those virtues, like his republicanism and his aggressive frontiersman's patriotism, are the heritage of his Lorraine birth. Of course, the real Frenchman is as unlike the swaggering, fussy, amorous American stage specimen as can be. He is prudent, thrifty, shrewd, industrious, matter-of-fact. He has none of the verbosity and sentimentalism of Babbitry. The Lorrainer is a true Frenchman in this respect, only more so. He is to the Parisian what the Scot is to the Londoner.

Poincaré comes from a respectable and prosperous family of Bar-le-Duc, a little town which has given to France, beside the world-famous jelly, two marshals and fifty generals in a hundred years. His father was a successful civil engineer. The family was a singularly happy and harmonious one. Poincaré's affection for his mother remained a leading influence of his life. It was at her advice that on leaving secondary school Raymond gave up his plans for a literary career and studied for the bar. His aim was financial independence; and he achieved it, and more, before he was thirty-five.

That he was an insatiable prize-winner at school goes without saying. His almost inhuman relish for work was manifest already in the schoolboy. In a poem, entitled *"Première Séparation,"* which he wrote at 15, he speaks of "hideous leisure"—surely a juxtaposition unique in world literature.

His industry was only exceeded by his cautiousness. Young Poincaré was never seen without his umbrella. His classmates teased him. "Leave it at home—it won't rain today," they said. "But it might," was Raymond's answer. It earned for him the nickname *prudence lorraine*. He disliked it.

At the age of 29 he was deputy, and he was not over 32 when he became Minister of Education. Up to his election to the Presidency he was in the Government, off and on, five times; he was Premier in 1911, at the head of the "National Cabinet," comprising an unusual array of talent.

As a deputy he specialized in finances. His parliamentary manner was his manner at the Bar—crystalline clarity, light without heat, dry elegance, the humour and imaginativeness of a railroad time-table. His great strength was reiteration—a kind of logical drumfire. The same traits characterize his writing. He was elected to the Academy in 1909.

His political creed was simple. He was a Republican and a conservative on a groundwork of nineteenth century liberalism and middle class prosperity. His pre-war foreign policy was based on firmness toward Germany and the cementing of the Entente. He was avowedly a militarist. He was, first and last, a Lorrainer; he could never forget the spiked helmets he had seen in his home town when he was ten years old. To make him responsible for the world war, as some of his English and German critics do, is exaggeration; but he worked, if not for it, toward it, and when it came, he congratulated himself on his foresight.

IIis honesty as a politician is of the highest order. He has been charged with being the tool of the *Comité des Forges,* the French steel trust, who needed the coal of the Ruhr to work the iron of reconquered Lorraine. When at the Bar he had among his clients some of the great industrialists of France, and he has been accused of playing into the hands of his old friends. Mr. Huddleston disposes of the charge.

The suggestion is that his policy has been influenced by personal interests. This is a calumny which is unworthy of any opponent of M. Poincaré in England or in France. That he has striven for what he conceived to be the material interests of France, and that he may have confused the material interests of France with the Comité des Forges is another matter.

He received no retainer for invading the Ruhr.

VII

President Grévy said once that the presidency of the French Republic was an honourable retirement for an old servant of the country. According to Sir Henry Maine, the King of England reigns but does not govern, the President of the United States governs but does not reign, and the President of France neither reigns nor governs. Yet, on paper at least, his powers are not negligible. He can dissolve or prorogue the Chamber, and in conjunction with a sympathetic Foreign Minister he can do almost anything over the heads of Cabinet and Parliament. But under the long series of presidential nonentities these prerogatives have fallen into disuse, so that today applying the letter of the Constitution would almost look like a *coup d'état.*

In 1912 the nomination of the Republican groups went to an amiable rubber stamp, M. Pams. He was a Radical Senator of the South, of Catalan extraction, great wealth, unimpeachable honesty,

and a kind heart. Whenever a deputy or a senator stopped him in the lobby with "M. Pams, may
I speak to you for a moment?", he simply said,
"How much?" and reached for his chequebook.
His candidacy loosened the dykes of wit. "He was
nominated because of his cook—why not elect the
cook?" asked one. "There is nothing really absurd about M. Pams, except his name," said
another. M. Dimnet wrote: "The nation asked
for a man—the Radicals offered it a Pams." Clemenceau said: "I am for the stupidest."

M. Pams merely smiled. His weakness was his
strength. It endeared him to Clemenceau, Cail-
laux, Combes, Briand. Being nominated by the
Republican groups was as good as being elected.

Great was his, and his sponsors', consternation
when M. Poincaré announced his candidacy. The
Left would not have him—he was that arch-bogey
of French politics, a Strong Man. M. Clemenceau
took an unprecedented step. Accompanied by four
other ex-Premiers—Five Characters in Search of
a Dummy—he called on Poincaré and asked him
to withdraw. Poincaré refused.

On the evening of the election an anxious party
awaited the result at the Poincaré residence in the
Rue Marbeau. It was getting late, and there was
no news. An old lady said: "If Raymond misses
it, it will be for the first time in his life that he does
not get what he wants."

At last Poincaré arrived. He had asked his
friends not to telephone to his home—he wanted

to break the news himself. Once more he got what he wanted.

Clemenceau's visit sealed the old feud, and the Tiger's vicious claws had their revenge. In 1917, when the war seemed all but lost, the cry went up for Clemenceau. He alone could save France. A reconciliation had to be contrived. Clemenceau said he was sorry. Poincaré said he did not recollect any offence. Clemenceau became Premier. The result is known.

The fear of the Radicals was not substantiated. Poincaré—the first man-size President in thirty years—proved a most scrupulous respecter of the Constitution. He served his country with credit in the most difficult period of its history.

VIII

Politically Raymond Poincaré is as much of a democrat as, say, Alexander Hamilton. In his social relations he is the most democratic of men. This is in keeping with French tradition. The government of England is much more democratic than that of France; but French society is much more democratic than the English. There are plenty of snobs in France, but snobbery is not the French national vice.

There is, however, the thing called etiquette. Frederick the Great once said, "If I were King of France I'd keep a man to do all the etiquette." There are no more Kings in France, but the President keeps a man whose only duty is to make the President do all the etiquette. He is the Chef du Protocol, or master of ceremonies, and he is the greatest tyrant between Calais and Caen.

Poincaré was not long President before he discovered a great game—one very popular with American schoolboys under the name of playing hookey. He ran away from the august gentleman who would squeeze him into evening dress at nine A.M. It is the gala uniform of French Presidents, and the fact that they survive going about in it in broad daylight proves the wonderful vitality of the French race. An Englishman would die of less.

Poincaré as President insisted on being treated like a human being. He went with Mme. Poincaré to picture galleries, exhibitions, theatres, just like an ordinary citizen. He instructed the police not to allow the Presidential car precedence unless under military escort. He cut the expenditure for "representation" to a minimum.

One day President Poincaré was to make a speech at the unveiling of a monument in a provincial town. There was the usual solemn crowd—mayor, council, guard of honour, awe-struck citizens. Poincaré was just about to begin, when he suddenly descried an old schoolmate among the spectators. He exclaimed: "Well, well—is that you, Larousse? How are you? Haven't seen you for years." He used the familiar *tu*—the untranslatable second person singular.

Would Mr. James Ramsay Macdonald, first

Labour Premier of Great Britain, do a thing like that? He would not.

IX

M. Poincaré has lived a virtuous and richly rewarded life under the spiritual shadow of the schoolboy's umbrella. Many excellent qualities found shelter under that modest convenience.

But there are limits to the capacity of even the roomiest umbrella.

Lack of humour, lack of imagination, lack of sympathy are Poincaré's most serious, but inevitable, defects. They are qualities which are the better for a little rain of adverse circumstance.

Unlike Clemenceau, unlike Briand, Poincaré never knew one of the greatest delights in this world, which consists in sitting down to a square meal after you had gone without one for some days.

X

Once he was asked by the editor of the *Revue des Revues* to contribute to a symposium on the French Genius. He introduced his paper with a joke. He wrote: "We legislators are not competent to discuss this question. To do so would be a violation of the separation of powers."

The reader may wonder how I found out that this was a joke. Well, it's simple. He could not mean it seriously, for he goes on discussing the question.

He asks: "Is the French genius an attribute of

the race or of the soil? Does it come in under *ius
sanguinis* or *ius soli*—the law of descent, or the law
of the land?" No foreigner, he continues, can become genuinely French in spirit. The Swiss, Rousseau, is an apparent exception. But then, "Rousseau has lent more to the French spirit than he has
borrowed from it."

Eight hundred words on the French Genius.
Separation of powers. Law of descent. Law of
land. Lending. Borrowing.

Poincaré.

XI

Yet it would be wrong to conclude that this cold
legalist, this hardened logician, this political efficiency engineer is devoid of feeling. His letters
to early friends bespeak a cool but appealing tend-
erness. His love for animals is perhaps his most
lovable trait.

It is a survival of his earliest childhood. His
biography by Girard, to date the standard work,
contains about a dozen photographs of animals—
pets of different periods. There is a majestic St.
Bernard, and crouching in his shadow a baby in
long clothes and with a most pathetic, scared expression—the President of the French Republic,
aged three. The dog looks much more presidential
than the baby. There is an intensely serious black
poodle named Bravo, guardian of the President's
country home at Sampigny. There are pictures
of cats and birds.

When as President he had to give official shooting parties for foreign celebrities, he walked with his guests carrying a cane instead of a gun. As a little boy he kept rabbits, and he remembers them.

He once complained to a friend that one of his difficulties was training kittens so that they should not eat the canaries and parrots when they grew up. He has since met with a still greater difficulty. He tried to kill the German goose and at the same time to preserve the supply of golden eggs. It could not be done.

It will not surprise psychologists that Poincaré, this dyed-in-the-wool rationalist, should extol instinct over reason. He says:

I owe priceless delights to animals, these mysterious creatures whom we call our inferior brothers. Inferior—why? The instinct that guides them—though I am convinced there is more than instinct to guide them—isn't it superior to our subtlest reasoning? I find in them a sense of logic more profound than that of many men, and a refinement of sensibility of which men are incapable. I love to lean on the obscurity of their souls.

He always speaks of the superiority of intuition to intellect—a typical attitude of the tired, thoroughbred rationalist. One loves what one hasn't got.

By the same token Poincaré, most unromantic of lawyers, delights in the novels of Dumas and Scott.

His taste in painting and music requires no such

sophisticated clue.   He loves Meissonier and Gounod.

XII

In 1912, when his candidate M. Pams was defeated, everybody spoke of Clemenceau as a beaten and finished man.   Five years later he was premier once more, and won the greatest war in history.

Nobody thinks of Poincaré, whose defeat at the elections was a severe one, as a beaten and finished man.   He is twenty years younger than Clemenceau; he is in good health; and he is the most terrific worker of his day.   He has survived the political death of the Presidency.   He will survive anything.

Poincaré is bound to come back.

In the interest of France and Europe let us hope it will be long before he does.

BIBLIOGRAPHY

Henry Girard	Raymond Poincaré. Paris, 1913.
H. Seeholzer	Raymond Poincaré. Zürich, 1922.
Sisley Huddleston	Poincaré. London, 1924.
Anonymous	Raymond Poincaré: a Sketch. London, 1914.
Anonymous	The Pomp of Power. London, 1922.
Anonymous	Ceux qui nous mènent. Paris, 1922.
Albert Thibaudet	Les Princes Lorrains. Paris, 1924.
Charles Dawbarn	Makers of the New France. London, 1923.
Raymond Poincaré	Idées contemporaines. Paris.
Raymond Poincaré	How France Is Governed. London, 1913.
Raymond Poincaré	The Origins of the War. London, 1922.

BENITO MUSSOLINI

BENITO MUSSOLINI

I

"LIFE," writes Samuel Butler, "is a fugue. Everything must flow from the theme, and there must be nothing new." At the age of twenty Mussolini, son of the village blacksmith at Predappio, was a Socialist candidate for Parliament. He was defeated by a wealthy opponent. In a fit of rage he smashed the ballot-box.

Everything in Mussolini's life was to flow from that theme, and for twenty years of the most romantic external events there has been nothing really new. Seldom was a *leitmotiv* in a human story carried out more consistently. Whatever one may think of Mussolini as a statesman, one must admit that his life has the unity of a true work of art. In 1904 the ballot-box was the stronger of the two, and Mussolini, in order to escape arrest, had to flee to Switzerland. In 1924 the Prime Minister of Italy—since Napoleon probably the least restrained possessor of personal power in Western Europe—issued the order, on the eve of the elections, to his fanatical following: "Take care of the ballot-boxes, and don't forget to look after those who vote against the Government." The order was enthusiastically obeyed, and the Fascist victory crowned twenty years' vendetta.

Among the numerous misconceptions current about Mussolini in America and England the most fatal is the notion that he is a leader of democracy. The mistake arises from confounding "popular" with "democratic." Mussolini is a popular leader—but the leader of a people tired with democracy. He is popular because he is anti-democratic. He is the symbol of the passionate Latin protest against the Anglo-Saxon fiction of fair play which is the very foundation of democratic parliamentarism; he is the *gonfaloniere* of the Italian return to roaring, violent, despotic normalcy from the alien interlude of an imported, unsympathetic and therefore ineffective theory of government. He is a repercussion, a reversion to type, a bucketful of cold water over the nineteenth-century infatuation with democratic Progress.

It is the great paradox of the nineteenth century that while it invented the historic sense and for the first time constructed a truly perspectivic view of the past, it also elevated its own pre-occupations into absolute laws, its moment-bound, once-occurring solutions into eternal patterns of evolution. It is as if Copernicus had applied his system to the universe while expressly exempting the earth. A fine example of the political miscarriage of evolutionary ideology is Benjamin Kidd's

PREMIER MUSSOLINI

statement that the supreme result of the century was the final triumph of the principles of the French revolution. It was confidently assumed that by way of the extension of suffrage, of universal education, and of a gradually humanized industrialism mankind would infallibly arrive in the paradise of super-democracy.

The native land of this liberal philosophy was England, but its—posthumous—patron-saint was a Frenchman. The nineteenth century believed that every day, in every way, the world was getting better and better. Even Marx, who rejected the valuation, accepted the process—he held that every day, in every way, the world was getting worse and worse, until it suddenly collapsed and turned good.

The facts had no patience with this political Couéism. By the beginning of the twentieth century the very babies whispered the open secret that parliamentarism on the continent proved a failure. A failure less spectacular and noisy, but hardly less real, than that of the counterfeit American constitutions in Spanish America. Corruption, terrorism and lying at the elections—underhand bargaining, favouritism and lying in parliament— such is the story of the imported democracy on the continent. In France parliamentarism was a thin disguise for the rule of the stock exchange; the Chamber was a combination of financial first aid and jumping-off board for ambitious young men and a doubtful counterweight for the ever-present possibility of a military *putsch*. In Austria the *Reichsrat* was a rather low-grade burlesque show. In Hungary the House of Representatives was a safety valve for excess hot air. In Germany the *Reichstag* was a self-adjusting doormat for the Kaiser's muddy boots.

This failure of parliamentarism on the continent affords some interesting lessons. One of these is that parliamentarism is not an article of exportation. It thrives in England where it is indigenous; it does not work elsewhere. The exceptions are only apparent. Parliamentarism was successful in the Scandinavian countries, in Holland and in Switzerland. But in none of these nations was it a mere importation; it had its roots in the past. These countries possess, like England, a continuous tradition of representative institutions, social equilibrium, and reasonable safety from foreign aggression. There exists in them that margin for political trial and error without which parliamentarism is either a sham or a danger—or both.

But the success of parliamentary democracy postulates a still deeper and subtler condition—a certain psychological disposition called spirit of sportsmanship. The very essence of parliamentarism is to accept the result of a toss-up as final; not to hit below the belt; and not to kick your enemy once he is down. Now to the logically-minded Latin or Teuton these notions appear as sentimental weakness. Supposing you lose in the toss-up—why not knock your opponent down and get what you want anyway? And of course the best time to kick him is when he is down. It may not be elegant but it is convenient.

Democracy is impossible without a cheerful acquiescence in periodic defeat. But the habit of that acquiescence presupposes centuries of training. The majority of continental peoples lack that training. Their history, unlike the English, moved not by gradual evolution but by violent jerks.

Parliamentarism on the continent was essentially a game with loaded dice. By and by the idea was conceived by certain bright intellects that the loser's remedy lay not in talking nicely to the dice, but in throwing them out the window. This idea was expounded in the philosophy of Direct Action, chief among whose advocates was Georges Sorel.

Then came the war. It showed up shams and demolished pretences. It provided millions of the common people with rifles, and offered the greatest university extension course of all times. The principal subject taught was Direct Action. The governments spared no effort in convincing people that to shoot straight was much more important than to think straight; that the short cut to the object of your desire was a cut across the throat of your rival.

Two major peoples decided to go in for postgraduate study. One was the Russian under Lenin. The other was the Italian under Mussolini.

The disagreements between Bolshevism and Fascism are many, but they are all dwarfed by one fundamental agreement. Both stand and fall with Direct Action. They *are* Direct Action. There is, to adapt Lord Melbourne's famous saying, no damned nonsense of discussion, persuasion, fair play about either. Both have for their motto, Bullets Beat Ballots.

It is recorded about the great Napoleon that he always cheated at cards whenever he could make reasonably sure that he would not be found out. Sometimes he was found out, but there was no one to tell him. Napoleon is the supreme instance of the man who never worries about the rules of the game. The Austrian and Prussian generals complained that he won all his battles by breaking the rules of strategy.

I do not know at what moment of his career Benito Mussolini made up his mind that he would be like Napoleon, but it must have been early. The broken ballot-box was only a start. The ascent of the Fascist dictator is marked by the *débris* of broken rules and broken skulls.

II

Mussolini was raised on a diet of revolution. His father was a local leader of the Socialist party. After the incident of the ballot-box the young schoolmaster in his Swiss refuge fought starvation by working as a bricklayer's labourer. At the same time he attended lectures in the university of

Lausanne and gained a diploma as a professor of French. His revolutionary activities caused his expulsion, and he proceeded to Trento, then under Austrian rule. Here he edited an irredentist newspaper, and even found time to write an historical novel, advocating tyrannicide as a patriotic duty. In 1908 an amnesty enabled him to return home. He founded a little revolutionary newspaper at Forli, called *La Lotta di classe* (Class War). His brilliancy as writer and speaker, and his efficiency as organizer attracted attention, and in 1912, at the age of twenty-nine, he was appointed editor-in-chief of the *Avanti,* organ of the Italian Socialist party, and one of the great journals of Europe.

It was at this juncture that Georges Sorel uttered a prophecy which has been quoted at least a thousand times within the past two years. He said:

Our Mussolini is not an ordinary socialist. Believe me, you will yet see him at the head of a sacred battalion, saluting with his uplifted sword the Italian flag. He is an Italian of the fifteenth century. It is not yet known, but he is the only man capable of mending the weaknesses of his Government.

When the world war broke out Mussolini was among the first to demand that Italy should join the Allies. His motive was twofold. He saw the opportunity to free the unredeemed provinces from Austrian rule, of which he had had first-hand experience. And he believed that the war was merely a prelude to a world-wide proletarian revolution, and that an Allied victory would really be a stepping-stone to the triumph of international socialism.

The leaders of the Italian Socialist party thought differently, and Mussolini was expelled. He founded at Milan a revolutionary newspaper called *Popolo d'Italia,* and conducted a ruthless campaign against neutralists. In 1915 he enlisted as a private in the infantry.

A few weeks later he was wounded by shrapnel. The Moiras sometimes display a sense for copy that would make them invaluable as sob sisters on the staff of Mr. Hearst. At the field hospital of Ronchi the King of Italy inspected the wounded. He stopped at—or merely passed by; no matter— Mussolini's bed. It had to be.

Seven years later [writes an enthusiast] Sovereign and corporal were to meet again—at the Quirinal, when Mussolini kissed hands as Prime Minister of Italy.

Honourably discharged, Mussolini returned to his desk and devoted himself to hunting traitors. The political division between neutralists and interventionists covered an industrial conflict. The so-called "old" industries—textiles and silk— grouped under the Banca Commerciale were, or rather had been, neutralist. The "new" industry —steel—was hundred per cent. bitter ender. Italian steel as represented by the Perrone brothers, and the neutralist-baiter editor of the *Popolo d'Italia* became friends. It proved a lasting friendship.

III

The war was won. But the troubles of Italy
were not yet over. In the dispute with the new
Jugoslav kingdom over Fiume, Istria and Dalmatia, Italy found her aspirations thwarted by her
own Allies. The Paris conference became the
Caporetto of Italian diplomacy.

At home things were worse still. The war had
laid bare the ravages of half a century of misgov-
ernment, of corruption, of makeshift husbandry.
The administration was in tatters; industry, commerce, agriculture were dishevelled; the currency
plunged downwards; the cost of living shot to the
skies. The disbanded armies found unemployment and hunger in lieu of the promised millennium. Life in the trenches had not been without
its dangers; but there were compensations. For
the first time in centuries masses of Italian peasants ceased to worry about their food; and they experienced a delicious release of all the instincts of
violence. War had meant plenty to eat and plenty
of Austrians to shoot at. Peace meant the return
to slow starvation under police supervision. And
those who had not risked their lives, the slackers
and profiteers, were now wallowing in luxury.

The demobilized soldier is a grave problem even
under the best circumstances. And in Italy circumstances were extremely bad. For all practical
purposes Italy at the end of 1918 was a defeated
country. And at the end of 1918 the wages of
defeat was Communism.

IV

Fascism was born at Milan in the spring of 1919 as the embodiment of the Italian protest against defeat in victory.

The fundamental idea of Fascism [writes Gorgolini] is that our victorious war is to be fruitful and productive of the corresponding good, whether moral, spiritual, or material.

Consolidation of the Italian victory is put forward by all its protagonists as the prime aim of the Fascist revolt. But there is in all this talk about consolidation just a little unconscious avowal of something lacking solidity. There is in all this exuberance about national triumph and strength and courage just a faint echo of somebody whistling in the dark. The extreme self-assertiveness of Fascism is the noise of an inferiority complex.

True enough—Italy had won the war. But the memory of Caporetto rankled. That terrible defeat was expiated, its effects were checked by Italian heroism on the Piave, the Carso and the Grappa; but the battle of Vittorio Veneto was won over the running army of a shadow Empire. Italians felt somehow that they had to tell the world about their wonderful victory in the field. The Italian defeat at the conference table needed no telling.

The young officers, students and intellectuals who returned from the Grappa and the Carso to the drab uncertainties of demobilization were torn by despair. They had a keen sense of their own sacrifices, of the incompetence and ingratitude of their Government. They saw themselves as well as their country robbed of the fruits of victory. They had tasted that intoxication of power which changed every little second lieutenant into a demigod. They claimed responsibility and privilege. And they had just received a most thorough schooling in direct action.

Had it not been for President Wilson's anti-Italian stand at Paris it is not inconceivable that the disgust and discontent from which Fascism sprung might have emptied their energy into the reservoir of the Socialist revolt. It was Woodrow Wilson who, without knowing it, dealt the decisive blow to the Red cause in Italy. As far as Western Europe is concerned, Lenin was beaten at Fiume.

The despair of the peace was reinforced by the surplus hate of wartime. Among the leftover supplies that had to be dumped after the sudden termination of the struggle the vast stores of canned hatred, manufactured by propaganda, were overlooked. In the defeated countries this hate could be comfortably spent on the victors. The sufferings of invaded France continued to drain the local supply into Germany. In uninvaded America, where the immediate suffering was negligible in comparison and where the Committee on Public Information had done an excellent job, the hate dumps were brought up, as it were, by the

Ku Klux Klan. Negroes, Jews, Catholics and immigrants served as *Ersatz* for the geographically unavailable Germans.

In Italy this "free" hate precipitated on President Wilson, the Jugoslavs and the Communists, and was absorbed by Fascism.

The war had kindled the youth of Italy, as of other countries, to a sense of romance and adventure. Fascism now unconsciously undertook to canalize the revolt against the dulness of modern middle class existence. It made possible the gratification of warlike impulses, while diminishing the risks of war; for the hitting average of Communists was lower than that of the Austrians, and the hitting average of innocent bystanders and of the Communists' wives and children was nil.

Mussolini did not invent Fascism. He merely discovered its material, and vitalized it by injecting one idea, brilliant in its very simplicity. It was the idea that it takes two classes to make a class war.

The Italian bourgeoisie was dazzled. So was the Italian proletariat. No one had thought of this before.

It remained only to organize the inevitable.

V

The years 1919 and 1920 form the period of Communist ascendency in Italy, and of the abdication of the official state. It is also the period of Fascist growth, and of civil war waged by small nuclei of Fascists against a numerically stronger enemy. The story of this civil war has been told many times. It shall not be retold here.

The Fascist methods were eclectic. In plain Saxon this means that the Fascists took those methods where they found them, without bothering much about the copyright. They were the methods of vendetta, of the old Italian inter-city feud; also, the methods of the Germans in Belgium, of Horthy's detachments in Hungary, of Trotzky's shock troops in Russia. In a word, they were the methods of Terror.[1]

To this assortment the Fascists added an innovation of their own. Another brilliantly simple idea. Castor oil.

VI

The most remarkable thing about Fascism is the incredible rapidity of its growth. By the end of 1919, we are told, there were no more than 1,000 Fascisti, scattered over Northern Italy. In January, 1921, when the military organization was formed, there were over 100,000. In October, 1922, at the time of the March on Rome, the armed cohorts contained 300,000 men, and the various non-fighting auxiliaries another million and a half.

[1] Sir Percival Phillips, the correspondent of the *Daily Mail*, put the number of victims killed by the Fascists at twenty-five hundred in two years. Seeing that the wars for the liberation of Italy, stretching over a period of thirty years, only claimed six thousand dead, the above number may seem rather large, but Sir Percival does not think so. He says the Bolsheviki killed much more—in Russia.

The explanation of these astonishing gains touches the innermost core of the Fascist revolt. Fascism is nothing new. It is the revival, with modern methods, of the central fact of Italian history, which is civil war. The history of Italy for the past thousand years is a history of feuds. In the centuries when the English fought the French, the French fought the Germans, the Spaniards fought the Moors, Italians fought one another. Throughout the Italian past runs the red thread of vendetta. The identity, both physiognomic and functional, of the Fascist revolt with the inter-city, inter-party, inter-clan feuds of medieval Italy becomes obvious when one reads, in Phillips, in Godden, in Beals, the accounts of the early Fascist forays.

It should not be forgotten that civil war in Italy was never the tragic affair it used to be in England or France or the United States. In the fourteenth century as in the twentieth it consisted in surprise raids, ambushes and duels of diminutive groups, with the populace looking on and gesticulating excitedly. The special feature of an Italian civil war is the sudden disappearance of the defeated. They go over to the victors as soon as the shooting has stopped and the result is announced.

When the tide turns in Italy it turns with a vengeance. In 1919 the ranks of Communists swelled overnight from a few thousands to a few millions. After the great Fascist victories in 1921 the Socialist and Communist locals joined the Fascists wholesale. They literally stood in long queues in front of the Fascist headquarters, and the organizers had to hang out a sign, "Admission by appointment only." There was a good deal of abominable bullying at work; but there was also the great Italian passion for climbing on the bandwagon.

Sir Percival tells the story of a Neapolitan labourer, Giovanni Esposito by name

He wrote to the King, begging to be allowed to change the name of his infant son, an act possible only by a Royal Decree. He explained . . . that when the child was born in December, 1919, Bolshevist propaganda was sweeping through Italy, and the peasant had to embrace revolutionary doctrines or starve. Now that the Fascisti have made the country safe for patriots . . . he begged to be allowed to change the name of young Esposito from Lenin to Benito Mussolini. Which has been done.

Sir Percival is a good propagandist. A good propagandist does not know a joke on his cause when he sees one. If he did he would not be a propagandist.

VII

In the summer of 1922 the Socialists and Communists called a general strike. Mussolini gave the Facta Government two days to settle it. He was not disappointed. The government did nothing. Whereupon the Fascists settled the strike, if not in two days, at any rate in two weeks.

On the twenty-fourth of October 40,000 armed

Fascisti congregated at Naples. Mussolini addressed a twenty-four hour ultimatum to the Government. The Government did nothing. On the twenty-seventh Mussolini ordered general mobilization and the march on Rome. On the twenty-eighth, three hundred thousand Fascists converged on the capital from three directions. The best Bolshevist precepts were followed: post offices, telephone exchanges, telegraph and railway stations were seized. The Government awoke and decreed martial law. The King, being an intelligent person and a realist, refused to sign the decree.

In this hour of fate Mussolini was at his headquarters, the editorial office of the *Popolo d'Italia* in Milan. The office was transformed into a fortress. The journalists sat at their desks in black shirts. Carbines were stacked in the corners. They remained there.

Mussolini, we are told, "preserved the characteristic disciplined calm of Fascism." He refused to deviate from his daily routine, and found time to play on his beloved violin, and to practise with the foil. He, too, wore a black shirt.

The climax came on Sunday, the twenty-ninth. It is graphically described by the Fascist writer, Piero Mozzucato.[1]

We are in Milan, in the Via Laviano, in the office of the *Popolo d'Italia*. It is exactly 2 P.M. when Benito Mussolini comes in. His face is full of light. Turning to his brother he says:

[1] Quoted by G. M. Godden in "Mussolini: The Birth of the New Democracy," from Giachetti's "Fascismo Liberatore."

"Arnaldo, we must issue a supplement. The King has asked me to undertake the formation of a cabinet."

·He says no more, turns from his brother with a bright smile, and leaves the room.

Twenty hours later, on Monday morning, Mussolini arrived in Rome and went straight to the Royal Palace. He still wore his black shirt, in which he had played the violin, exercised with the rapier, and issued a special supplement. He said to the King:

Your Majesty will excuse me if I come here in my black shirt, as I have just left the barricade on which I was obliged to engage in a conflict, fortunately without bloodshed. I bring to your Majesty the victory of Vittorio Veneto, consecrated afresh; and I am happy to call myself your Majesty's faithful servant.

Next day he and his cabinet took the oath of office.

VIII

Mussolini and his literary general staff never tire of emphasizing that Fascism has no system, no philosophy. It is, they say, empirical, pragmatic, eclectic. Fascism was born as a negative movement, a movement of protest. It was anti-Wilsonian, anti-Jugloslav, anti-liberal, anti-government, anti-socialist. Its technique was determined by the emergency and by the psychology of its personnel. It invented, or borrowed, its doctrinal justification by the way.

Our programme is simple [Mussolini says]. We wish to govern Italy. They ask us for programmes, but there are already too many. It is not programmes that are wanting for the salvation of Italy, but men and will power.

And again:

We are a movement, not a museum of dogmas and principles. We have a living and plastic programme of action, which we offer in place of the present fossilized policy; and we mean to fight for it.

The first principle in this "living and plastic programme of action" is the contempt for democracy.

Fascismo represents [says Mussolini] a reaction against the democrats who would have made everything mediocre and uniform, and tried in every way to conceal and to render transitory the authority of the state. . . . We shall not give . . . universal liberty, not even if it assumes the garb of immortal principles. It is not electoral subterfuges which divide us from democracy. If people wish to vote, let them vote. Let us all vote until we are sick of it.

The point is that as long as one has an armed following of 300,000 men, "fired by an almost mystic spirit of obedience," it does not really matter how people vote.

Perhaps the clearest exposition of Mussolini's theory of government is to be found in an article he contributed to the Fascist review *Gerarchia* in April, 1923. He starts out with the declaration that liberalism and democracy are obsolete. What

the world wants is dictatorship. "This is a truth
grasped only by Russian Communism and Italian
Fascism." He continues:

Mankind is tired of liberty. They have had an orgy of it.
Liberty is not the chaste and severe virgin for whom the
generations of the first half of the nineteenth century fought
and died. . . . The new watchwords are to be order, authority, discipline. . . . Let it be known once for all that Fascism
has already passed and, if necessary, will calmly turn to
pass again, over the putrescent corpse of the Goddess of
Liberty.

Another obsolete watchword that must go over-
board is equality. Fascism believes that all Fascists are born free, and all men are born inequal.
It founds its practice on the distinction between
Fascist and non-Fascist, the capable and the incapable, those born to lead and those born to obey.
This idea of inequality is expressed in the Fascist
concept of hierarchy, which implies the quasi-
divine authority of Mussolini, military discipline,
blind obedience, a stepladder of ranks, promotion
of the faithful according to merit and political re-
liability, and an outside mass that exists only on
sufferance. It is fundamentally the idea of a
black-shirted Khalifate.

Inasmuch as Fascism has any central doctrine
at all, it is the doctrine of syndicalism, of direct
action. Indeed, Fascist writers declare that Fascism is a blend of Italian nationalism and of syndicalism. Corradini calls it national syndicalism.
According to Gorgolini, there is no great difference

between the principles of Fascism and of Sorelian socialism.

What does direct action mean? It means that parliamentarism is a fraud, because it rests on argument. Now, argument is futile, because your oppressor will not yield to it unless you can show that you are stronger than he; but if you are stronger, argument becomes unnecessary. Democracy is thus nothing but a narcotic, a means of fooling the oppressed into acquiescence. The only way of shaking off oppression is to knock the oppressor on the head.

This, of course, is the doctrine underlying all revolutions. Sorel distinguishes between force, by which the oppressor imposes his domain, and violence, whereby the oppressed fight oppression. Force is immoral; violence is moral.

Mussolini worships violence. In 1921, *à propos* of the Fascist victory in the elections, he wrote in *Popolo d'Italia:*

The fact can be best explained by applying the concepts of violence that Sorel developed magnificently. It was the prestige of violence that gave victory to the Fascist candidates. The great popular mass submitted to the fascination of violence, which is the creator of valour and the resuscitator of enthusiasm. . . . . At the bottom of the present Facist victory one encounters a case of force that creates right. . . . .

The same idea recurs in all his speeches and writings. Its natural corollary is the principle of dictatorship. Mussolini maintains that the people are incapable of governing themselves; that it is the determined self-conscious minorities that make history; and that no government can succeed that is not based on armed force.

Here, obviously, is an inconsistency. Fascism advocates the morality of violence and the righteousness of armed revolt. It also advocates the strong state's right to crush opposition by force. In other words, the Fascist rebellion against the state was right; a rebellion against the Fascist state would be wrong.

Fascist theorists meet this difficulty by declaring that the morality of violence is determined by its purpose. Also, they reserve to themselves the right of defining that purpose. Which comes down to a very simple thesis: "My violence is right; your violence is wrong."

The argument about the morality of violence is an old one. There are those who hold that it has been settled once for all nineteen hundred years ago. It was a tranquil spring night in an eastern garden. All of a sudden there was a commotion. Sharp words cleft the darkness. Scabbards clanged against shields. A blade flashed—a man fell, bleeding. Some one said in a quiet voice: "Put up again thy sword into his place; for all they that take the sword shall perish with the sword."

IX

To sum up: Fascism has no system, only methods and tendencies. The methods are direct action and dictatorship. The tendencies are anti-liberalism, anti-socialism, anti-Catholicism, nationalism and imperialism. Fascism demands that the state shall relinquish all economic functions. It proposes to restore to private ownership and management not only the railways, the telegraph and the telephone, but even the postal service.

There is in this insistence on the purely political state, and also in the vehement advocacy of individualistic organization of industry, just an echo of the hated Liberal creed. But then, Fascism, after smashing the Socialist labour unions, peasant leagues, and co-operative societies, organized its own unions, peasant leagues, and co-operatives. It annexed all the property, most of the membership, and some of the principles, of its rivals, and set up in business on its own account. This is what Fascists call eclecticism. In English it is called stealing somebody else's thunder.

Fascist activities, at least in the early days, were financed by some big industrialists and landowners, and by tribute levied on the raided districts. To-day most of the deserving Fascists are cared for in governmental and municipal offices, and there is a well-paid Fascist militia of eighty thousand men, formed to replace the so-called Guardie Regie, or royal gendarmerie, which was forty thousand strong. Economy is a cardinal item in the Fascist schedule.

That Fascism, its bloody and detestable methods,

its unscrupulous opportunism, and its intellectual muddle notwithstanding, has achieved no little good for Italy, is unquestionable. It has swept away a dishonest and paralytic system of government and dragged the Italian people out of its age-old rut. It broke open sealed windows and let in fresh air; it quickened up the drowsy pace of Italian life; it restored the fundamental public services to a working basis. It put Italy on the international map. Above all, it probably prevented Bolshevism, in 1919, from overflowing Western Europe and putting an end to a civilization which, with all its shortcomings, is the only one we have.

Apart from that outstanding merit, Fascism for America and England is important chiefly as a warning and a deterrent.

X

Mussolini is eminently a man of action. His principle is to hit first and find out afterwards. He has intuitive shrewdness, but not much reasoning power. Theory is his weakness, and he hates weakness. He is an avowed enemy of reflection.

Yet this man lives surrounded by mirrors. He never acts but he watches himself acting. He combines a phenomenal unity of purpose and fitness with a pathological dualism of personality. There are two Mussolinis—Mussolini the performer and Mussolini the audience.

Men like that are not rare. Life as well as

literature swarms with them. But they usually achieve nothing beyond a doubtful eminence as heroes of neurotic fiction. Their self-consciousness paralyzes them; they are so intent on observing what they are going to do next that they forget doing it.

Mussolini never forgets doing anything. Yet he never forgets looking at himself either. His past is ever-present. At the Lausanne conference he points out to a friend the spot where he worked as a bricklayer. He goes home to Predappio to accept the cottage where he was born as a gift of the villagers; he stands in the room with his head bowed, absorbed in meditation, in full view of all the reporters. He addresses the workers of the foundry where he worked as a lad; he muses on the fact, and rubs it in.

He is an actor in the most thrilling of melodramas: the life of Benito Mussolini. But he is an actor who feels his part. Mussolini was once called the greatest operatic tenor Italy ever produced; but that *mot,* while it overestimates his voice, does not do justice to his character. It should not be forgotten that he is an Italian. An Anglo-Saxon can be dramatic only when he feels nothing; emotion stifles and numbs him. The average Latin is more articulate in the throes of passion than the average Englishman when executing a problem in differential calculus.

Mussolini is a sincere man. He sincerely works for the weal of his beloved Italy. He sincerely be-

lieves that the weal of his beloved Italy is insepara-
ble from the weal of Benito Mussolini.

XI

In *The Prince* Machiavelli, discussing those
rulers who attained their position by their own efforts, Moses, Cyrus, Romulus, Theseus, writes:

> Examining their lives and actions, one does not see that
> they had other fortune than that of the opportunity which
> gave them the material and enabled them to shape it as seemed
> best to them; and without that opportunity the virtue of their
> souls would have been lost, and without that virtue the oppor-
> tunity would have come in vain.

Once Mussolini quoted that passage in a speech.
As he pronounced it the words must have flashed
up in his mind like mirrors down the dark corridors
of his life.

"There is a veiled quality to his eyes," writes one
of his keenest critics, "not a dreaming expression,
but the indefinable smouldering haziness that one
may observe in the eyes of a person who has enjoyed some new and delicious emotional experience
and is still slightly intoxicated."

The new age which dawned on August 1, 1914,
gave Mussolini his material. The virtue of his soul
responded to the opportunity. His eager hand
responded to the beckoning of an over-ripe fruit.

His great qualities have won for him great successes. A great man he is not.

There is no charity in him. He cannot forget

the bitterness of his youth.   Victorious, he is unrelenting to the beaten enemy.   A favourite phrase of his is: "I shall not forgive unto those who . . ." And he does not.

Lincoln was made of other stuff.

BIBLIOGRAPHY

Mussolini   As revealed in his political
                             speeches. Selected, translated
                             and edited by Barone Bernardo
                             Quaranta di San Severino.
                             New York, 1923.

G. M. Godden   Mussolini. London, 1923.

Pietro Gorgolini   The Fascist Movement in Italian
                             Life. London, 1923.

Carleton Beals   Rome or Death. New York,
                             1923.

Sir Percival Phillips   The "Red" Dragon and the Black
                             Shirts. London.

Georges Sorel   Reflections on Violence. London,
                             1916.

International Relations Section of The Nation. New York,
    1919-1923.